# SCIENCE EXPERIMENTS
## in food and textiles

Kevin Howard
BSc, PhD, Cert Ed, FRSH, MIHEc, MIBiol, MIHE
Deputy Director, School of Education and
Community Studies
Liverpool Polytechnic

Elaine Prisk
BSc, MSc, Cert Ed, MIFST, MSAB, MIHEc
Head of Home Economics
Liverpool Polytechnic

fp  FORBES PUBLICATIONS

## Acknowledgements

The authors would like to express their sincere thanks to Dr Peter Borrows, chairman of the ASE Safety Committee, for checking the experiments for safety, and to Sue Sevaglia, Jeannette Kelly and Helen Sprawson for their careful testing of the experiments, as well as teachers involved in trials who have contributed many useful suggestions. Thanks are also due to James Reed for checking sections of the text, and to Mary Harris and Jean Howard for typing the manuscript.

**Kevin Howard**
**Elaine Prisk**
*Liverpool 1984*

Published by
**Forbes Publications Limited**
120 Bayswater Road, London W2 3JH

© **Forbes Publications Limited**
All rights reserved
First published 1984
Second revised edition 1989
ISBN 0 901762 80 6

The equipment shown in our cover photograph was kindly loaned by Griffin & George Ltd. It does not, however, represent the apparatus required for any of the experiments described in this book.
*Photograph by Steve Marwood*

Printed in Great Britain by
St Edmundsbury Press Limited, Bury St Edmunds, Suffolk

# CONTENTS

# INTRODUCTION

Following the success of the first two-volume edition of *Science Experiments in Food and Textiles*, many teachers indicated that they would welcome a format where the pupils' material and teachers' notes are contained in the same book. This suggestion has been adopted in this combined new edition where teachers' notes are given on the page adjacent to the experiment to which they apply.

As in the first edition, *Science Experiments in Food and Textiles* contains detailed instructions to pupils for carrying out 74 experiments on foods, textiles, detergents and dyes arranged in sections. In addition the suggestions for further work provide a basis for experimental design of further investigations by the pupil. It is intended that teachers should photocopy each set of pupil instructions for class use.

The experimental procedures have been clearly set out to enable pupils with little experience of scientific practical work to carry out the experiments with the minimum of instruction from the teachers. The authors benefited greatly from the suggestions of home economics teachers who tested the feasibility of the procedures for classroom use.

Each experiment has been graded alongside its title as follows:
\* indicates simpler experiments needing little specialised equipment
\*\* needs more specialised equipment and greater practical skills
\*\*\* requires familiarity with laboratory work; probably better carried out by sixth form pupils

The aims and objectives of the book are the development of an investigatory, critical attitude of mind; an understanding of the science and technology of foods and materials; a practical approach to experimental design and problem-solving; and a numerate as well as a descriptive approach; these are some of the demands made of home economics teaching as a result of changes in examination syllabuses where the advent of GCSE has laid an increased emphasis upon scientific content and skills. It is to help meet these demands that this book has been compiled.

In addition, the intention behind the book is that pupils with little scientific background should be able to carry out experimental work successfully, paying attention to the need for appropriate controls, so giving immediacy, relevance and interest to some of the theoretical aspects of home economics covered in GCSE and A level syllabuses.

The book will also be extremely useful to all science teachers, at all levels in the school, who wish to teach laboratory skills using experiments which will have relevance and meaning for the student.

At the end of the book, sample questions from several examining boards have been included to illustrate the relevance of experiment and observation to home economics. They comprise both A level questions selected from recent past papers, and specimen questions published by the Examining Groups offering GCSE Home Economics syllabuses.

Reference to the teacher's notes will enable the teacher to give additional guidance to pupils. The notes contain practical information on procedure and equipment and reagents used. They also give sufficient theoretical background and explanation of results to enable the text questions to be answered and the practical work to be seen in its theoretical context.

## How to use this book
### Structure of the experiments
Each experiment is set out under the following headings: *Purpose* or *Introduction*; *Materials*; *Method*; *Result*. In addition, many of the experiments are followed by a section headed 'Suggestions for further work'. These headings are used to subdivide both the pupils' instructions (to be photocopied as class sets) and the teachers' notes (on adjacent pages).

## Introduction
This section in the teachers' notes expands on the brief purpose given in the pupils' material. It introduces the experiment, pointing out its relevance in the wider context of the subject, and, where appropriate, mentions related experiments.

## Materials
All materials required for each experiment have been listed to facilitate preparation and to enable pupils to see at a glance what is required.

In the pupils' instructions reagents are listed first, but otherwise materials are listed in the order they will be required in the experiment. The teachers' notes give useful additional information as well as referring to the appropriate pages of the Appendix. The number of each piece of apparatus required for each pupil or group is also indicated in the pupils' instructions. For small items like test tubes, however, although the numbers suggested give a good indication, it would be wise to have spares just in case.

## Method

The numbered step-by-step presentation of the method in the pupils' instructions has been found to be popular in trials as an aid to systematic working, although the pupils should be advised first to read through the whole of the method before commencing.

This section of the teachers' notes contains useful hints on the carrying out of the experiment and attempts to anticipate some of the common specific practical errors which are made. The teacher can judge the best time to bring some of these details to the pupils' attention. A general point can be made here. The volumes suggested in the method section of many of the experiments are preceded by the word 'about' eg 'place about $2cm^3$ of the solution into a test tube'; in these cases the volume need only be approximate, and it may be useful to point out that $1cm^3$ of liquid in a standard test tube is about 1cm in depth.

## Result

Here the expected results are summarized and explained, and the opportunity has been taken to give some of the theoretical background needed to increase the pupils' understanding. Ideally, the theory and practical work should be taught in conjunction, when one will reinforce the other. The theoretical treatment given here has necessarily been restricted, the aim being simply to give some ideas as to how the experimental work can be used to stimulate discussion of the appropriate theory. Other more detailed texts can be used in conjunction. Some of these are mentioned in the teachers' notes and listed in the bibliography in Appendix IV.

## Suggestions for further work

This section of many of the experiments is intended to provide the basis of individual or small-group project work. As such, the method is indicated but not described in as much detail as in the standard experiments. The onus will therefore be much more on the pupils to design the investigation in a practical, logical way, including compiling a list of the materials required a few days prior to the experiment.

## Appendix

The Appendix, starting on *page 146*, is in four parts.

*Part I* lists details of all reagents required for all experiments, including suggestions for further work. An indication of specific hazards associated with certain reagents is given.

*Part II* lists details of equipment required for all experiments, including suggestions for further work. Certain items, marked with an asterisk, are commonly available in home economics rooms or in local shops. Very little explanation of these items is included except where they may have to be adapted for special purposes.

*Part III* gives names and addresses of some suppliers of materials – equipment and reagents – required for the experiments. This list is by no means exhaustive, and local sources should be explored. In any case, it is hoped that the co-operation of the Science Department, who will have relevant catalogues, will be sought.

*Part IV* lists books referred to in the texts and from which further information on the topics covered in the pupils' material and the teachers' notes may be obtained.

## Nomenclature

Both traditional names for chemicals, and those recommended in the Association for Science Education booklet *Chemical Nomenclature, Symbols and Terminology* are included. Within the text of the *Pupils' Worksheets*, however, the name which is considered to be the most useful for the student to remember is used.

## Safety

Although many of the experiments can be performed in a standard home economics room, timetabling the work in a properly equipped laboratory is strongly recommended (except where any tasting is required). It is, of course, the responsibility of the teacher to ensure that standard laboratory safety procedures are followed. In a few cases the teacher will need to have appropriate scientific training (either initial or in-service) in order to supervise the handling of particularly hazardous chemicals or techniques. In these cases the warning sign ⚠ is given at the start of the experiment.

Attention is drawn to the use of the word **CARE** in the text where particular caution is needed with a reagent or part of a method. Potentially hazardous chemicals have been marked with the warning symbol ⚠.

It is expected that at all times normal laboratory safety precautions will be observed.
For example:

**Safety spectacles should be worn whenever chemical reagents are handled.**

**No eating or drinking must take place in the laboratory.**

**Large volumes of liquids such as Winchester bottles should not be carried about.**

**Concentrated acids and inflammable reagents should be used in a fume cupboard.**

Difficult or potentially dangerous procedures are indicated in the pupils' instructions and further information given in the teachers' notes. It is inadvisable for young or inexperienced pupils to carry out these procedures without close supervision by a teacher with appropriate scientific training. As an alternative, many of the experiments may be performed as demonstrations by the teacher. If in doubt, discuss the particulars with your LEA adviser.

In addition, potentially hazardous reagents have been indicated in the pupils' instructions by a danger symbol so that teachers can advise pupils to take extra care with these chemicals. Further information about specific hazards associated with each reagent can be found in consulting Part 1 of the Appendix.

**Health and Safety at Work Act**  The purpose of the Act is to secure as far as possible the health, safety and welfare of persons at work. To this end the duties of both employers and employees are stated (Sections 2 and 7 respectively). Teachers come within the scope of that Act as employees of the LEA and Section 7 of the Act is specifically concerned with their duties as employees.

In addition, Section 4 imposes duties on those who are not employees but use non-domestic premises, for example, schools, made available to them as a place of work. Pupils come into this category.

It is beyond the scope of this book to give a detailed account of the responsibilities placed on LEAs, teachers and pupils in order to ensure safe working. However, if teachers act in their traditional 'in loco parentis' role, including encouraging pupils to use their common sense, this will certainly be in keeping with the spirit of the Act. Specifically, in relation to this book, it follows that there is obviously a duty on teachers to set an example of safe scientific practice and to encourage this in their pupils.

Inspectors of the Health and Safety Executive set up under the Act have the right of entry to schools for the purposes of the Act. In addition, they are very willing to give technical advice on safety matters when it is sought. If you do not know the address of your local Health and Safety Inspector, it can be obtained from the Health and Safety Executive, Baynards House, 1–13 Chepstow Place, Westbourne Grove, London W2 4TF.

# SECTION A

# Observation of food structure

## Experiment 1**

## Microscopic examination

### Purpose

To observe and draw the appearance of meat, plant foods, cereals and emulsions under the microscope.

### Materials

foods, eg:

    small piece of lean meat

    onion

    carrot

    potato (raw, partly cooked and cooked)

    whole wheat grain

    starch (rice, potato, maize, wheat, arrowroot)

    breadmaking flour

    milk (pasteurized and homogenized)

    margarine and low-fat spread

glycerol

⚠ Sudan III

methylene blue solution *or* malachite green solution

solution of iodine in potassium iodide

microscope with x10 eyepiece and x10 and x40 objective lenses

microscope slides

coverslips

singled-edged razor blade (or ordinary razor blade embedded in cork) **CARE**

mounted needles **CARE** (or sharpened pencil)

dropping pipettes (or eye droppers)

small spatula (or blunt knife)

grease pencil

filter paper (or blotting paper)

### Method

#### First prepare the food:

Be very careful with blades and needles. Your teacher will count them out to the class and count them back.

**Meat** Cut a very thin small slice 'along the grain'. Place on the microscope slide and tease out the fibres with the mounted needles. Add a drop of water and carefully lower the coverslip on to the specimen (Fig. 1.1) so that air bubbles are not introduced.

**Fig. 1.1**

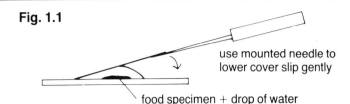

use mounted needle to lower cover slip gently

food specimen + drop of water

**Onion** Take a small piece of the paper-like tissue from between the onion layers. Place on a microscope slide, add a drop of water and lower a coverslip as in Fig. 1.1. Because this tissue is only one cell thick, this slide may be taken as the thinness to aim for when cutting sections.

**Carrot** Cut a very thin section from a carrot: it should be transparent and can be quite small in area. Place the section on a microscope slide, add a drop of water and lower a coverslip as in Fig. 1.1.

**Potato** Cut very thin sections from raw, partly cooked and cooked potato. Place on separate, labelled microscope slides. Add a drop of water and lower a coverslip as in Fig. 1.1.

**Whole wheat grain** Soak some grains in cold water overnight. Cut sections both lengthways and across the grain (Fig. 1.2.). The sections must be very thin indeed. Place the sections on separate microscope slides, add a drop of water and lower a coverslip as in Fig. 1.1.

**Fig. 1.2**      cut thin sections along the planes indicated by the broken lines

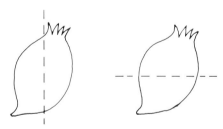

**Starch** Put a very small quantity of each type of starch on separate labelled microscope slides. Add a drop of glycerol and lower a coverslip as in Fig. 1.1.

**Flour dough** Use breadmaking flour and observe immediately after mixing with a small amount of water, and also after kneading for five minutes. Place a very small amount of the dough (about the size of a grain of rice) on the microscope slide. Tease out the dough with the mounted needles. Add a drop of glycerol and cover with the coverslip as in Fig. 1.1.

**Milk** Simply place a drop of milk on a microscope slide and lower a coverslip as in Fig. 1.1.

*cont./*

© *Forbes Publications Limited 1989*

**Margarine and low-fat spread** Take a very small scraping of the fat from the centre of the packet or block. Put the scraping on a microscope slide, cover with a coverslip and gently press the coverslip to squash the fat.

## Then examine the food:

Place the slide on the stage of the microscope and observe using first the x10 objective and then the x40 objective. A clearer image can be obtained with some foods if the amount of light passing through the specimen is reduced.

Observe and draw the unstained specimen. Clear labelled drawings should be made of a representative field for each slide. State the magnification, eg eyepiece x10 and objective x10 means that the total magnification is x100.

**The foods listed below may be stained as described and further drawings made:**

**potato, wheat, starch and flour dough:** to stain the starch granules, place a drop of iodine solution to one side of the coverslip. Touch the liquid at the other side of the coverslip with a small strip of filter paper. The iodine will be drawn between the coverslip and the slide, staining the starch granule as it passes. With care, this can be carried out, and observed under the microscope.

**milk, margarine and low-fat spread:** fat droplets may be stained with Sudan III and water droplets with methylene blue or malachite green solution.

## Result

### Look for the following:

**Meat** muscle fibres; striations along fibres; fat cells.

**Onion** cell walls bounding rectangular cells.

**Carrot** cells; plastids containing carotene within the cell.

**Potato** cells containing starch granules; shape of starch granules in raw, partly-cooked and cooked potato.

**Whole wheat grain** shape of wheat grain, along and across the grain; the crease; cells in the outer bran layers; starch granules embedded in a protein matrix in the endosperm; the beard and the germ in longitudinal section.

**Starch** the distinctive shape of each type of starch; characteristic markings on the potato starch.

**Flour dough** starch granules; gluten, in the form of strands in the developed dough.

**Milk** oil-in-water emulsion; finely-dispersed small fat droplets; even size in homogenized compared with pasteurized milk.

**Margarine and low-fat spread** water-in-oil emulsion; fat droplets in different margarines vary in size but for a given margarine they should be small and even in size.

## Suggestions for further work***

a Using a graticule, measure the dimensions of cells, starch granules and fat droplets.

b Observe cooked foods microscopically, eg meat, bread, cake. Care must be taken to obtain very thin specimens.

See also *Experiments 29 and 30 (Starch gelatinization)*.

4

# Experiment 1**
# Microscopic examination

## Introduction

The behaviour and appearance of foods during and after cooking can often be related to their microscopic structure. This applies to cellular foods such as meat and vegetables as well as to dispersions like milk and margarine.

The macroscopic appearance of the food should first be described, then a hand lens or low-power binocular microscope should be used to take a closer look at the surface of the food and at a section through it.

Although this experiment draws together the microscopic examination of a whole range of foods, it is not necessary to carry out all the parts of the experiments. Instead, it may be desirable to choose the parts that are relevant when a particular food is being studied.

## Materials

### Foods

See notes by the individual foods in the *Method* below. *Very* little food is needed – the specimen should be as small and as thin as possible. The onion tissue is useful as a guide to the desired thickness of other specimens.

### Reagents

a   Sudan III *(page 149)*, supplied in alcoholic solution, which stains fats and oils orange.

b   Methylene blue and malachite green are water-soluble dyes, supplied as powder or solution (see *page 147*).

c   Solution of iodine in potassium iodide (see *page 147*).

### Apparatus

a   The microscope should have a x10 eyepiece, x10 and x40 objective lenses if possible, to give a final magnification of x100 and x400, respectively.

b   Microscope slides are reusable and should be dust-free. Clean them by immersing in 70 per cent alcohol.

c   Coverslips should be discarded after use. If care is taken that the objective lens does not touch the specimen, a coverslip is not essential. In this case, however, there is a possibility of the specimen drying out unless the observations are made quickly.

d   Instead of a single-edged razor blade, a very sharp scalpel or an ordinary razor blade embedded in a cork may be used. For satisfactory results and for safety (to lessen the chance of slipping) all must be very sharp – a blunt blade is more dangerous than a

sharp one. They should be counted out and counted back.

e   Mounted needles are essential for teasing out meat fibres, useful for spreading dough, recommended for lowering coverslips. A sharp pencil or a long fingernail will perform this last task equally well. Again, needles must be counted out and counted back.

f   A small spatula is suggested for putting very small quantities of starch or margarine onto the slide, but with care a normal spatula or the pointed end of a kitchen knife could be used.

g   Filter paper or blotting paper will be used for drawing liquid between coverslip and slide. A small piece, about 5 cm by 1 cm, is needed.

## Method
### Preparation of the food

**Meat**   Best results will be seen if the raw meat (preferably beef) is very fresh. Cooked meat may be observed for comparison.

**Onion**   There is no need to cut a section. The papery tissue (epidermis) from between the layers is a very convenient example of a preparation one cell thick.

**Carrot and potato**   Very thin sections are needed. It is almost impossible to cut a section from a cooked vegetable – take a piece as small and thin as possible and spread on a slide without squashing.

**Wholewheat grain**   Other grains may be used, but all are difficult to section – they should be soaked in water overnight prior to sectioning. The grains could be cut in half first and observed under a binocular microscope or with a hand lens.

**Starch**   Use cornflour or arrowroot from a grocer; rice, potato and wheat starch from chemicals' suppliers (see *Appendix III*). Put a tiny amount on the slide, then, holding the other end of the slide, tap the narrow side on the bench. This will remove most of the starch but will leave enough for observation.

**Flour dough**   Sufficient dough must be available for kneading. This experiment is best done when gluten balls *(Experiment 49)* or bread are being made so that dough is not wasted and results can be linked.

**Milk**   Compare pasteurized and homogenized.

**Margarine and low-fat spread**   The fat should be squashed evenly – it takes practice to press the coverslip (with a non-greasy finger) the required amount without cracking it. Two types of fat can be studied on the same slide, with separate coverslips.

## Examination of the food

See notes on *page 5 and 154* about the use of a microscope. The most likely hazards here are:

a  the objective may touch, and perhaps crack, the coverslip. When focusing, always move the objective lens and the specimen away from each other while looking through the lens.

b  moisture, glycerol or fat will get onto the lens. Hands should be washed after preparing the food and there should be a good supply of lens tissues available. If the lens is too dirty to be cleaned with a tissue alone, use a drop of xylene.

Drawings *must* be made while the specimen is being observed. Look through the microscope with one eye and at the paper on which the drawing is being made with the other. It is tempting to make a rough sketch during the lesson, copying it later. If this is done the finished drawing will, at best, be simply a representation of what the specimen *should* have looked like.

## Result

**Meat**  Muscle fibres should be seen clearly (Fig. 1.1). Connective tissue is to be found between and around the fibres as well as forming sheets that are all too visible to the naked eye in some cuts. Fat cells can sometimes be seen within the muscle (marbling).

**Fig. 1.1**
Raw beef
(x100)

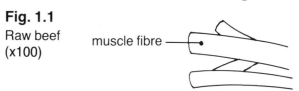
muscle fibre

With x400 total magnification, striations can be seen along the fibres (Fig. 1.2). These are bands of actin and myosin that, by sliding over each other, enable muscle to contract.

**Fig. 1.2**
Raw beef
(x400)

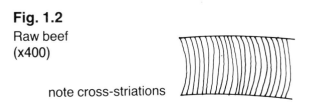
note cross-striations

**Onion**  Observe the cell walls around regular, rectangular cells (Fig. 1.3).

**Fig. 1.3**
Onion cells
(x400)

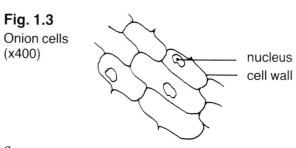
nucleus
cell wall

**Carrot**  Observe the cell walls and the bright orange inclusions in otherwise clear cells (Fig. 1.4). These are plastids, containing water-insoluble carotene which gives carrot its colour, and is a valuable source of vitamin A.

**Fig. 1.4**
Carrot cells
(x100)

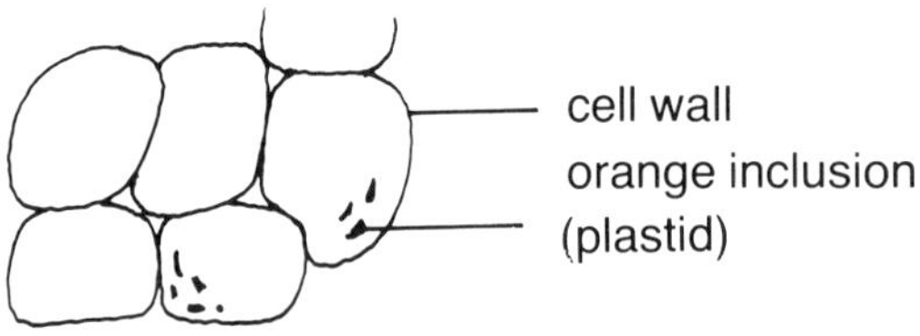

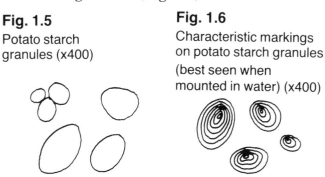
cell wall
orange inclusion (plastid)

**Potato**  Note the characteristic shape of potato starch granules (Fig. 1.5). Move the fine-focusing knob to observe the markings on the unstained granules (Fig. 1.6).

**Fig. 1.5**
Potato starch
granules (x400)

**Fig. 1.6**
Characteristic markings on potato starch granules (best seen when mounted in water) (x400)

Observe the cell walls and the shape of the raw cells (Fig. 1.7). Count the number of starch granules in each of, say, ten cells.

**Fig. 1.7**
Potato cells
(x100)

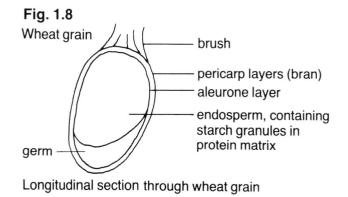
starch granule
cell wall

Note the swelling of starch granules in stained and unstained, partly cooked and fully cooked specimens. The starch molecules – amylose and amylopectin – have taken up water, mainly from within the cell.

**Wholewheat grain**  It will be a fortunate (and skilful) student who observes all the items mentioned in the *Pupils' Material*. Fig. 1.8 shows the type of drawing that should be made.

**Fig. 1.8**
Wheat grain

brush
pericarp layers (bran)
aleurone layer
endosperm, containing starch granules in protein matrix
germ

Longitudinal section through wheat grain

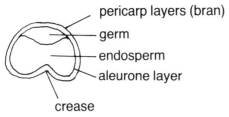

cross section
through wheat grain

**Starch** Students should first observe known samples (Fig. 1.9) then attempt to identify unknown samples.

**Fig. 1.9**
Starch granules

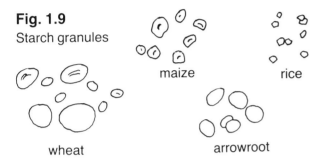

maize

rice

wheat

arrowroot

Disintegration of the granules may be observed by boiling them and removing samples for microscopic observation at one minute intervals.

**Flour dough** Starch granules and gluten strands should be seen in the developed dough. Relate this to the macroscopic and microscopic structure of cooked bread – when the bread rises the gluten expands, surrounding gas bubbles. The starch granules hydrate and eventually the heat causes the gluten to set.

**Milk** Note the fat globules in a watery solution. The globules in pasteurized milk vary in size, but in homogenized milk they are smaller and of even size.

**Margarine and low-fat spread** Observe different margarines – soft, hard, polyunsaturated, as well as low-fat spreads. These are water-in-oil emulsions; look for density and evenness in size of water droplets.

## Suggestions for further work***

To measure the size of cells, starch granules etc. an eyepiece graticule and a stage graticule will be needed (see *page 153* for details of their use).

# SECTION B

# Tests for food constituents

## Experiment 2** ⚠

# Molisch's test

This experiment must be carried out in a laboratory under the supervision of a teacher with appropriate scientific background.

## Purpose

A general test for carbohydrates.

## Materials

1% glucose solution

1% sucrose solution

1% starch solution

Molisch's reagent

⚠ concentrated sulphuric acid

4 test tubes

test tube rack

grease pencil

dropping pipettes

length of narrow glass tubing (about 25 cm)

## Method

Make sure you are wearing eye protection before starting this experiment. Should you spill any acid on yourself or your clothes, **quickly** apply copious amounts of water.

1 Place about 1 cm$^3$ of each carbohydrate solution in separate labelled test tubes.

2 Set up a control tube containing about 1 cm$^3$ water.

3 Using a dropping pipette, add 3 drops of Molisch's reagent to each tube (Fig. 2.1). Mix well by swirling.

**Fig. 2.1**

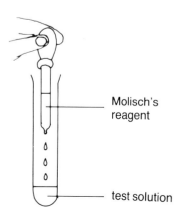

Molisch's reagent

test solution

4 Slowly and **CAREFULLY**, using a glass tube, add about 1 cm$^3$ concentrated sulphuric acid down the side of each tube (Fig. 2.2). **DO NOT MIX.**

**Fig. 2.2**

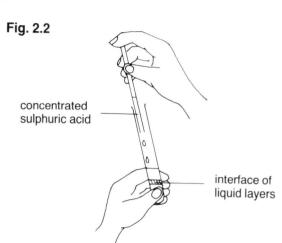

concentrated sulphuric acid

interface of liquid layers

## Result

Formation of a purple ring at the interface of the liquid layers shows the presence of carbohydrate.

## Suggestions for further work*

Carry out Molisch's test on a protein (eg egg white) and a fat (eg olive oil).

8

# Experiment 2\*\*
# Molisch's test

## Introduction

This is a sensitive test for all carbohydrates, whether free or combined. A positive reaction may also be given by some proteins containing a carbohydrate grouping in their molecule. Egg-white contains such a protein and will give a weakly positive reaction.

This experiment involves the use of concentrated sulphuric acid, which must be handled with care. Eye protection **must** be worn. In the event of a spillage, gallons of water must be applied **quickly** – this acid can penetrate clothes in seconds and burn the skin. With younger pupils, the teacher may prefer to carry out this experiment as a demonstration.

## Materials

a  See Appendix I for the method of making up percentage solutions and of preparing a solution of starch.

b  Molisch's reagent, *page 148*.

## Method

a  More control of dropwise addition is obtained using a glass tube as suggested, rather than a dropping pipette, so this method is advised when adding concentrated sulphuric acid.

b  Disposal of the acid should be carried out by slowly tipping the contents of the tube a little at a time into the sink and flushing away with plenty of water.

c  Treat acid spillage on bench, clothes or skin immediately with copious amounts of water.

## Result

Glucose, sucrose and starch all give a positive result with Molisch's test.

On treatment with concentrated sulphuric acid, carbohydrates are partially dehydrated to form the substance furfural, or one of its derivatives. The furfural, or furfural derivative, then condenses with the $\propto$-naphthol present in Molisch's reagent to form a purple compound.

## Suggestions for further work\*

Proteins (with some exceptions as indicated in the *Introduction* above) and fats do not give a positive result.

# Experiment 3*

# Benedict's test

## Purpose

To distinguish between reducing and non-reducing sugars.

## Materials

1% glucose solution
1% fructose solution
1% maltose solution
1% lactose solution
1% sucrose solution
Benedict's solution

$250\,cm^3$ beaker
bunsen burner
tripod
gauze
flameproof bench mat
6 test tubes
test tube rack
grease pencil
test tube holder

## Method

1 Half-fill the beaker with water and bring to the boil.

2 Place about $1\,cm^3$ of each carbohydrate solution in separate labelled test tubes.

3 Set up a control tube containing about $1\,cm^3$ water.

4 Add about $5\,cm^3$ Benedict's solution to each tube.

5 Put the test tubes in the boiling waterbath for about 2 minutes (Fig. 3.1).

## Result

Production of a green, yellow or red precipitate shows the presence of a 'reducing' sugar.

**Note** The term 'reducing' does not mean that the sugar is an aid to slimming. The word refers to the sugar's chemical property of being able to reduce the amount of oxygen in some substances during a chemical reaction.

**Fig. 3.1**

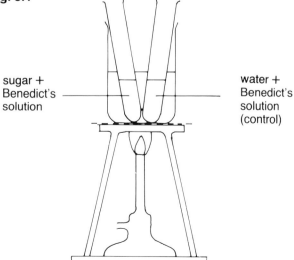

sugar +
Benedict's
solution

water +
Benedict's
solution
(control)

# Experiment 3*
# Benedict's test

## Introduction

Benedict's test is a more reliable, convenient and safer test for reducing sugars than the alternative and commonly used Fehling's test. Fehling's test suffers from the fact that Fehling's solution deteriorates on standing and so must be freshly prepared by mixing the constituents (Fehling's A and B) together shortly before the test is carried out. Also, Benedict's solution is not only less liable to reduction by substances other than sugars but is only mildly alkaline and therefore less caustic than Fehling's solution. For this reason a description of Fehling's test has not been included in the *Pupils' Material*. However, the theory underlying both these tests is similar and is explained in the *Results* section below.

Incidentally, the term 'reducing sugar' can often cause confusion in pupils' minds. Of course, it refers to the property of such sugars as chemical reducing agents, and does not indicate a low calorific value and suitability for inclusion in a reducing diet!

## Materials

a  See Appendix I for the method of making up percentage solutions.

b  Note that the common monosaccharide sugar galactose is not included as it does not normally occur except combined with glucose to form lactose.

c  Benedict's solution, *page 146*.

## Method

Often the results will become clear before the two minute period suggested has elapsed.

## Result

All the sugars tested, with the notable exception of sucrose, which is a non-reducing sugar, give a positive Benedict's test.

The basis of Benedict's (and Fehling's) test is that the sugar reduces copper(II) sulphate, a blue solution, to insoluble yellow or red copper(I) oxide. Sometimes, with very low sugar concentrations, the yellow precipitate can be partially masked by the blue coloration to give a greenish appearance – this is also a positive indication of reducing sugar.

All monosaccharide sugars (glucose, fructose) and the disaccharides maltose and lactose possess a potential free reducing group (either aldehyde or ketone) and are therefore reducing sugars. However, the nature of the glucose–fructose bond in the disaccharide sucrose obscures its reducing potential. Hence, sucrose is a non-reducing sugar.

# Experiment 4*

## Barfoed's test

### Purpose

To distinguish between monosaccharide and disaccharide sugars.

### Materials

1% glucose solution
1% fructose solution
1% maltose solution
1% lactose solution
Barfoed's reagent

$250 \, cm^3$ beaker
bunsen burner
tripod
gauze
flameproof bench mat
5 test tubes
test tube rack
grease pencil
test tube holder

### Method

Make sure you are wearing eye protection.

1 Half-fill the beaker with water and bring to the boil.

2 Place about $1 \, cm^3$ of each carbohydrate solution in separate labelled test tubes.

3 Set up a control tube containing about $1 \, cm^3$ water.

4 Add about $5 \, cm^3$ Barfoed's reagent to each tube.

5 Put the test tubes in the boiling waterbath for 3-4 minutes.

### Result

Formation of a green, yellow or red precipitate shows the presence of monosaccharide.

# Experiment 5*

## 'Clinistix' test

### Purpose

A specific test for glucose.

### Materials

1% glucose solution
1% sucrose solution
'Clinistix' reagent strips

dropping pipette
white tile

### Method

1 Place a few drops of glucose solution on the white tile.

2 Dip a reagent strip into the solution and remove immediately. Do not contaminate the strip with your fingers or the bench top before or after the test.

3 Repeat the test with sucrose solution, using a fresh reagent strip.

4 Carry out a control using water instead of sugar solution.

### Result

After 10 seconds observe any colour change. Darkening of the light pink reagent to purple shows the presence of glucose.

# Experiment 4*
# Barfoed's test

## Introduction

This test is specific for monosaccharide sugars only. It is very sensitive, and can be used to detect very small concentrations.

## Materials

a See Appendix I for the method of making up percentage solutions.

b Barfoed's reagent, *page 146.*

## Method

Although, as stated in the *Introduction,* this test is very sensitive, if only minute concentrations of the monosaccharide sugar are present, the precipitate may not be visible until the tube has been allowed to stand undisturbed for about 15 minutes to allow the precipitate to settle.

## Result

A positive test is given by the monosaccharides glucose and fructose but not by the disaccharides maltose and lactose.

In alkaline solution, as in Benedict's (and Fehling's) tests, all reducing sugars precipitate copper(I) oxide from copper(II) salts. However, in acid solution, only the more strongly reducing monosaccharides will do this. This is the basis of Barfoed's reagent which is a solution of copper(II) acetate in acetic acid.

# Experiment 5*
# 'Clinistix' test

## Introduction

'Clinistix' reagent strips provide a rapid and convenient method for the specific detection of glucose in solution. They are very sensitive, and will give a positive result at glucose concentrations as low as 0.1%. The test reagent will not react with other reducing sugars such as lactose, maltose, fructose and galactose.

## Materials

a See Appendix I for the method of making up percentage solutions.

b 'Clinistix' reagent strips (see *page 146*). The suppliers provide full instructions and a colour checking chart with the strips.

## Method

The extreme sensitivity of the test means that every precaution must be taken to ensure that the control or sucrose tests do not give spurious results due to contamination with minute amounts of glucose.

## Result

Only glucose will give a positive result. The test papers are impregnated with a dye and with glucose oxidase, an enzyme which acts specifically on glucose only. When glucose is present, the resulting complex series of reactions produce the colour changes observed. The test is semi-quantitative – comparison with the colour charts supplied with the reagent strips provide an approximation of the glucose concentration of the test solution.

# Experiment 6*

## Iodine test

### Purpose

Test for starch.

### Materials

1% starch solution
solution of iodine in potassium iodide

2 test tubes
test tube rack
grease pencil
dropping pipette

## Method

1 Put about $2\,cm^3$ starch solution into a labelled test tube.

2 Set up a control using about $2\,cm^3$ water.

3 Add 2 drops iodine solution to each tube.

## Result

A deep blue colour shows the presence of starch.

## Suggestions for further work*

Carry out the iodine test on starch powder, glycogen solution, sucrose solution.

# Experiment 7**

## Identification of carbohydrates

### Purpose

To identify an unknown carbohydrate.

### Materials

unknown 1% carbohydrate solutions, labelled
   $A, B, C$, etc.
Benedict's solution
Barfoed's reagent
'Clinistix' reagent strips
solution of iodine in potassium iodide

$250\,cm^3$ beaker
bunsen burner
tripod       or small pan of water
gauze         on a hotplate
flameproof bench mat
8 test tubes for each unknown solution
test tube rack
grease pencil
dropping pipettes (or eye dropper)

### Method

1 Divide each unknown solution into 5 portions, in labelled test tubes.

2 Using separate portions of the unknown solution and controls when necessary, work through the following scheme. Record the results very carefully.

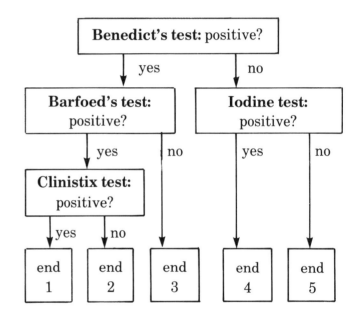

## Result

The unknown solution should correspond with one of the **'end'** boxes shown on the scheme:

End 1   monosaccharide: glucose

End 2   monosaccharide other than glucose, eg fructose

End 3   reducing disaccharide: maltose, lactose

End 4   non-reducing carbohydrate: starch

End 5   non-reducing carbohydrate other than starch, possibly sucrose

# Experiment 6*
# Iodine test

## Introduction
The well-known iodine test can be conveniently used to demonstrate the presence of starch, both in solid form as well as in solution.

## Materials
a The method of making up a starch solution is described on *page 148*.

b Iodine in potassium iodide, *page 147*.

## Method
The test is sensitive so every precaution should be taken to ensure that the control tube is not contaminated with traces of starch.

## Result
The characteristic blue–black coloration is due to the presence of amylose. Starch consists of two constituents, amylose and amylopectin. Amylose is a long straight-chain polymer of glucose units with a molecular weight of 10 000–20 000. These chains are so long that they form spirals. Although it is the minor component of starch (about 25% by weight), it is largely inclusion of the iodine molecules in the turns of these spirals which alters the light absorption properties of the starch, giving the blue–black colour. On the other hand, the major component of starch, amylopectin, is a branched chain polymer of glucose units. Although a much larger molecule than amylose (molecular weight 500 000 – 1 million), the extensive branching means that no individual chain is long enough to form a spiral. Hence, with iodine, a slightly different absorption complex is formed which produces a reddish–black colouration, masked by the blue–black amylose-iodine complex.

## Suggestions for further work*
A positive result is obtained with starch powder.

Glycogen (sometimes called 'animal starch') is the storage polysaccharide of most mammals including humans. It is a branched molecule of glucose units, soluble in cold water, and gives a red–brown colour with iodine solution. In fact, it is similar in structure and reaction with iodine to amylopectin.

Sucrose solution will not, of course, give a positive iodine test.

# Experiment 7**
# Identification of carbohydrates

## Introduction
By following the scheme systematically, an unknown carbohydrate can be identified. Any carbohydrate solution can be given as an unknown. A suggested combination of unknowns would be:

*A* sucrose or maltose, *B* starch and *C* glucose or fructose.

In addition, if desired, the pupils could initially confirm the presence of carbohydrate using Molisch's test. In this case, a non-carbohydrate unknown such as salt solution or plain water could be given for comparison.

Of course, it is expected that the pupils will previously have performed the Benedict's, Barfoed's, 'Clinistix' and iodine test on known solutions *(Experiments 3-6)*. When these practicals are coming to an end it is a good idea to have a number of unknowns to reinforce the practical technique of pupils who finish early.

As an exercise in scientific working and logical deduction this experiment provides a useful way of assessing pupils' understanding of the tests for carbohydrates.

## Materials
All reagents and apparatus used have already been mentioned – see *Experiments 3-6*.

## Method
The tests used are described in *Experiments 3-6*.

Since many practical steps need to be performed, it is vitally important that the need for very careful labelling of test tubes and recording of results is impressed upon the pupils. Similarly, it is essential to use perfectly clean apparatus and to avoid sources of contamination – for example, a common error is to use a dropping pipette to transfer one solution and then inadvertently dip it into another solution. Confusing and misleading results could occur unless adequate precautions are taken.

## Result
Correct identification of a variety of unknown solutions depends on the factors already mentioned. Note that the scheme cannot distinguish between maltose and lactose, and that sucrose cannot be positively identified as such but only as a non-reducing carbohydrate other than starch.

# Experiment 8*

## Grease spot test

### Purpose

A test for fats and oils.

### Materials

olive oil

dropping pipettes
filter paper

### Method

1 Place a drop of olive oil on the filter paper.

2 Place a drop of water on to a second piece of filter paper.

3 Hold both pieces of paper up to the light and observe.

4 Leave the papers to dry and again examine.

Record your observations.

### Result

A *permanent* translucent stain indicates fat or oil.

### Suggestions for further work***

Try washing out the oil-stain from the filter paper with (a) water and (b) ether.

**CARE:** Ether is poisonous and flammable – use small quantities from a dropping pipette, preferably in a fume cupboard. There must be no naked flame or hotplate in the room, as the heavy vapour can creep a considerable distance along benches and ignite far from its source.

# Experiment 9*

## Sudan test

### Purpose

A selective stain for fats and oils.

### Materials

olive oil
⚠ Sudan III solution
2 test tubes
test tube rack
grease pencil
dropping pipettes (or eye droppers)

### Method

1 Add 12 drops of olive oil to a labelled test tube one-third full of water

2 Shake the mixture briskly – note that an unstable emulsion is formed.

3 Add 5 drops Sudan III to the emulsion and also to a control test tube containing water only.

4 Shake both tubes vigorously, place in the test tube rack. Examine the contents after 10 minutes.

### Result

The red dye is taken up selectively by the oil droplets which form a surface layer on standing.

### Suggestions for further work*

Use a dropping pipette to suck up the red-stained oil layer. Add to a large volume of water in a test tube and shake vigorously. Observe the retention of the dye by the oil droplets.

# Experiment 8*
# Grease spot test

## Introduction

This experiment and *Experiment 9* describe two methods of showing the presence of fats. The production of a permanent translucent stain is the simplest test for fats and oils. If solid fat is used instead of an oil the stain is made by simply rubbing the meat fat, lard, etc onto the filter paper.

## Materials

a  Olive oil – see *page 148*.

b  If filter paper is not available, any absorbent material can be used, for example, any unglazed paper such as typing paper or newspaper.

## Method

Use separate dropping pipettes for the oil and water.

## Result

A translucent stain, when compared to the surrounding filter paper, appears lighter when viewed against a bright background. The essential feature of this test is that fats and oils leave a permanent stain. (Water also temporarily renders the filter paper translucent, but this disappears on drying.)

## Suggestions for further work***

The oil stain cannot be removed with water as the two liquids are immiscible, hence an organic solvent such as ether is required. The inflammability of ether means that there should be no naked flames or hot plates in the room. Care must be taken to ensure that the toxic vapour is not inhaled.

Cloth fragments can also be used to test the removal of fatty stains using ether. Other organic solvents such as alcohol (fat is sparingly soluble in cold alcohol) and proprietary cleaners can be tested in this way.

# Experiment 9*
# Sudan test

## Introduction

Sudan III is a red dye which is selectively taken up by fats and oils so providing the basis of the test.

In order to understand the method, the pupils will need to know that an emulsion is a fine dispersion of minute droplets of one liquid in another. When oil is shaken in water the emulsion is unstable, the oil droplets coalescing at the surface after a few minutes.

## Materials

a  Olive oil, *page 148*.

b  Sudan III solution, *page 149* (there are, in fact, other Sudan stains, such as Sudan black, which could be used as alternatives). The solution should be handled with care as it is flammable.

## Method

a  It is important to use the quantities suggested. In particular, if too much dye is added, its selective uptake by the oil will be masked by the presence of excess dye in the water.

b  For reasons given above, a control tube containing water only is needed for comparative purposes, and exactly the same amount of dye must be added to this as to the experimental tube.

## Result

When the dye is added to the emulsion it is dissolved in oil droplets. When the droplets coalesce at the surface on standing, this concentrates the dye, giving a darker red appearance in this region. In the absence of fat the dye will be evenly distributed in the water, as in the control. Providing the same amount of dye and water has been used in each case, the aqueous phase of the experimental tube should be lighter in colour than the control due to concentration of the dye in the surface oil layer.

## Suggestions for further work*

The purpose of this experiment is to show that the oil droplets will retain the dye even when they are shaken up in a large volume of clear water. On standing, the oil will coalesce at the surface with the dye and the water will remain unstained.

It is important that only the oil layer is used, so it is advisable to use a dropping pipette with a very fine tip.

# Experiment 10*

# Biuret test

## Purpose

Qualitative test for proteins.

## Materials

raw egg white

⚠ dilute sodium hydroxide solution

1% copper sulphate solution

$100\,cm^3$ beaker

stirring rod

grease pencil

2 test tubes

test tube rack

dropping pipette (or eye dropper)

## Method

Wear eye protection.

1 Dilute the egg white with an equal volume of water in a beaker and stir vigorously.

2 Pour about $5\,cm^3$ of this diluted egg white into a labelled test tube. Pour an equal volume of water into a similar test tube.

3 To each tube add about $1\,cm^3$ of dilute sodium hydroxide solution and shake the tube.

4 Add 1% copper sulphate solution to each tube, a drop at a time, shaking after the addition of each drop.

## Result

Development of a violet colour indicates the presence of protein.

## Suggestions for further work*

Carry out the Biuret test on saliva. This contains the enzyme salivary amylase.

# Experiment 10*
# Biuret test

## Introduction

This experiment and *Experiment 11* describe two good general tests for proteins. This book, however, does not include Millon's test, another traditional test for proteins, for safety reasons which are explained below. A positive Biuret test is given by nearly all compounds containing two or more peptide bonds, for example, proteins and the substance biuret (after which the test is named, see Fig. 10.1 below) but not by free amino acids.

**Fig. 10.1** Biuret

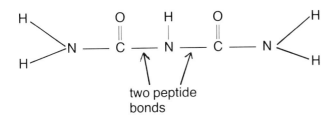

two peptide bonds

## Materials

**a** Dilute sodium hydroxide solution (harmful) see *page 148*.

**b** 1% copper sulphate solution, see *page 147*.

**c** Suppliers stock 'Biuret reagent', which, in addition to copper sulphate and sodium hydroxide, contains sodium potassium tartrate (rochelle salt) and potassium iodide as stabilizers. The method of carrying out the test described here is just as sensitive, and it is not necessary to incur the expense of purchasing the ready-made reagent from a dealer.

## Method

**a** The control tube is necessary for comparison with any positive result, especially with very small protein concentrations, when the violet colour may be very delicate indeed.

**b** Because the violet colour may be very faint with small protein concentrations, the copper sulphate must be added dropwise, shaking and observing after the addition of each drop. If this is not done, a blue coloration due to excess copper sulphate may mask the positive result.

**c** Spare egg-white solution can be retained and used in *Experiment 11*.

## Result

The chemistry involved in the test is quite complex, but basically the characteristic violet colour is formed due to complexes with copper II ions.

## Suggestions for further work*

Saliva gives a good positive Biuret test due to the presence of the enzyme salivary amylase (all enzymes are, of course, proteins). The pupils can be reminded of this when carrying out *Experiment 27* using this enzyme.

### Note on Millon's test

This traditional test for proteins involves boiling the protein with Millon's reagent, when a red precipitate is formed. However, Millon's reagent is prepared by dissolving mercury in fuming nitric acid to give a solution of mercuric and mercurous nitrates in nitric and nitrous acids, and its use is *not* recommended due to possible hazards of laboratory contamination by the mercury salts. Mercury vaporises readily and is a cumulative heavy-metal poison. Its use in schools is to be strongly discouraged.

In fact, as Millon's test is a reaction given by tyrosine, free or combined in protein, *Experiment 11* is a perfectly good substitute and, although not without its own hazards, is suggested as a safer alternative.

# Experiment 11***

## Xanthoproteic test

This experiment must be carried out in a laboratory under the supervision of a teacher with the appropriate scientific background.

## Purpose

A qualitative test for protein.

## Materials

raw egg white solution, diluted 1:1 with water

⚠ concentrated nitric acid

⚠ concentrated (0.880) ammonia solution

250 cm³ beaker
bunsen burner
tripod                          } or small pan of water on a hotplate
gauze
flameproof bench mat
2 test tubes
test tube rack
grease pencil
length of narrow glass tubing (about 25 cm)
dropping pipette (or eye dropper)
test tube holder

## Method

Make sure you are wearing eye protection before starting this experiment.

Spillages of nitric acid or ammonia must be treated immediately with copious amounts of water.

1  Half-fill the beaker with water and bring to the boil.

2  To about 1 cm³ of the egg white solution in a labelled test tube add about 1 cm³ concentrated nitric acid. **CARE** – use glass tubing to transfer the acid as shown in Fig. 11.1.

**Fig. 11.1**

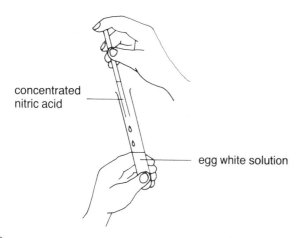

concentrated nitric acid

egg white solution

3  Carry out a control experiment, using 1 cm³ water instead of the egg white solution.

4  Heat by placing the tubes in the beaker of boiling water for 1 minute.

5  **Cool well** under running water and **cautiously** add concentrated ammonia dropwise to form a layer on the surface. **Do not mix.** Allow the tubes to stand.

## Result

On adding the nitric acid a yellow coloration appears. When the ammonia is added an orange ring at the interface shows the presence of protein.

## Suggestions for further work***

Carry out the Xanthoproteic test on hair or fingernail clippings. These contain the protein keratin.

# Experiment 11***
# Xanthoproteic test

## Introduction

Strictly speaking, this is a test for aromatic amino acids, that is, those amino acids which contain a benzene ring – for example, phenylalanine, tyrosine and tryptophan. A positive result is therefore given by all proteins containing an aromatic amino acid. It is also given by free aromatic amino acids. Hence, to be reasonably certain that an unknown substance is, in fact, protein, it is wise to perform more than one test. The combination of a positive Xanthoproteic test together with a positive Biuret test (described in *Experiment 10*) provides good evidence that protein is present.

## Materials

Great care must be taken in performing this test due to the highly corrosive and toxic nature of concentrated nitric acid *(page 148)* and 0.880 ammonia *(page 147)*. Spillages of either of these solutions on the bench or on the skin must be treated immediately with a large volume of water. In addition, pupils must be warned on no account to sniff the ammonia solution which gives off an extremely unpleasant, irritating vapour. For the same reason, the solution must be kept in a small bottle with a secure stopper which is only removed for the few seconds necessary to dispense it.

## Method

a   As in *Experiment 2,* a glass tube is suggested – this gives better control when transferring concentrated acids. Another tube may be used, if desired, for dropwise addition of the ammonia solution.

b   Again the need for a control for comparison should be emphasized. Apart from being good scientific practice when pupils start testing unknown solutions or foods, it is important that they should know that a negative result may still produce discernible changes.

c   The test tube and its contents must be cooled well before adding the ammonia, otherwise a more vigorous reaction and spitting will result.

## Result

This reaction depends on the nitration of the benzene ring (see *Introduction* above) to form yellow nitro-compounds which turn orange on the addition of ammonia.

## Suggestions for further work***

Hair and nails will give a positive result.

# Experiment 12**

## Protein combustion

### Purpose

To demonstrate that protein contains nitrogen.

### Materials

raw egg white

red litmus paper
bunsen burner
flameproof bench mat
ignition tube
test tube holder
forceps (or tweezers)

### Method

Make sure you are wearing eye protection before starting this experiment.

1 Place a small portion of the egg white in the ignition tube and heat strongly. **CARE.**

2 During heating, use the forceps to suspend a dampened piece of red litmus paper over the mouth of the tube (Fig. 12.1).

**Fig. 12.1**

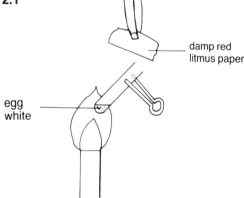

damp red litmus paper

egg white

3 Waft the fumes towards you and smell cautiously. **Do not** point the test tube directly at your nose or face.

### Result

Record what you see and smell. Note the charring and 'burning flesh' odour characteristic of proteins. Evolution of ammonia will turn the red litmus blue. What does this indicate about the nature of ammonia? Why does evolution of ammonia indicate the presence of nitrogen in the protein?

### Suggestions for further work**

Perform the experiment with a carbohydrate (starch or sucrose) and a fat.

# Experiment 13**

## Sulphur test

### Purpose

To show that proteins contain sulphur.

### Materials

raw egg white solution
⚠ 40% sodium hydroxide solution
⚠ lead acetate solution

$250 \, cm^3$ beaker
bunsen burner
tripod                    or small pan of water
gauze                     on a hotplate
flameproof bench mat
test tube
test tube rack
dropping pipettes (or eye droppers)
test tube holder

### Method

Make sure you are wearing eye protection before starting this experiment.

1 Half-fill the beaker with water and bring to the boil.

2 To about $1 \, cm^3$ of the egg white solution in a test tube add about $2 \, cm^3$ sodium hydroxide solution (**CARE** – use a dropping pipette).

3 Heat by placing the tube in the beaker of boiling water for 3 minutes.

4 Place the tube in the test tube rack and add 2–3 drops of lead acetate solution.

### Result

A black or brown colour shows the presence of sulphur.

### Suggestions for further work**

Repeat the experiment with a carbohydrate (starch or sucrose solution) and a fat.

# Experiment 12**
# Protein combustion

## Introduction

This demonstration, that proteins contain nitrogen, is based on the evolution of ammonia, so obviously pupils will need to have prior knowledge that ammonia itself is a compound of nitrogen and hydrogen, $NH_3$.

For some proteins, the evolution of ammonia on heating can be increased by the addition of soda lime. This has not been described in the present experiment as egg-white evolves ammonia readily on heating without the need for soda lime.

## Materials

a  Litmus paper, see *page 147*.

b  An ignition tube (see *page 153*) is necessary – an ordinary test tube would shatter if the contents were heated strongly to dryness in this way.

## Method

a  The litmus paper needs to be damp so that the gaseous ammonia will dissolve, with the production of the ammonium ion which turns the litmus blue.

b  The use of the hand to waft gaseous fumes gently towards the nose is a safe scientific practice which should be encouraged – many chemicals (for example 0.880 ammonia used in *Experiment 11*) give off extremely pungent fumes and incautious sniffing can have distressing effects.

## Result

Initially, water vapour (steam) will be observed, then the charring, accompanied by the characteristic odour. Litmus turns blue, indicating an alkaline gas. The only common alkaline gas is ammonia. As ammonia itself contains nitrogen this provides good evidence that the protein from which it is derived on combustion also contains nitrogen.

## Suggestions for further work**

Starch, sucrose and fats contain the elements carbon, hydrogen and oxygen only, and do not release ammonia on combustion.

# Experiment 13**
# Sulphur test

## Introduction

The vast majority of proteins contain sulphur due to the presence of sulphur-containing amino acids, whereas carbohydrates and fats very rarely contain this element. The nature of the chemicals in this experiment make it preferable to carry it out in a properly equipped laboratory.

## Materials

a  The method of making up percentage solutions is given in Appendix I

b  40% sodium hydroxide (see *page 148*) is extremely caustic and should be used with care. Spillages and splashes on skin and clothing should be treated with large quantities of water.

c  To prepare the egg-white solution, dilute raw egg-white with an equal volume of water in a beaker and stir vigorously.

d  The lead acetate solution (see *page 147*) must be freshly prepared just prior to the practical session. Lead is a cumulative poison and the danger of accidental ingestion of the solution (eg spillage on the hand being transferred to the mouth) must be emphasized very strongly indeed.

## Method

Because of the danger of large-scale spillage, pupils must be discouraged from pouring caustic liquids directly from the bottle, hence the use of a dropping pipette is recommended.

## Result

The strongly alkaline sodium hydroxide liberates sulphur from the amino acids cystine and cysteine (which are present in virtually all proteins) and forms sodium sulphide. On adding lead acetate solution, insoluble lead sulphide is precipitated, giving the black or brown coloration.

The reaction is negative for the other sulphur-containing amino acid methionine – its sulphur is not converted to inorganic sulphide.

# Experiment 14**

# Tests for macronutrients

## Purpose

To test a variety of foods for the presence of carbohydrate, fat and protein.

## Materials

selection of foods eg

*liquid/semi-liquid foods* – milk, egg white, egg yolk, fruit juices, jam/honey/syrup

*solid foods* – meat, fish, bread, biscuits, butter, lard, cheese, cereals, fruit, vegetables, seeds (eg sunflower)

Benedict's solution
Barfoed's reagent
'Clinistix' test papers
solution of iodine in potassium iodide
⚠ dilute hydrochloric acid
⚠ dilute sodium hydroxide solution
1% copper sulphate solution
⚠ Sudan III

| | |
|---|---|
| sharp knife | grease pencil |
| chopping board | boiling tubes |
| filter paper | test tubes |
| filter funnel | test tube rack |
| conical flasks | glass stirring rod |
| pestle and mortar | dropping pipettes or |
| silver sand | eye droppers |
| 250 cm³ beaker | |
| bunsen burner | |
| tripod | or small pan of water |
| gauze | on a hotplate |
| flameproof bench mat | |

## Method

Make sure you are wearing eye protection. Prepare the chosen food sample and test as follows:

### Liquid/semi-liquid foods

1 Dilute semi-liquid or strongly coloured foods with water and shake well prior to testing – in some cases it may be necessary to filter first in order to remove solid debris.

2 Apply the tests directly. Test for carbohydrate using the scheme shown in *Experiment 7*. Use the *Sudan test (Experiment 9)* to investigate the presence of fat and the *Biuret test (Experiment 10)* for protein.

### Solid foods

3 Try the *Iodine test* for starch *(Experiment 6)* and *Grease spot test* for fat *(Experiment 8)* on slices of the solid food. (Use a clean knife and separate chopping board to cut up each type of food so as to avoid any mixing of different foods which could confuse the results.)

4 Next crush fragments of the food in a mortar. In the case of 'soft' foods the addition of some silver sand will provide the necessary abrasive to help reduce the food to a finely divided state.

5 Add some of the crushed food to a boiling tube one-third full of water and boil, stirring briskly with a glass rod.

6 Place in the test tube rack and allow to stand for 10 minutes. Use a dropping pipette to remove a drop of the upper layer for retesting the food for fat, this time using the *Sudan test (Experiment 9)*.

7 Filter the remaining solution and test the filtrate for carbohydrate using the scheme in *Experiment 7* and for protein using the *Biuret test (Experiment 10)*.

## Result

Copy the table below and record your results as + (present) or − (not found) in each column.

**Table of results for Experiment 14**

| Food | Carbohydrate | | | | | Fat | Protein |
|---|---|---|---|---|---|---|---|
| | Monosaccharide sugar | | Disaccharide sugar | | | | |
| | glucose | other | reducing | non-reducing possibly sucrose | Starch | | |
| | | | | | | | |

# Experiment 14**
# Tests for macronutrients

## Introduction

Testing for carbohydrates, fats and proteins in actual foods is the culmination of the tests on the 'pure' substances carried out in *Experiments 2 – 11*. Now that the pupils know what the various positive (and negative) results look like they should be able to apply this knowledge to testing foods.

The various tests are carried out as described in the *Pupils' Material* under the relevant experiment. However, for reliable results it is first necessary to treat particular foodstuffs in different ways prior to testing. Suggestions on suitable treatments are given in the method.

## Materials

a The foods listed are simply suggestions, any other food may be included. Care must be taken to keep the different foods completely separate from each other. For example, it is necessary to keep chopping boards and knives scrupulously clean to avoid contamination of one food with another. Similarly, if pupils have touched one food they must wash their hands thoroughly before handling another.

b Details of all reagents can be found in Appendix I.

c Silver sand is useful as an abrasive when grinding up some solid foods.

d Obviously the number of boiling tubes, test tubes, dropping pipettes, etc., required will depend on the number of foods to be tested which, in turn, will depend on the time available.

## Method

a **Liquid/semi-liquid foods** These are the easiest to deal with as they merely need diluting with water before applying the tests. In fact, milk can be tested directly without dilution. Reddish-coloured foods will need considerable dilution in order that the red precipitate produced from a positive Benedict's or Barfoed's test is not masked by the original colour.

b **Solid foods** The iodine and grease-spot tests can be carried out directly on the food. However, a food may *contain* fat but still not give a translucent stain when rubbed onto filter paper. In this case, extraction of the fat with boiling water as described in steps 5 and 6 in the *Pupils' Material* will enable the fat droplets to be detected using the Sudan test. Note that an alternative method of extracting fat from food in sufficient quantities to be tested is by using ether, in which it is very soluble. However, in view of the dangers inherent in the use of ether in schools, this method has not been included. Filtration, step 7, can be very time consuming and can be greatly speeded up by the use of a Buchner funnel if available (see *page 150*). The suspension could also be centrifuged and the supernatant tested.

## Result

Table 14.1 lists most of the foods given in the *Materials* section, together with the expected results. It must be emphasized that the tests in this experiment are *qualitative*, simply showing the presence or absence of a nutrient.

## Table 14.1 Carbohydrate, fat and protein content of some foods

| Food | Carbohydrate g/100 g | Fat g/100 g | Protein g/100 g | Notes |
|---|---|---|---|---|
| Milk | 4.7 | 3.8 | 3.3 | carbohydrate: lactose (reducing disaccharide) |
| Egg white | 0.7 | 0.03 | 9.0 | several of the protein fractions in egg albumen contain carbohydrate |
| Egg yolk | trace | 30 | 16 | |
| Fruit (orange) | 8.5 | trace | 0.8 | relative proportions of sucrose and reducing sugars (glucose and fructose) vary with the fruit tested and with maturity. Avocado and olive contain appreciable amounts of fat (about 20%) |
| Jam | 69 | 0 | 0.5 | carbohydrate: mainly sucrose but boiling in the presence of acid hydrolyses the sucrose |
| Raw minced beef | 0 | 16 | 19 | |
| Raw fish (cod) | 0 | 0.7 | 17 | |
| Bread, white | 50 | 2 | 8 | carbohydrate: mainly starch |
| Butter | trace | 82 | 0.4 | carbohydrate: lactose but quantity probably too small to be detected by these tests |
| Cheese (cheddar) | trace | 33 | 26 | carbohydrate: as for butter |
| Cottage cheese | 1.4 | 4 | 14 | carbohydrate: lactose |

*(taken from Paul, A. A. and Southgate, D. A. T.)*

# Experiment 15*

## Test for water

### Purpose

To find whether a food contains an appreciable amount of water.

### Materials

a range of foods such as biscuits, cakes, jelly, meat, fruit
cobalt chloride papers

bunsen burner
flameproof bench mat
forceps (or tweezers)
spatula or blunt knife

### Method

1 Dry a cobalt chloride paper by warming it over a small bunsen flame until it is blue.

2 Using a blunt knife or spatula (**not** fingers – why not?) press the paper on to the food.

3 Observe the colour change.

4 Repeat for other foods.

### Result

A colour change from blue to pink indicates the presence of water.

26

# Experiment 15*
# Test for water

## Introduction

The amount of water a food contains determines, to a large extent, the way in which it should be stored. A quantitative method of finding the water content of food is given in *Experiment 21;* what follows is a very simple, very rapid way of indicating whether a food may be considered 'dry' or not.

## Materials

a Use a selection of dry, wet and intermediate moisture foods.

b Cobalt chloride papers, see *page 147.*

## Method

a Care must obviously be taken not to singe or to ignite the cobalt chloride papers.

b If fingers are used to press the cobalt chloride papers on to the food, the paper is likely to turn pink because of moisture from the fingers.

## Result

An appreciable amount of water is shown to be present if the cobalt chloride paper turns pink when in contact with the food. Conclusions should be drawn about methods of storage, eg, biscuits are 'dry' and are likely to gain moisture if they are not stored in an air-tight tin; meat is 'wet' and is likely to dry out unless it is covered. Food spoilage and food poisoning bacteria need high levels of available water to multiply. Results could be tentatively related to possible spoilage of food and its prevention.

See *Experiment 21* for a list of the water content of common foods.

# Experiment 16***

# Tests for minerals

This experiment must be carried out in a laboratory under the supervision of a teacher with appropriate scientific background.

## Purpose

To find whether certain elements are present in food.

## Materials

selection of foods, eg cheese, bacon, bread

⚠ dilute nitric acid

⚠ ammonium hydroxide

⚠ ammonium oxalate (ammonium ethanedioate) solution

⚠ ammonium thiocyanate solution

⚠ hydrogen peroxide solution (6% – 20 volumes)

⚠ barium chloride solution

⚠ silver nitrate solution

⚠ ammonium molybdate solution

| | |
|---|---|
| crucible or silica dish | silica rod |
| pipe-clay triangle | blue glass |
| tripod | 5 test tubes |
| bunsen burner | test tube rack |
| flameproof bench mat | 2 dropping pipettes |
| boiling tube | 250 cm$^3$ beaker |

## Method

Make sure you are wearing eye protection before starting this experiment.

**First ash the food:** In a fume cupboard

1 Place a small amount of the food in a crucible or silica dish on a pipe-clay triangle supported on a tripod (**CARE – goggles must be worn**).

2 Heat gently at first. The food will turn black and fumes will be produced.

3 Carry on heating gently until the fumes no longer appear.

4 Increase the heat at this stage and continue heating strongly until only a very pale grey or white powder is left.

5 Allow to cool.

**Next, bring the ash into solution:**

6 In a boiling tube, dissolve the ash in dilute nitric acid: about 12 cm$^3$ of the solution will be needed for all the tests.

## Then test for the minerals:

7 For *sodium, potassium* and *calcium,* heat a silica rod in the hottest part of a hot bunsen flame until the flame no longer changes colour.
Dip the rod into the test solution and heat it again in the flame. Note the colour of the flame.

**Result** Yellow flame – sodium present

Red flame – calcium present

Lilac flame (pale blue when viewed through blue glass) – potassium present.

8 For *calcium,* neutralize about 2 cm$^3$ of the test solution with ammonium hydroxide.
Add about an equal volume of ammonium oxalate solution.
Allow to stand.

**Result** White precipitate – calcium present.

9 For *iron,* add a few drops of ammonium thiocyanate solution to about 1 cm$^3$ of the test solution.

**Result** Red colour – iron (III) present.

10 If step 9 is negative, oxidize any iron (II) that might be present by warming about 1 cm$^3$ of the solution with a few drops of hydrogen peroxide. Then repeat step 9.

**Result** Red colour after oxidation – iron (II) present.

11 For *sulphate,* to about 1 cm of the test solution add about 2 cm$^3$ barium chloride solution.

**Result** White precipitate – sulphate present.

12 For *chloride,* add a few drops of silver nitrate solution to about 1 cm$^3$ of the test solution.

**Result** White precipitate – chloride present.

13 For *phosphate,* add about 3 cm$^3$ ammonium molybdate solution to about 2 cm$^3$ of the test solution. Heat in a water bath (a 250 cm$^3$ beaker half-full of boiling water).

**Result** Yellow colour or precipitate – phosphate present.

Record all the results in a table.

### Table of results for Experiment 16

| Food | Record as + (positive) or – (not found) | | | | | | | | |
|---|---|---|---|---|---|---|---|---|---|
| | Flame tests | | | | iron | | | | |
| | sodium | calcium | potassium | calcium | (III) | (II) | sulphate | chloride | phosphate |
| | | | | | | | | | |

# Experiment 16***
# Tests for minerals

## Introduction
This experiment must be carried out in a properly equipped laboratory.

Foods are made up of many complex chemicals but they contain only four major elements: carbon, hydrogen, oxygen and nitrogen. Four further elements are present in much smaller quantities: calcium, potassium, sodium, and phosphorus. Very small amounts of many more elements are found in foods. These 'trace elements' are essential in minute amounts but may be toxic if consumed in excess – examples are copper, zinc, magnesium, iron, sulphur, chromium, selenium, cobalt, chlorine, iodine.

Quantitative tests for these elements are time-consuming and need sophisticated equipment but simple tests, such as those described here, can show whether the element is present or not.

## Materials
a Any food can be used but it must be ashed before the tests are carried out. The ashing is easier if the water content of the food is not too high, for example, cereals and meats, although with care fruits and vegetables can be ashed.

b See Appendix I for details of making up solutions.

c For safety, eye protection is *essential* both when ashing food, due to the danger of 'spitting', and when carrying out the tests.

d It is preferable that ashing is carried out by the teacher prior to the lesson. The crucible, pipe-clay triangle and tripod will not then be needed.

e A platinum wire is a good – but very expensive – substitute for a silica rod.

f The blue glass is not essential but, if available, provides a useful confirmatory test for potassium.

## Method
a For ashing, it is easy to underestimate the amount of food needed, for example, 100 g cheese will form about 5 g ash. It is also easy to underestimate the smell and the fumes that will be produced. Use a fume cupboard if possible, or open doors and windows. **Take care** not to set the food on fire or to cause spitting. If large quantities are needed, use a small crucible or silica dish and add small quantities of the food (chopped, crumbled or grated) as required. The ash will keep indefinitely, if kept in a stoppered, labelled bottle.

b Only a very small quantity of ash should be dissolved in the nitric acid – a pinch, or sufficient to cover the end of a small spatula.

c When conducting flame tests it is important to heat the rod long enough to remove sodium which produces a characteristic yellow flame.

## Result
Results should be recorded as positive or not found, rather than negative. Pupils should be encouraged to check these qualitative results with figures in Paul, A. A. and Southgate, D. A. T., *The Composition of Foods*. For guidance, some are given in Table 16.1. Phosphorus, sulphur and chlorine are found in ashed food in the form of phosphate, sulphate and chloride.

**Table 16.1 Inorganic constituents of some foods**

|  | Sodium | Potassium | Calcium | Phosphorus | Iron | Sulphur | Chlorine |
|---|---|---|---|---|---|---|---|
|  | (milligrams in 100 g food) | | | | | | |
| **Wholemeal flour** | 3 | 360 | 35 | 340 | 4.0 | * | 38 |
| **White plain flour** | 2 | 140 | 150 | 110 | 2.4 | * | 45 |
| **Cheddar cheese** | 610 | 120 | 800 | 520 | 0.4 | 230 | 1060 |
| **Raw lean beef** | 61 | 350 | 7 | 180 | 2.1 | 190 | 59 |
| **Raw potato** | 7 | 570 | 8 | 40 | 0.5 | 35 | 79 |
| **Curry powder** | 450 | 1830 | 640 | 270 | 75 | 86 | 470 |

*(taken from Paul, A.A. and Southgate, D.A.T.)*                    *No figure given

# Experiment 17*

# Test for ascorbic acid (1)

## Purpose

To show the presence of ascorbic acid (vitamin C) in fruits and vegetables.

## Materials

fruits and vegetables such as orange, lemon, apple, plum, cucumber, potato, carrot

1% ascorbic acid (vitamin C) solution

dichlorophenolindophenol (DCPIP) papers

dropping pipette (or eye dropper)

sharp knife

chopping board

## Method

1 Put a few drops of ascorbic acid solution on to the DCPIP-impregnated filter paper to observe a strongly positive result.

2 Cut through the fruits and vegetables provided and press the cut surface on to the paper for a few seconds, then remove.

## Result

If vitamin C is present the DCPIP will be decolorized. A pink colour merely indicates the presence of fruit acid, *not* ascorbic acid.

# Experiment 17*
# Test for ascorbic acid (1)

## Introduction

This is a very simple, qualitative test for the presence of ascorbic acid (vitamin C) in fruits and vegetables. The result depends on the reducing action of ascorbic acid, so care should be taken only to test foods which do not contain other reducing agents. Meat, for example, gives a false positive result because the protein, containing the amino acid cysteine, acts as a reducing agent. Dried fruits and preserved fruit juices may contain sulphites which are also reducing agents.

## Materials

**a** See Appendix I for making up percentage solutions of ascorbic acid and 2,6-dichloro-phenolindophenol (DCPIP).

**b** DCPIP papers may be made as follows:
  1 Put a piece of filter paper on a small beaker (Fig 17.1).

**Fig. 17.1**

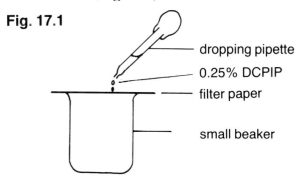

— dropping pipette
— 0.25% DCPIP
— filter paper

small beaker

  2 Drop 0.25% DCPIP solution onto the paper, a little at a time, allowing the paper to dry between additions. An unstained area should be left round the perimeter of the filter paper.
  3 Allow the paper to dry completely.
  4 Store the papers in a plastic bag, excluding as much air as possible, in a refrigerator. The papers should stay blue, and therefore usable, for up to six months.

## Result

DCPIP is blue in neutral and alkaline solutions, pink in the presence of acids and colourless in the presence of reducing agents. Because of the acidic juice the filter paper will turn pink when, for example, an orange is pressed on it. However, ascorbic acid, although a very weak acid, is a strong reducing agent, so where ascorbic acid is present in reasonable concentration the DCPIP is reduced and the blue filter paper becomes colourless.

# Experiment 18*

# Test for ascorbic acid (2)

## Purpose

To find whether foods contain ascorbic acid (vitamin C). This method will distinguish between rich sources and poor sources.

## Materials

foods to be tested, eg parsley, Brussels sprouts, apple, potato, turnip, pear, green grapes, bread

2,6-dichlorophenolindophenol (DCPIP) tablets

dilute acetic (ethanoic) acid

⚠ acetone (propanone)

$100\,cm^3$ measuring cylinder

$100\,cm^3$ beaker

stirring rod

chopping board

sharp knife

$25\,cm^3$ measuring cylinder

pestle and mortar

small filter funnel

small filter papers

test tubes (one for each food)

test tube rack

dropping pipette (or eye dropper)

## Method

1 Dissolve 2 DCPIP tablets in $50\,cm^3$ water.

2 Grind, chop or mix about 3 g (about a level half-teaspoonful) of the food with $10\,cm^3$ acetic acid. Choose a method according to the food: the aim is to get as much ascorbic acid as possible into solution.

3 Filter the solution into a test tube.

4 If the food is from a package which states that the food contains preservative, add about $1\,cm^3$ acetone.

5 Using a dropping pipette, add the DCPIP solution to the extract a drop at a time. Count the number of drops necessary to produce a pink colour.

## Result

The DCPIP is first decolorized by the ascorbic acid then, when no more ascorbic acid is in the solution, it turns pink because of the presence of acetic acid. The more ascorbic acid in the solution, the more DCPIP will be needed to reach a pink end-point.

Record your results in a table.

### Table of results for Experiment 18

| Food | Volume of DCPIP needed to produce a pink colour:<br>  * less than 2 drops<br>  ** 3 – 10 drops<br>  *** 11 – 20 drops<br>  **** more than 20 drops | Comments |
|------|------|------|
|      |      |      |

# Experiment 18 *
# Test for ascorbic acid (2)

## Introduction

Like *Experiment 17,* this is a qualitative test but it is rather more complicated and needs more apparatus. If the method is carefully worked through, a rough comparison of ascorbic acid content can be made.

## Materials

a  Very small quantities of foods are needed.

b  See Appendix I for details of reagents.

c  It is recommended, but not essential, to use acetic (ethanoic) acid – see notes under **Method** below.

d  This experiment can be carried out with very little laboratory equipment, though test tubes are certainly necessary. Volumes can be estimated, and the food suspensions can be allowed to stand then decanted into the test tube.

e  Propanone (acetone) is flammable: it should be kept well clear of any naked flame.

## Method

a  While it is recommended that the experiment is carried out as stated, acetic (ethanoic) acid is not absolutely necessary. It has two advantages:

1  it helps to prevent oxidation of ascorbic acid, and

2  the pink end-point, due to the low pH, is easy to see.

If the experiment is quickly worked through, however, the ascorbic acid should remain stable for the times involved here. In the absence of acetic acid, dichlorophenolindo-phenol (DCPIP) would be added drop by drop until a drop is no longer decolorized by the ascorbic acid. This can be difficult to see in strongly green liquids such as parsley extract. A pink end-point is much more obvious.

b  Sulphur dioxide is sometimes used as a preservative in fruit juices or preserved fruit and vegetable products. This is a reducing agent and will decolorize DCPIP. Acetone forms a complex with the sulphur dioxide so that it cannot react with the DCPIP.

## Result

Comment should be made about whether the food is a poor, moderate or rich source of ascorbic acid. A list could be made, with the foods in descending order of ascorbic acid content. The accuracy of the list could be checked against figures in *The Composition of Foods* or *Manual of Nutrition,* some of which are included in Table 18.1.

**Table 18.1  Ascorbic acid content (mg/100 g) of some vegetables**

| | Ascorbic acid mg/100 g | |
| --- | --- | --- |
| | Average | Range |
| **Vegetables** | | |
| Boiled French beans | 5 | |
| Fresh beansprouts | 30 | |
| Raw Brussels sprouts | 90 | 70–140 |
| Boiled Brussels sprouts | 40 | 30–90 |
| Raw winter cabbage | 55 | 40–70 |
| Boiled winter cabbage | 20 | 10–40 |
| Raw cauliflower | 60 | 50–90 |
| Boiled cauliflower | 20 | 15–40 |
| Parsley | 150 | 100–200 |
| Raw fresh peas | 25 | 15–35 |
| Boiled fresh peas | 15 | |
| Raw frozen peas | 17 | |
| Boiled frozen peas | 13 | |
| Raw green peppers | 100 | 60–170 |
| Boiled green peppers | 60 | |
| Raw green plantain | 20 | |
| Boiled green plantain | 3 | |
| Old raw potatoes | | 8  20 |
| Boiled raw potatoes | | 4–14 |
| Potato chips | | 5–16 |
| Raw sweet potatoes | 25 | |
| Boiled sweet potatoes | 15 | |
| Raw yam | 10 | |
| Boiled yam | 2 | |
| **Fruits** | | |
| Eating apple | 3 | |
| Raw cooking apple | 15 | |
| Stewed apple | 11 | |
| Banana | 10 | |
| Grape | 4 | |
| Fresh lemon juice | 50 | 40–60 |
| Raw mango | 30 | 10–180 |
| Orange and orange juice | 50 | 40–60 |
| Pear | 3 | |
| Fresh pineapple | 25 | 20–40 |
| Canned pineapple | 12 | |

*(Paul, A. A. and Southgate, D. A. T. 1978)*

Distinction should be made between a 'good source' of ascorbic acid such as parsley and a 'major source' such as potato. Parsley (150mg/100g) is used mainly as a garnish and is not eaten at all by many people, whereas 400 g potatoes (about 10 mg/100g) may be eaten in one meal.

# Experiment 19***

# Estimation of ascorbic acid in orange juice

## Purpose

Using 2, 6-dichlorophenolindophenol (DCPIP) tablets to determine the ascorbic acid (vitamin C) content of fresh orange juice.

## Materials

2, 6-dichlorophenolindophenol tablets (1 tablet is equivalent to 1 mg ascorbic acid)

dilute acetic (ethanoic) acid

small funnel (burette filler)

1 orange

lemon squeezer

2 x 100 cm³ beakers

filter funnel

stirring rod

funnel stand

wash bottle containing distilled water

muslin

2 x 100 cm³ volumetric flasks *or* stoppered measuring cylinders

2 x 10 cm³ pipettes

pipette filler

3 x 100 cm³ conical flasks

100 cm³ burette

burette stand

white tile or sheet of white paper

## Method

### First prepare the DCPIP solution

1  Crush 4 DCPIP tablets in a beaker and dissolve in a little distilled water.

2  Transfer to a 100 cm³ volumetric flask or measuring cylinder, washing the solution into the flask with distilled water (Fig. 19.1).

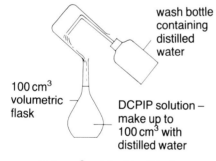

**Fig. 19.1**

wash bottle containing distilled water

100 cm³ volumetric flask

DCPIP solution – make up to 100 cm³ with distilled water

3  Make up to 100 cm³ with distilled water, stopper and mix by inverting several times.

4  Fill the burette with this solution (1 cm³ is equivalent to 0.04 mg ascorbic acid).

### Next, prepare the orange juice

5  Squeeze the orange and strain through double muslin, supported in a filter funnel, into a small beaker.

6  Using a safety filler, pipette 10 cm³ juice into a 100 cm³ volumetric flask or measuring cylinder (Fig. 19.2).

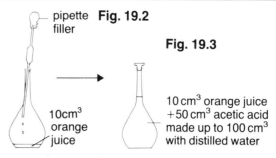

pipette filler  **Fig. 19.2**

**Fig. 19.3**

10cm³ orange juice

10 cm³ orange juice +50 cm³ acetic acid made up to 100 cm³ with distilled water

7  Add 50 cm³ dilute acetic acid to the flask or cylinder and make up to 100 cm³ with distilled or tap water (Fig. 19.3). Stopper and mix by inverting.

## Carry out the titration

8  Using a safety filler, pipette 10 cm³ of the diluted solution into a 100 cm³ conical flask.

9  Record the initial burette reading and then titrate (Fig. 19.4), adding DCPIP from the burette until a faint pink colour persists for 15 seconds. Record the final burette reading.

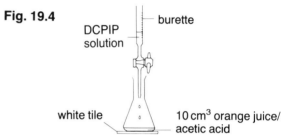

**Fig. 19.4**

DCPIP solution

burette

white tile

10 cm³ orange juice/ acetic acid

10  Repeat the titration twice.

## Result

If $T$ cm³ is the average volume of DCPIP needed, 10 cm³ of the diluted juice contain 0.04 x $T$ mg ascorbic acid.

The original juice was diluted 1:10, so 1 cm³ of the fresh juice contains 0.04 x $T$ mg ascorbic acid.

Therefore 100 cm³ fresh juice contain 4 x $T$ mg ascorbic acid.

## Suggestions for further work***

a  Compare your results with those in *Manual of Nutrition* or *The Composition of Foods*.

b  Measure the volume of juice from the orange (step 5) and calculate the ascorbic acid content of the whole orange. Compare this with the recommended daily amount of ascorbic acid for your age group.

c  Compare your value for the ascorbic acid content of fresh orange with the stated ascorbic acid content of canned and bottled orange (look on the label). It is possible to estimate the ascorbic acid content of these juices by adapting *Experiment 19*. Acetone (propanone) (**CARE** – flammable) must be added immediately prior to the titration if the juice contains preservative (about 2 cm³ per 10 cm³ portion).

# Experiment 19***
# Estimation of ascorbic acid in orange juice

## Introduction

Oranges are an important source of ascorbic acid. An orange can, as this experiment shows, supply the whole of a day's recommended daily amount. Ascorbic acid is the only vitamin that can be estimated accurately and easily in a school laboratory. Since the results are obviously of practical importance, it is a popular experiment with pupils who have some experience of titrations and is easily adapted to show the effects of heating on the vitamin or the amount lost to the water when cooking vegetables (see *Experiment 20*). For the principle of the titration, see *Pupils' Material, Experiment 18*.

## Materials

a  For details of 2,6-dichlorophenolindophenol tablets see *page 147*.

b  Acetic (ethanoic) acid stabilizes the vitamin C, preventing oxidation during the course of the experiment.

c  If preserved orange juice is to be tested, about $2\,cm^3$ propanone (acetone) must be added to the contents of each conical flask immediately before filtering. This removes preservatives that might decolorize DCPIP. (Propanone is flammable.)

d  For safety, a pipette filler must be used at all times – **no mouth pipetting should be allowed.**

e  The small funnel must be used for filling the burette, but it should be removed before titrating. Remember to turn the burette tap with the left hand, pulling the stopcock in at the same time.

f  One conical flask can be used, if it is thoroughly washed between titrations.

## Method

a  Care must be taken to dissolve the DCPIP tablets completely or blockage of the burette may occur. The accuracy of the result depends on this solution being correctly made up.

b  Fresh orange juice is diluted ten times. If the experiment is adapted for any other juice or liquid, for example cabbage water, this proportion may need to be adjusted.

c  Step 9: the DCPIP is decolorized by the ascorbic acid. When no further ascorbic acid remains, the DCPIP simply drops into an acid solution and will therefore turn pink.

d  It is likely that the first end point will be overshot; the two succeeding titrations should be within $1\,cm^3$ of each other.

## Result

The ascorbic acid content of 'fresh orange juice', raw oranges and frozen reconstituted orange juice is given in *The Composition of Foods* as $50\,mg$ per $100\,g$. This is an average, however, and individual samples may vary considerably.

## Suggestions for further work***

The volume of orange juice (step 5) may easily be measured; this, too, varies but it is usually about $60\,cm^3$. The ascorbic acid content of an orange can be calculated by:

$$\frac{\text{volume of juice x mg/100 g vitamin C}}{100}$$

Recommended daily amounts of ascorbic acid are.

| | |
|---|---|
| 0 – 8 years | 20 mg |
| 9 – 15 years | 25 mg |
| 15 years and adult | 30 mg |
| pregnant and lactating women | 60 mg |

While this experiment can be carried out on other juices and vegetable cooking water, it is not possible to find the ascorbic acid content of blackcurrant juice or tomato juice because the colour masks the end point of the titration.

# Experiment 20***

# Estimation of ascorbic acid in Brussels sprouts

## Purpose

Using dichlorophenolindophenol (DCPIP) tablets to determine the quantity of ascorbic acid in 100 g of cooked and uncooked sprouts.

## Materials

Brussels sprouts

dilute acetic (ethanoic) acid

2, 6-dichlorophenolindophenol tablets (1 tablet is equivalent to 1 mg ascorbic acid)

| | |
|---|---|
| balance | grease pencil |
| liquidizer | 2 x 250 cm$^3$ conical flasks with corks |
| 2 x 100 cm$^3$ measuring cylinders with stoppers | 250 cm$^3$ beaker |
| filter funnel | clock glass or large petri dish for lid |
| funnel stand | |
| filter paper | |
| bunsen burner | |
| tripod | |
| gauze | or a small pan with a lid on a hotplate |
| flameproof bench mat | |
| 100 cm$^3$ beaker | |
| glass rod | 6 x 100 cm$^3$ conical flasks |
| 100 cm$^3$ volumetric flask | |
| 100 cm$^3$ burette | 10 cm$^3$ pipette |
| burette stand | pipette filler |
| white tile or sheet of white paper | |

## Method

### First prepare the uncooked sample
(Fig. 20.1)

1 Homogenize 20 g sprouts with 50 cm$^3$ dilute acetic acid in the liquidizer.

2 In a measuring cylinder, dilute the suspension to 100 cm$^3$ with distilled water. Insert stopper and mix by inverting.

3 Filter the suspension into a 250 cm$^3$ conical flask, cork and label 'sample 1'. (Fig. 20.1)

**Fig. 20.1**

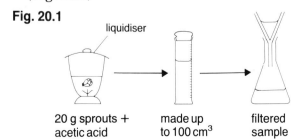

20 g sprouts + acetic acid    made up to 100 cm$^3$    filtered sample

## Next prepare the cooked sample

4 In a 250 cm$^3$ beaker, boil two sprouts for 15 minutes or until cooked.

5 Follow steps 1, 2 and 3 (Fig. 20.1) with the cooked sprouts, labelling the filtrate 'sample 2'.

## Estimate the ascorbic acid in each sample (Fig. 20.2)

**Fig. 20.2**

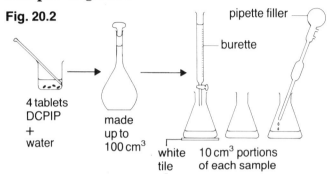

4 tablets DCPIP + water    made up to 100 cm$^3$    white tile    10 cm$^3$ portions of each sample    pipette filler    burette

6 Dissolve 4 DCPIP tablets in distilled water in a small beaker. Transfer with washing to a 100 cm$^3$ volumetric flask and make up to the mark with distilled water.

7 Fill a burette with the DCPIP solution. Titrate three 10 cm$^3$ portions of samples 1 and 2 against DCPIP until a faint pink colour persists for 15 seconds. Record the volume of DCPIP used and calculate the average volume for each sample.

## Result

If $T$ cm$^3$ is the average volume of DCPIP needed for the sample,

10 cm$^3$ of the sample contain 0.04 x $T$ mg ascorbic acid.

100 cm$^3$ of the sample contain 0.4 x $T$ mg ascorbic acid.

100 cm$^3$ of the sample contained 20 g sprouts.

Therefore 20 g sprouts contain 0.4 x $T$ mg ascorbic acid.

100 g sprouts contain 2 x $T$ mg ascorbic acid.

## Suggestions for further work***

a Carry out a similar experiment on cabbage, potato or other vegetable which is normally cooked before eating.

b By adapting this method, study the effects of different methods of preparing and processing fruits and vegetables.

c If cooked sprouts contain less ascorbic acid than raw sprouts, what might have happened to the vitamin? Design and carry out an experiment to investigate your theory.

# Experiment 20***
# Estimation of ascorbic acid in Brussels sprouts

## Introduction

The principle of titration with 2,6-dichloro-phenolindophenol (DCPIP) to estimate ascorbic acid is explained in the *Pupils' Material, Experiment 18,* and titrations are described in the *Teachers' Guide, Experiment 19*. This experiment aims to find the ascorbic acid content of Brussels sprouts, but it can easily be adapted to other vegetables or fruits.

Ascorbic acid is the most heat-labile vitamin so it is of practical importance in cookery to find the difference between the ascorbic acid content of cooked and uncooked vegetables, as described here.

## Materials

a Only two sprouts are needed for the 'uncooked' estimation, and a further two for the 'cooked'.

b Acetic acid, see *page 146;* DCPIP, *page 147*.

c The acetic acid stabilizes the ascorbic acid, preventing oxidation during liquidizing. It also enables the end point to be seen more clearly.

d The balance should be accurate to one decimal place.

e Kitchen equipment may be used for some parts of this experiment. As long as the balance is accurate for small quantities, a laboratory balance is not essential. The liquidizer may be of any type. Dilution of the suspension is most accurately carried out using a measuring cylinder, but a measuring jug could be used. The suspension can be stored in any stoppered container, after filtering through muslin as an alternative to filter paper.

## Method

a Formation of a foam during liquidizing can be a problem: liquidize as briefly as possible, allow the suspension to stand for a few minutes then ignore the foam when measuring the volume.

b A double layer of muslin may be used instead of filter paper.

c The DCPIP tablets are diluted in such a way that $1\,cm^3$ solution is equivalent to $0.04\,mg$ ascorbic acid.

d The first titration will probably be inaccurate due to 'overshooting' the end point; repeat at least twice – the repeat titrations should be within $1\,cm^3$ of each other. Calculate the average of the two closest titrations.

## Result

As can be seen from Table 20.1 there is a considerable loss of ascorbic acid from sprouts on cooking, less than half of the vitamin remaining.

## Suggestions for further work***

a Table 18.1, *page 14,* shows ascorbic acid contents of some cooked and uncooked vegetables.

   Cooking losses, and the amount of each vegetable that will supply one-third of the *Recommended Daily Amount,* are shown in Table 20.1.

**Table 20.1**
**Effect of cooking on ascorbic acid and quantity needed to supply one-third of Recommended Daily Amount**

| Food | % of original ascorbic acid *remaining after boiling* (figures taken from Paul, A.A. and Southgate, D.A.T. (1978) | Weight of cooked vegetable supplying ⅓ Recommended Daily Amount of ascorbic acid (10 mg) |
| --- | --- | --- |
| Brussels sprouts | 44 | 25g |
| Cabbage | 36 | 50g |
| Potato | 60 | 83g |
| Runner beans | 25 | 200g |
| Carrots | 66 | 250g |
| Peas (frozen) | 76 | 77g |
| Plantain | 15 | 333g |
| Sweetcorn | 75 | 111g |
| Yam | 20 | 500g |

b Potatoes, especially boiled potatoes, are very slow to filter. It is not necessary to filter the whole sample, just enough for titration. Alternatively, the suspension may be centrifuged, the supernatant being titrated.

c If dried potatoes are to be tested, add $2\,cm^3$ acetone to each aliquot immediately prior to titrating, to prevent decolorization of the DCPIP by preservative.

d To test the water in which vegetables have been cooked, first measure the volume of liquid before boiling, and then make the liquid up to the same volume after the vegetable has been cooked. Adapt *Experiment 19* to find the amount of ascorbic acid in the cooking water, diluting the liquid 1:1 with acetic (ethanoic) acid. Or simply carry out a qualitative test, as in *Experiment 18,* on the cooking water to show the presence of the vitamin.

# Experiment 21***

# Estimation of water content

## Purpose

To find the amount of moisture in a food by the application of heat to drive off water vapour.

## Materials

food such as finely minced meat, finely chopped
vegetables, margarine, lightly beaten egg

oven

glass petri dish

short glass rod

tongs

desiccator

balance

## Method

1 Place the glass petri dish and the short glass rod in the oven at 105°C for about 20 minutes, cool in a desiccator and weigh. Record the weight.

2 Accurately weigh about 10 g of the sample into the dish.

3 Using the glass rod, arrange the sample in the dish so that the maximum surface area is exposed.

4 Dry at 105°C for about 1½ hours, cool in desiccator and weigh.

5 Return to the oven for 30 minutes, cool in desiccator and weigh.

## Result

Percentage water

$$= \frac{\text{weight lost (g)}}{\text{weight of sample taken (g)}} \times 100$$

# Experiment 21***
# Estimation of water content

## Introduction

Many methods of finding the water content of foods are available to the analyst, but this is the simplest. Finely-divided food is weighed into a dish and heated at a temperature just above the boiling point of water. When the water has been driven off, the food is re-weighed and the amount of water is calculated.

Most foods consist mainly of water, but this is not always obvious just by looking at the food. Boiled peas, for example, are four-fifths water; lettuce is 96 per cent water. Some 'slimming' foods are low in energy simply because they contain a high proportion of cunningly-disguised water; low-fat spread is over half water. The water content of foods may, as explained in *Experiment 15*, determine the storage conditions for a food. In advanced work, though, it should be pointed out that in a food like jam (30 per cent water), very little of it is available to spoilage organisms because the sugar lowers the water activity of the food.

## Materials

**a** The foods *must* be as finely-divided as possible, to provide a large surface area from which moisture can be lost.

**b** Any oven may be used, as long as the temperature does not exceed 105°C.

**c** A saucer could be used instead of a petri dish.

**d** For accurate work a desiccator is essential, as is drying and cooling the dish and glass rod before weighing. These may only be dispensed with if a great degree of accuracy is not considered to be of major importance.

## Method

**a** The amount of food is not critical, but the *exact* weight must be known.

**b** The food must not cook and dry quickly on the outside or water will not be lost from the centre. If the food contains fat, take care to avoid it spitting or volatilizing.

**c** If the weight after step 5 is not the same as after step 4, dry for a further 30 minutes then cool and weigh again. Only by heating to a constant weight can one assume that all the water has been driven off.

## Result

Compare results for the food tested with data in *The Composition of Foods;* some representative figures are given in Table 21.1. These are averages, however, and a single determination for a food will vary, perhaps considerably from

these. Meat is especially variable because of sampling problems and the presence of fat.

**Table 21.1**
**Water content of some foods**

| Food | % Water |
|---|---|
| Plain white flour | 13 |
| White bread | 39 |
| Cheddar cheese | 37 |
| Egg | 75 |
| Cooking oil | trace |
| Margarine | 16 |
| Low fat spread | 57 |
| Raw lean bacon | 67 |
| Raw minced beef | 64 |
| Raw haddock | 81 |
| Raw cabbage | 90 |
| Raw frozen peas | 79 |
| Raw potatoes | 76 |

# SECTION C

# Properties of food constituents

## Experiment 22***

# Non-enzymic browning

## Purpose

To demonstrate the effect of heat on sugars alone and in the presence of amino acids.

## Materials

sugar, eg glucose

amino acid, eg lysine

2 test tubes

test tube rack

grease pencil

test tube holder

bunsen burner

flameproof bench mat

safety goggles – be certain to wear them!

### Sugar alone:

## Method

1 Place a pinch of sugar in a labelled test tube.

2 Heat, gently at first then more strongly until a change in colour is noticed.

3 Allow to cool and smell the contents, but do not point the tube directly at your face.

## Result

Characteristic odour and colour of caramel. This would be followed by charring and eventually complete combustion.

### In the presence of amino acid:

## Method

4 Place a pinch of the sugar and a pinch of the amino acid in a labelled test tube.

5 Heat very gently until a change in colour is noticed.

6 Allow to cool and smell the contents.

## Result

Note rapid browning and the savoury smell.

## Suggestions for further work***

Repeat steps 4, 5 and 6 with other amino acids. Different amino acids produce subtly different odours.

40

# Experiment 22***
# Non-enzymic browning

## Introduction

Browning of foods is fundamental to cookery – toast, cakes, meat, rice pudding are all more appetizing when they are a rich shade of brown. This type of browning is caused by heat. Another type of browning, enzymic browning, is not so desirable – apples, bananas and potatoes all brown during preparation – and this is investigated in *Experiment 23*.

## Materials

a Any sugar may be used, depending on the teaching purpose. Use sucrose, for example, to illustrate caramelization; use sucrose or lactose to illustrate browning in milk puddings. Ideally, reducing sugar should be used for the second part of this experiment (steps 4, 5 and 6). If sucrose is used, the heat will cause enough hydrolysis to supply the reducing sugar.

b Any amino acid can be used, although lysine best illustrates the principle of the experiment, explained in the results section below.

c For safety, goggles should be worn when heating sugar in test tubes.

## Method

a Heating, in both parts of the experiment, should be extremely gentle initially, over a small blue bunsen flame. Increase the height of the flame slowly. Do not use a yellow flame or the carbon deposit on the outside of the test tube will mask the browning.

b Smelling the contents of a test tube is not, in general, advisable. If care is taken (using the hand to waft the fumes to the nose) and the test tube is cool, it is quite safe in this experiment.

## Result and Suggestions for further work***

**Sugar alone** The odour and colour characteristic of caramel should be related to preparation of dishes such as creme caramel. A complicated series of reactions occurs beginning with dehydration of the sugar molecules and leading to formation of brown polymerization compounds. These reactions occur only at high temperatures because they have high energy requirements.

**Sugar and amino acid** More rapid and more intense browning should be seen, compared with caramelization. This is given the name *Maillard reaction* and is found when sugars are heated in the presence of amines such as an amino acid or a protein containing lysine residual groups.

This type of browning occurs at the surface of dry-cooked foods containing protein and sugar: egg custard, milk pudding, bread, roast meat (the traces of sugar in the meat are sufficient). There may be some nutritional damage: up to 15 per cent of the lysine in bread can be lost by crust browning.

Caramel used to be produced for food colouring by heating sugar alone, but is now generally made by heating sugar in the presence of ammonia, ie, by the Maillard reaction.

# Experiment 23***

# Enzymic browning

## Purpose

To investigate the control of browning in fresh apple slices.

## Materials

apple

sucrose syrup

lemon juice

1% salt (sodium chloride) solution

1% sodium disulphate (IV) (sodium metabisulphite) solution

1% ascorbic acid solution

sharp knife

9 white tiles

refrigerator

3 small beakers

2 x 250 cm$^3$ beakers ⎤

bunsen burner      |

tripod              ⎬ or pans on hotplates

gauze              |

flameproof bench mat ⎦

stop clock

balance

dropping pipettes

cling film

## Method

1 Peel an apple and cut it into 12 approximately equal segments.

2 Treat the segments as follows:

 a  leave exposed to the air (control).

 b  bruise then leave exposed to the air.

 c  place in refrigerator.

 d  immerse in tap water.

 e  immerse in boiled and cooled tap water.

 f  immerse in boiling water for 30 seconds, remove and leave exposed to the air.

 g  immerse in syrup

 h  immerse in lemon juice, remove and leave exposed to the air.

 i  immerse in salt solution, remove and leave exposed to the air

 j  immerse in sodium metabisulphite solution, remove and leave exposed to the air.

 k  immerse in ascorbic acid (vitamin C) solution, remove and leave exposed to the air.

 l  wrap cling film tightly around the segment and leave at room temperature.

3 Examine the apple segments at 5 minute intervals for 30 minutes or, if possible, 1 hour.

## Result

Record the degree of browning on a four point scale 0-3 where:

0  indicates no browning.

1  indicates slight browning.

2  indicates moderate browning.

3  indicates an unacceptable degree of browning – the apple would be considered inedible.

Make a table of your results:

### Table of results for Experiment 23

| Time | Treatment | | | | | | | | | | | |
|---|---|---|---|---|---|---|---|---|---|---|---|---|
|  | a | b | c | d | e | f | g | h | i | j | k | l |
| zero |  |  |  |  |  |  |  |  |  |  |  |  |
| 5 minutes |  |  |  |  |  |  |  |  |  |  |  |  |
| 10 minutes |  |  |  |  |  |  |  |  |  |  |  |  |
| etc. |  |  |  |  |  |  |  |  |  |  |  |  |

Comment on the effectiveness, practicality and safety of each treatment.

Relate each treatment to methods of food preparation and processing, and to your knowledge of the theory of enzymic browning.

## Suggestions for further work***

Cut slices of various fruits and vegetables, including other varieties of apple, and leave exposed to the air to see if browning occurs.

If it does, suggest ways of preventing the browning that would be appropriate for the particular fruit or vegetable.

# Experiment 23***
# Enzymic browning

## Introduction

Both in the home and in industry, browning of certain fruits and vegetables during peeling, washing, cutting, slicing, etc., is responsible for much wastage. It is relevant to a study of fruits and vegetables, and of food preparation and processing, to investigate methods of preventing such browning.

While the results can be appreciated and applied by all pupils, the underlying theory requires a knowledge of enzyme action.

## Materials

a Sucrose syrup should be made in the usual way for a fruit salad – boil 50 g of sucrose in 150 cm$^3$ water for 10 minutes.

b Fresh or bottled lemon juice may be used.

c See Appendix I for the method of making up percentage solutions.

d Saucers may be used instead of white tiles; cups instead of small beakers; a cooker hob instead of a bunsen burner.

## Method

The experiment simulates as many common methods of preventing browning during preparation of fruits and vegetables as possible. The pupils may like to suggest alternatives.

## Result and Suggestions for further work***

Browning is not always enzymic (see Experiment 22 for a demonstration of non-enzymic browning). Darkening in fruits such as apples and bananas, and vegetables – notably potatoes – during preparation, however, is due to the presence of an enzyme (an oxidase), a substrate present in the cells and oxygen (Fig. 23.1). Little can be done about the substrate; prevention of enzymic browning depends on exclusion of oxygen or inhibition of the enzyme.

**Fig. 23.1**  Enzymic browning

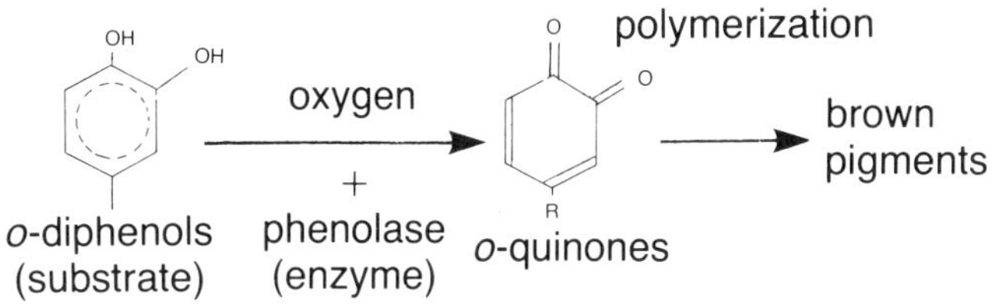

The treatments in this experiment affect browning for the following reasons:

a **Leave exposed to the air**  This is the untreated control – substrate, enzyme and oxygen are all present. It should show an appreciable degree of browning in the time available for the experiment, but it is a good idea for the teacher to pre-test the particular type of apple being used in order to confirm this.

b **Bruise then leave exposed to the air**  Similar to a except that some cells have been deliberately crushed, mixing substrate and enzyme and exposing more of the substrate to oxygen. The greatest degree of browning should occur with this treatment.

c **Place in refrigerator**  Enzyme activity is slowed down at low temperatures but the enzymes are not destroyed so they will act again when the temperature is raised. This applies also to freezing, with the added effect of possible cell rupture as in b. (Vegetables are blanched to prevent enzymic action on thawing.)

d **Immerse in tap water**  A simple, quick household method of preventing browning. Oxygen from the air does not reach the apple, but the water contains a small amount of oxygen in solution.

e **Immerse in boiled and cooled tap water**  The result should be compared with d. Oxygen has been partially removed from the water by boiling (some will redissolve on cooling). There will still be oxygen between the plant cells, and as enzyme and substrate are unaltered, some browning will take place.

f **Immerse in boiling water for 30 seconds, remove and leave exposed to the air**  The apple is blanched, the method used in the home and industry to prevent browning during freezing and thawing. Enzymes are destroyed at high temperatures. Protein denaturation begins at about 65°C and occurs more quickly as the temperature rises. Without the enzyme, this type of browning cannot take place.

g **Immerse in syrup**  A fresh fruit salad is made with a syrup like this. It is an effective way of preventing browning because the syrup has been boiled to remove oxygen. The syrup penetrates the apple slices, reducing the level of dissolved oxygen.

h **Immerse in lemon juice, remove and leave exposed to the air**  Most proteins are denatured at low pH, and the oxidase that causes enzymic browning is no exception. The optimum pH is 6–7; there is virtually no activity below pH3. The apple is exposed to the air after immersion to show that it is not lack of oxygen that prevents browning.

i **Immerse in sodium chloride solution and leave exposed to the air**  Salt inhibits

cont./

# Experiment 24**

# Acid hydrolysis of sucrose

## Purpose

To demonstrate that sucrose (a non-reducing disaccharide) can be hydrolyzed to reducing monosaccharides.

## Materials

1% sucrose solution
Barfoed's reagent
⚠ dilute hydrochloric acid
dilute sodium carbonate solution
red litmus papers

$250\,cm^3$ beaker
bunsen burner
tripod ⎫ or small pan of
gauze ⎬ water on a hotplate
flameproof bench mat ⎭
2 test tubes
test tube rack
grease pencil
2 dropping pipettes

## Method

Make sure you are wearing eye protection.

1 Half-fill the beaker with water and bring to the boil.

2 Carry out *Barfoed's test* on the sucrose solution *(Experiment 4)*.

3 To about $2\,cm^3$ sucrose solution add 2 drops of dilute hydrochloric acid.

4 Place the tube in the boiling waterbath for two minutes.

5 Cool the tube under running water.

6 Add dilute sodium carbonate solution, one drop at a time, until the contents of the tube are just alkaline to litmus. Then carry out *Barfoed's test* on this solution.

## Result

Record your results and conclusions.

## Suggestions for further work**

Carry out another test that would indicate more precisely a sugar present after hydrolysis of the sucrose.

44

enzyme action, though the concentration needed for complete inhibition of browning may be so high that the food is unpalatable. It is sometimes recommended, however, that cooking apples are immersed in salt water if there is a delay between peeling and cooking. This should be more effective than water alone, but the apples must be well rinsed before cooking.

**j Immerse in sodium metabisulphite solution, remove and leave exposed to the air** Sulphur dioxide and sulphites are powerful inhibitors of polyphenoloxidase, but they have an unpleasant odour and flavour, they are toxic at high levels and they destroy thiamin. The 'off' flavours will be removed by cooking.

**k Immerse in ascorbic acid solution, remove and leave exposed to the air** Ascorbic acid (vitamin C) prevents browning because it acts as a reducing agent rather than as an acid. It reduces the o-quinones, being oxidized itself in the process. It also uses up dissolved oxygen in the apple.

**l Wrap cling film tightly around the segment and leave at room temperature** Oxygen is excluded at the surface of the apple, but enough will be between the cells to cause some browning.

---

# Experiment 24**
# Acid hydrolysis of sucrose

## Introduction

Sucrose, whilst itself not a reducing sugar (see *page 4)*, can be hydrolyzed by dilute acids to the reducing sugars glucose and fructose. The presence of these monosaccharides can then be demonstrated using *Barfoed's test*. Other disaccharides, such as maltose and lactose, can also be hydrolised in this way, as can starch. Hence, this is not a specific test for sucrose. However, if a known carbohydrate (positive *Molisch test*) has been shown not to be a reducing sugar (negative *Benedict's test*) or starch (negative *Iodine test*), then it is likely to be sucrose if hydrolysis yields monosaccharides.

Hydrolysis of sucrose can also be performed enzymically *(Experiment 25)* and it may be useful to draw the pupils' attention to the differing conditions necessary to produce its breakdown to its constituents, ie boiling temperatures (100°C) with acid, 40°C only with enzyme. This obviously relates to the need for enzymes in human digestion, where hydrolysis must be carried out at a body temperature of 37°C. The presence of acid from the fruit in jam making hydrolyzes some of the sucrose during boiling. Since glucose and fructose are more soluble than sucrose, this helps to prevent crystallization of the sugar in the jam.

## Materials

**a** For method of making up percentage solutions see Appendix I.

**b** Barfoed's reagent, *page 146;* dilute hydrochloric acid, *page 147;* dilute sodium carbonate solution *page 148*.

**c** Universal indicator (pH) papers can be used as an alternative to litmus papers.

## Method

**a** As *Barfoed's test* needs to be performed on neutral (or at most slightly alkaline) solutions, it is necessary to add dilute sodium carbonate to neutralise the acid used to hydrolyze the sucrose. After each addition of sodium carbonate solution, the test tube should be swirled to mix the contents, and a drop of the mixture put on the litmus paper. This is easier and less messy than trying to immerse litmus paper each time into the contents at the bottom of the test tube, which may also lead to a dyeing of the contents, thus masking a subsequent positive *Barfoed's test*.

**b** Sucrose can, in fact, be hydrolised by prolonged (at least half an hour) boiling in the absence of acid. In this case, *Barfoed's test* could be performed directly without the need to neutralize with sodium carbonate solution.

## Result

Sucrose will not give a positive *Barfoed's test*. After boiling with acid, however, it is split into its constituent monosaccharides, so a positive result will be obtained. Hydrolysis (literally 'water splitting') involves splitting the glucose-fructose bond by the addition of a water molecule. See Fig. 24.1.

**Fig. 24.1** Hydrolysis of sucrose (the C atoms of the ring are not shown; vertical lines represent H atoms)

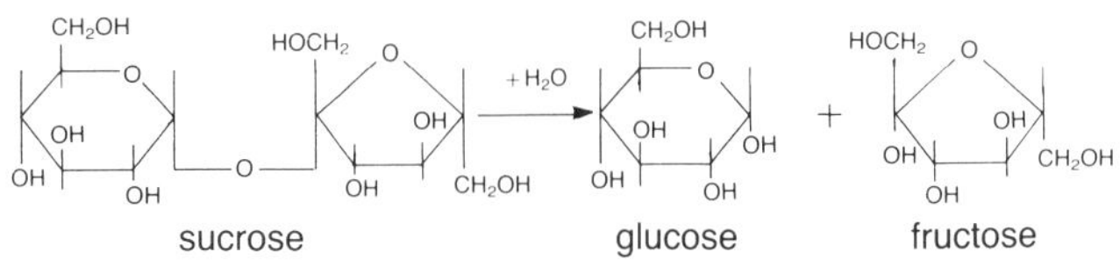

## Suggestions for further work**

The *'Clinistix' test (Experiment 5)* can be performed in order to indicate specifically glucose as being present in the sucrose hydrolysate. This test should also be carried out on the neutralized solution.

# Experiment 25**

# Invertase

## Purpose

To extract sucrase (invertase) from yeast cells and use it to hydrolyze sucrose.

## Materials

fresh yeast

2% sucrose solution

2% maltose solution

Barfoed's reagent *or* 'Clinistix' glucose testing strips

dilute sodium carbonate solution

red litmus papers

pestle and mortar

silver sand or clean fine sand

filter funnel

filter papers

boiling tube

250 cm³ beaker ⎫

bunsen burner ⎬ or small pan of

tripod ⎪ water on a hotplate

gauze ⎪

flameproof bench mat ⎭

12 test tubes

test tube rack

grease pencil

dropping pipettes or eye droppers

waterbath at 40°C or pan of water held at 40°C

## Method

1 In a mortar grind up approximately half a teaspoon of yeast with the same volume of silver sand, moistening slightly and gradually adding more water until a thin paste is formed (Fig. 25.1).

2 Filter into a boiling tube (Fig. 25.2), adding a little more water if necessary. It may be necessary to repeat the filtration until a fairly clear filtrate is obtained. This filtrate contains the enzyme invertase.

3 Add about a third of the invertase solution to a test tube and place in a beaker of boiling water for 10 minutes (Fig. 25.3). Cool thoroughly by holding the test tube under running water. This boiled enzyme will be used as a control.

4 Set up three labelled test tubes as follows (Fig. 25.4):

$A$ – 1 cm³ invertase + 5 cm³ sucrose solution

$B$ – 1 cm³ boiled invertase + 5 cm³ sucrose solution

$C$ – 1 cm³ invertase + 5 cm³ maltose solution

Shake each tube well.

5 Immediately take a small sample from each of tubes $A$, $B$ and $C$ and, after neutralizing with dilute sodium carbonate solution, carry out *Barfoed's test (Experiment 4)* or *'Clinistix' test (Experiment 5)*.

6 Place tubes $A$, $B$ and $C$ in the waterbath at 40°C for 30 minutes then, after neutralizing, carry out *Barfoed's test* again (or use the *'Clinistix' test)*.

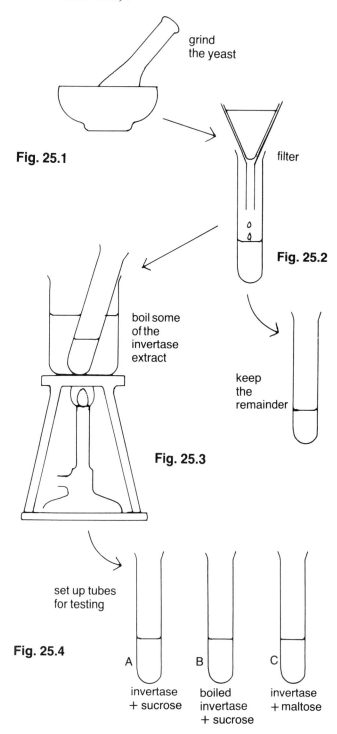

**Fig. 25.1**

grind the yeast

filter

**Fig. 25.2**

boil some of the invertase extract

keep the remainder

**Fig. 25.3**

set up tubes for testing

**Fig. 25.4**

A invertase + sucrose

B boiled invertase + sucrose

C invertase + maltose

## Result

Record your results and conclusions. What was the purpose of the tube containing boiled enzyme? How does the experiment show enzyme 'specificity'?

# Experiment 25**
# Invertase

## Introduction

As indicated in the teacher's notes to the previous experiment, enzymic rather than acid hydrolysis of sucrose can take place under milder conditions of temperature and pH. Invertase (sucrase) is a carbohydrase enzyme occurring in yeast. The name invertase is derived from the fact that it hydrolyses sucrose (sometimes called invert sugar), which rotates the plane of polarized light to the right, dextro-rotatory, to a mixture of glucose and fructose which is laevo-rotatory. The enzyme thus produces a source of glucose for respiration, which can include fermentation, by other yeast enzymes. This experiment introduces in a practical way the concept of catalytic activity by enzymes.

Further, it can be pointed out that the invertase has to be extracted from *within* the yeast cells by grinding them up, that is, it is an *intracellular* enzyme. This is an important aspect of the consideration of enzymes. Their study should not be restricted, as it often is, to the extracellular secretions of the human digestive system when, in fact, the vast majority of enzymes are intracellular.

## Materials

a  Fresh yeast can be obtained from chemists, 'home brew' sections of large department stores, bakers, delicatessens, etc.

Reconstituted yeast can also be used in this experiment. As an alternative, the enzyme invertase itself can be obtained from suppliers (see *page 156*). Although this would make the somewhat tedious extraction process unnecessary, we feel it is worthwhile showing that invertase is a naturally occurring substance, an intracellular enzyme, and not something only found in bottles on laboratory shelves.

b  See Appendix I for notes on making up percentage solutions.

c  Barfoed's reagent, *page 146.*

d  The silver sand provides the necessary abrasive to assist in grinding up the yeast cells.

## Method

The process of filtration may take some time and can be considerably speeded up if a Buchner funnel *(page 150)* is available. A little over $3 \, cm^3$ of filtrate will be sufficient for this experiment, remembering that some will be lost by evaporation when boiling a sample of the enzyme in step 3. If necessary, to save time in waiting for filtration, the quantities in tubes $A$, $B$ and $C$ (step 4) could be halved.

## Result

Tube $A$ should give a positive *Barfoed's test*, showing that the sucrose has been hydrolyzed to monosaccharides. (This tube will also give a positive *Clinistix test*, denoting the formation of glucose.)

The purpose of the control tube $B$ is to show that the sucrose does not spontaneously break down into its constituent monosaccharides, and neither *Barfoed's* nor *Clinistix tests* will prove positive. Boiling, of course, inactivates the enzyme.

Similarly the tests will be negative for tube $C$, giving the opportunity to draw attention to an important feature of enzyme action, namely, specificity. Although maltose and sucrose are both disaccharide sugars with similar structures (see Fig. 25.1 overleaf), only one of them will be hydrolyzed by invertase. A different enzyme, maltase, is required to hydrolyse maltose to two glucose molecules.

**Fig. 25.1**

Comparison of the structures of the disaccharides maltose and sucrose

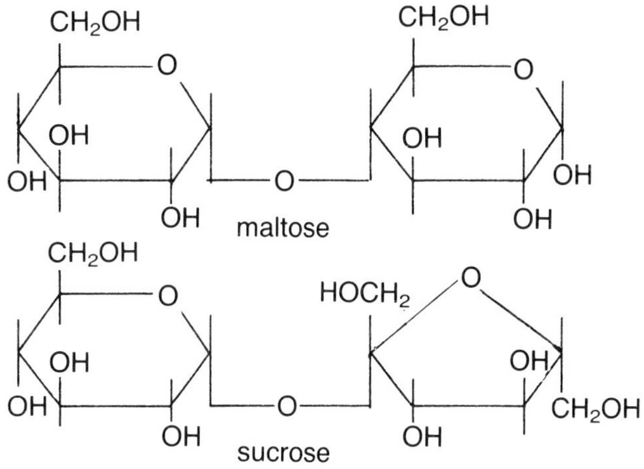

# Experiment 26**

# Acid hydrolysis of starch

## Purpose

To show that starch can be hydrolyzed to reducing sugars.

## Materials

1% starch solution

⚠ dilute sulphuric acid

dilute sodium carbonate solution

red litmus paper

Benedict's solution

solution of iodine in potassium iodide

250 cm³ beaker ⎤
bunsen burner ⎥
tripod ⎥ or small pan of
gauze ⎥ water on a hotplate
flameproof bench mat ⎦

100 cm³ beaker

25 cm³ measuring cylinder

stirring rod

12 test tubes

test tube rack

grease pencil

dropping pipettes (or eye droppers)

clock

## Method

Make sure you are wearing eye protection.

1 Half-fill the 250 cm³ beaker with water and bring to the boil.

2 In the small beaker mix 20 cm³ of the starch solution with 5 cm³ of dilute sulphuric acid and stir thoroughly.

3 Divide the mixture into six approximately equal portions in labelled test tubes.

4 Place five of the tubes in the boiling waterbath for the following periods: 2, 5, 10, 15 and 30 minutes.

5 *Immediately* divide the solution in the remaining tube into two parts. Carry out the *Iodine test (Experiment 6)* on one portion and, after neutralizing it with dilute sodium carbonate solution, *Benedict's test (Experiment 3)* on the other portion.

6 Repeat these tests with the contents of each of the other test tubes as soon as they are taken out of the water bath.

## Result

Draw up a table of results as shown below using + for a positive reaction and − for a negative reaction.

**Table of results for Experiment 26**

| Time | Iodine test | Benedict's test | Comment |
|------|-------------|-----------------|---------|
| zero | | | |
| 2 minutes | | | |
| 5 minutes | | | |
| 10 minutes | | | |
| 15 minutes | | | |
| 30 minutes | | | |

# Experiment 26**
# Acid hydrolysis of starch

## Introduction

Acid hydrolysis of starch produces a mixture of maltose and glucose. Just as it was useful to compare acid hydrolysis of sucrose *(Experiment 24)* with enzymic hydrolysis by invertase *(Experiment 25),* a similar teaching point can be the much milder conditions required to hydrolyse starch enzymically using amylase as described in *Experiment 27.* This emphasizes the need for enzymes in human digestion, where hydrolysis must be achieved at a temperature of 37°C and almost neutral conditions.

See *Experiment 30* for further investigation of the effect of acid on starch.

## Materials

**a** For method of making up starch solution see *page 148.* Other reagents, Appendix I. Note that dilute hydrochloric acid would work just as well as dilute sulphuric.

**b** Universal indicator (pH) papers can be used as an alternative to litmus papers.

## Method

The initial tests for starch and reducing sugar must be carried out immediately the acid is added to the starch, before any significant hydrolysis has occurred.

Subsequently, the *Iodine* and *Benedict tests* must be carried out as quickly as possible upon removal from the water bath, after cooling under the tap.

## Result

Initially *Benedict's test* will be negative, but as hydrolysis produces reducing sugar a positive result will be obtained. Conversely, a strong initial positive result with the *Iodine test* will gradually become less pronounced.

# Experiment 27**

# Amylase

## Purpose

To show that salivary amylase hydrolyzes starch.

## Materials

1% starch solution
solution of iodine in potassium iodide
Benedict's solution

$50\,\mathrm{cm^3}$ measuring cylinder
$3 \times 100\,\mathrm{cm^3}$ beakers with watch glass to cover
bunsen burner
tripod
gauze
flameproof bench mat
4 test tubes
test tube rack
grease pencil
$250\,\mathrm{cm^3}$ beaker containing ice
stop clock
white spotting tiles
dropping pipettes

## Method

1 Rinse your mouth out thoroughly with about $50\,\mathrm{cm^3}$ tepid water into a beaker (Fig. 27.1).

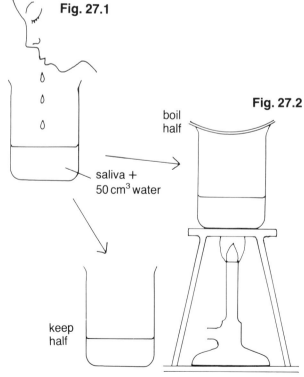

**Fig. 27.1**

**Fig. 27.2**

boil half

saliva + $50\,\mathrm{cm^3}$ water

keep half

2 Divide this solution into two equal parts (Fig. 27.2). Boil one half in a covered beaker for 10 minutes then cool thoroughly under running water.

3 Put the following labelled tubes in a beaker of ice (Fig. 27.3):

a tube containing about $2\,\mathrm{cm^3}$ salivary amylase solution.
a tube containing about $2\,\mathrm{cm^3}$ boiled amylase solution.
two tubes containing about $2\,\mathrm{cm^3}$ starch solution.

Leave the tubes in the icebath for 5 minutes.

**Fig. 27.3**

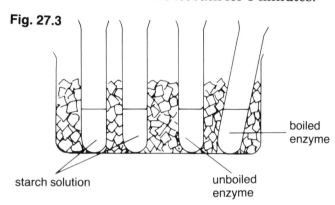

starch solution

boiled enzyme

unboiled enzyme

4 Pour one of the starch samples into the amylase solution and the other into the boiled enzyme (Fig. 27.4). **Immediately** start the stop clock and transfer a drop of each reaction mixture with a dropping pipette (use a separate pipette for each mixture) into cavities in a white spotting tile (Fig. 27.5). Immediately add a drop of iodine solution to each.

**Fig. 27.4**

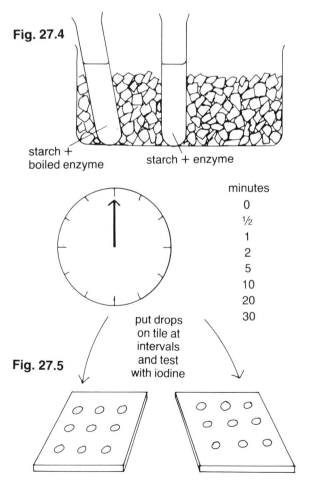

starch + boiled enzyme

starch + enzyme

minutes
0
½
1
2
5
10
20
30

put drops on tile at intervals and test with iodine

**Fig. 27.5**

5 Repeat step 4 after ½, 1, 2, 5, 10, 20, and 30 minutes.

50

**6** At the end of the experiment carry out *Benedict's test (Experiment 3)* on the remainder of each starch-amylase mixture (Fig. 27.6).

**Fig. 27.6**

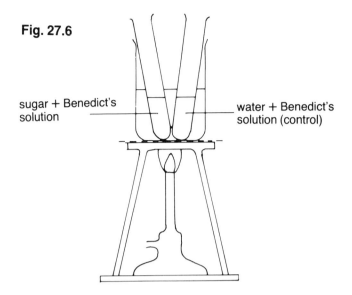

sugar + Benedict's solution

water + Benedict's solution (control)

# Result

Record your observations including the time to reach the end point, ie when no blue-black coloration occurs with iodine. What was the purpose of the control tube containing boiled enzyme?

# Suggestions for further work**

**a** Either chew a small piece of bread for about a minute or place a little starch gel on the tip of the tongue for the same period. Record any change in taste and relate this to the results obtained in the above experiment.

**b** Repeat steps 3 – 5 of this experiment but this time, instead of boiled amylase solution for the control, use 2 cm³ unboiled amylase solution to which a few drops of dilute hydrochloric acid (an irritant – **CARE**) have been added. Record your results. To aid your conclusions, test the pH of your saliva with indicator paper.

**c** Repeat the experiment (omitting the boiled enzyme control) at a series of temperatures, for example 0°C (icebath), 20°C (or room temperature), 30°C, 40°C, 50°C, 60°C, 70°C. Thermostatically-controlled waterbaths, if available, are ideal, otherwise use a controlled bunsen flame to maintain the appropriate temperature in a $1\,000\,\text{cm}^3$ beaker half-filled with water. It is not necessary that the temperatures used are precisely those suggested above, provided the actual temperature is taken accurately with a thermometer and it is held constant for the duration of each experiment. Take samples for testing with iodine every 30 seconds until the end-point is reached. Plot a graph of the time taken to reach end-point against the temperature – this will give an indication of the optimum temperature for the enzyme.

# Experiment 27**
# Amylase

## Introduction

This experiment is best carried out in the home economics room.

Amylase is an important human digestive enzyme, hydrolyzing starch to maltose. Starch digestion starts in the mouth due to the action of salivary amylase. However, once the food is swallowed the acid conditions of the stomach inhibit amylase activity. The alkaline conditions of the small intestine favour the later action of an amylase produced by the pancreas, and it is here that the bulk of starch is hydrolyzed to maltose. The enzyme maltase in the intestinal secretions subsequently hydrolyzes the maltose to glucose for absorption.

It is interesting to compare the mild conditions of temperature and pH employed in this experiment with the fierce conditions required for non-enzymic hydrolysis of starch (see *Experiment 26*).

## Materials

Watch glasses, or a sheet of ordinary glass on a white background could be substituted for white spotting tiles.

## Method

a The tubes need to be left in the ice bath for 5 minutes to equilibriate at 0°C.

b The method requires good organization in the early stages when the *Iodine test* has to be carried out at half- or one-minute intervals. It is tempting to spot out the iodine solution beforehand and then simply add the reaction mixture. This is satisfactory provided the iodine solution is not exposed for more than a minute or two before use as it tends to lose its iodine as vapour, thus giving a weaker response to starch.

## Result

With each successive test of the unboiled enzyme-starch reaction mixture the characteristic starch-iodine dense blue colour will become fainter, gradually changing via purple to brown due to enzymic hydrolysis of the starch by the salivary amylase. The purple colour is due to dextrins formed as intermediate breakdown products. The final product, maltose, will give a positive *Benedict's test*. The length of time taken to hydrolyze all the starch present varies according to the initial concentration of the amylase solution as well as individual differences. In fact, occasionally, individuals occur with an amylase deficiency in their saliva.

The control tube, containing boiled, therefore denatured, enzyme will persistently give a positive starch test. A control is necessary to demonstrate that starch will not spontaneously change in the duration of the experiment and, therefore, that the rapid changes in the experimental tube are brought about by the active enzyme. As no maltose is formed in the control tube, *Benedict's test* will prove negative in this case.

## Suggestions for further work**

a After a while a sweet taste will be noticed, owing to hydrolysis of starch to maltose by salivary amylase. Normally, of course, food is not in the mouth long enough for this to occur.

b The acidified enzyme will not catalyse the hydrolysis of starch as effectively since the pH optimum for amylase is slightly alkaline and the hydrochloric acid has an inhibitory effect. Saliva itself is usually slightly alkaline but sometimes dissolved substances taken into the mouth make it slightly acid. As pointed out in the introduction, the hydrochloric acid of the gastric juice will stop starch digestion once the food reaches the stomach, so the effect of salivary amylase in digestion of starch is negligible.

c In this experiment, it would save time if different groups employed different temperatures. However, if valid comparisons are to be made, a $2 \, cm^3$ aliquot of the same original saliva solution must be used by each group. If several thermostatically controlled waterbaths are available they can be held at different temperatures. If only one waterbath is available it can be set at 30°C (or thereabouts, provided the temperature is accurately recorded) and after each experiment the temperature can be increased, in 10°C steps, allowing sufficient time for equilibration; however, this is very time consuming. Do not rely on the dial setting of a thermostatically controlled waterbath as these are often inaccurate – always use a thermometer.

The temperature optimum of human salivary amylase is approximately 40°C (body temperature is 37°C) and at this temperature there will be a rapid hydrolysis of the starch and therefore the end point (no reaction with iodine solution) will be reached rapidly. At higher temperatures there will be a reduction in efficiency due to denaturation of the enzyme.

Although the actual times to reach the end point will vary according to the potency of the particular saliva solution, a graphical comparison of time against temperature should give an indication of the optimum temperature of amylase.

In addition, a graph of reaction rate against temperature should be plotted, as this is the standard way of expressing this information, where

$$\text{reaction rate (min}^{-1}) = \frac{1}{\text{time to reach end point in minutes}}$$

Fig. 27.1 indicates the general shape of such a curve.

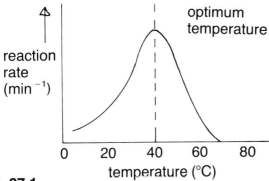

**Fig. 27.1**
Effect of temperature on the action of amylase

# Experiment 28**

# Dialysis

## Purpose

To separate a mixture of starch and glucose.

## Materials

2% starch solution

glucose powder

iodine in potassium iodide solution

'Clinistix' test papers

100 cm$^3$ beaker

25 cm$^3$ measuring cylinder

spatula or teaspoon

stirring rod

Visking tubing

filter funnel

thread

retort stand, clamp and boss

1 000 cm$^3$ beaker

clock

white spotting tile or flat plate

dropping pipettes or eye droppers

## Method

1 Stir about half a teaspoonful of glucose powder into about 25 cm$^3$ of the starch solution.

2 Soften a piece of Visking tubing (about 20 cm long) in water and open it.

3 Tie one end of the tubing with a very firm knot (do not use the thread at this stage).

4 Using the filter funnel pour about 20 cm$^3$ of the starch–glucose mixture into the open end of the length of Visking tube.

5 Tie a knot in the open end and suspend this Visking 'sausage' from the retort stand using the thread (Fig. 28.1).

**Fig. 28.1**

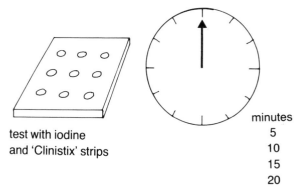

thread

stir continuously take samples

starch-glucose solution

water

knotted Visking tubing

6 Place the 'sausage' in a large beaker about half full of water. Take a sample of the water immediately and put half into each of two cavities of a white spotting tile (Fig. 28.2). Test for starch by adding a drop of iodine solution *(Experiment 6)* and for glucose using 'Clinistix' test papers *(Experiment 5)*.

**Fig. 28.2**

test with iodine and 'Clinistix' strips

minutes
5
10
15
20

7 Stirring the water continuously, take samples after 5, 10, 15 and 20 minutes. Carry out the *Iodine* and *'Clinistix' tests* on all the samples.

## Result

Draw up a table of results as shown below using + for a positive reaction and − for a negative reaction.

### Table of results for Experiment 28

| Time | Iodine test | Clinistix test | Comment |
|------|-------------|----------------|---------|
| zero | | | |
| 5 minutes | | | |
| 10 minutes | | | |
| 15 minutes | | | |
| 20 minutes | | | |

# Experiment 28**
# Dialysis

## Introduction

Dialysis is a technique for separating a mixture on the basis of differences in the molecular size of its components. The Visking tubing acts as a selectively permeable membrane. Small molecules can pass through the micropores of the membrane but large molecules are held back.

The experiment enables the teacher to draw a useful analogy between the Visking membrane and the intestinal lining, indicating the need for digestion of large molecules into smaller molecules before absorption can take place. Thus, for example, the carbohydrate in food must be hydrolyzed by digestive enzymes to monosaccharide sugars before it can pass through the selectively permeable intestinal lining into the blood.

In addition, the experiment provides opportunity for discussion of the physical phenomenon of diffusion.

## Materials

a For the method of preparing starch solution see *page 148;* iodine in potassium iodide, *page 148.*

b Visking tubing *(page 155)* is the brand name for a regenerated cellulose tubing. It is available in several different diameters.

c If a 1 000 cm³ beaker is not available, any large, clean vessel will do just as well.

## Method

a It is a good idea to let the pupils mix the glucose into the starch solution themselves (rather than give it to them already made up). This makes the subsequent separation of the glucose by dialysis much more convincing.

b If the Visking tubing proves hard to open, the end should be wetted under the tap. When the starch–glucose mixture has been introduced, and *before* placing the 'sausage' in the beaker of water, the outside of the Visking tubing must be thoroughly rinsed with tap water to remove any traces of starch or glucose.

c It may seem rather pedantic to ask the pupils to confirm that there is no starch or glucose in the water in the beaker at the beginning of the experiment, when they may have just run it from the tap. However, it should be emphasized that this is good scientific practice. The situation at the commencement of any experiment must be established in order to act as a control for changes which may later occur. After all, it is possible, for example, that the beaker itself could have been previously contaminated with traces of starch or glucose.

d Continuous stirring of the water is needed. There will be a net movement of glucose molecules along a diffusion gradient across the membrane from inside the 'sausage' to the water in the beaker. If this water was still, glucose would tend to accumulate as a concentrated layer just outside the membrane, thus reducing the diffusion gradient across it and considerably slowing down the process. Stirring will dissipate this glucose layer, thus maintaining a steady rate of diffusion.

## Result

The large starch molecules cannot pass through the membrane and the *Iodine test* will prove negative however long the experiment is run. Glucose will diffuse into the water in the beaker and eventually its concentration will be within the sensitivity range of the *Clinistix test* papers. The length of time this will take will depend on a number of factors such as the original concentration of glucose in the solution within the sausage, the volume of water in the beaker, and the efficiency of stirring.

Theoretically, if the water in the beaker was changed continuously, it is possible to achieve a starch solution of a very high purity. However, in practice, this would be a tedious and lengthy procedure, and it is considered sufficient to demonstrate the retention of starch molecules within the Visking tubing and the passage of the glucose molecules through it.

# Experiment 29**

# Starch gelatinization (1)

## Purpose

To find the temperature at which starch gelatinizes and to observe the effect of gelatinization on starch granules.

## Materials

starch

solution of iodine in potassium iodide

spatula

2 x 250 cm³ beakers

thermometer

5 boiling tubes with stirring rods

bunsen burner ⎤
tripod          ⎟  or small pan of
gauze          ⎟  water on a hotplate
flameproof bench mat ⎦

microscope

microscope slides

coverslips

lens tissues

grease pencil

## Method

1 Suspend about 5 g (1 heaped teaspoon) starch in about 100 cm³ water in a 250 cm³ beaker.

2 Put about 10 cm³ of the suspension in a boiling tube fitted with a stirring rod.

3 Put the boiling tube in a beaker of water at 50°C. Keep the water at this temperature for 10 minutes, stirring the starch suspension frequently, then remove the boiling tube. Examine the contents of the tube for evidence of gelatinization. (Take care if your thermometer contains mercury. Spilt mercury from a broken thermometer must be treated with lime and sulphur.)

4 Put a drop of the starch suspension on to a labelled microscope slide and observe under the microscope (see *Experiment 1*). Draw what you see.

5 Repeat steps 2, 3 and 4 at 60°, 70°, 80° and 90°C.

## Result

Record your results on a chart.

**Table of results for Experiment 29**

| Temperature | Type of starch _____ | |
| | macroscopic appearance | microscopic appearance (draw representative starch granules) |
| --- | --- | --- |
| 50°C | | |
| 60°C | | |
| 70°C | | |
| 80°C | | |
| 90°C | | |

At what temperature did the starch gel?

Relate the results to the cooking and setting of sauces and blancmange.

## Suggestions for further work**

Carry out the experiment with different starches, eg potato, rice, maize, wheat, arrowroot, and with cereals such as ground rice and semolina.

56

# Experiment 29**
# Starch gelatinization (1)

## Introduction

When starch is heated in water, the water gradually penetrates through the surface of each granule. Hydrogen bonds between the crystalline starch molecules are broken and increased water uptake, as heating proceeds, causes the granule to swell. Some starch molecules leave the surface of the granule. This, with suspension of the swollen granules, results in formation of a colloidal dispersion. The mixture therefore thickens – gelatinization has occurred. This happens in foods like custard, and also in bread and cakes. It occurs within the cell in potatoes.

## Materials

a Any starch may be used (see *Suggestions for further work*). Cornflour is convenient and easily available from grocers. Other starches may be bought from chemicals suppliers.

b Iodine in potassium iodide solution, see *page 148*.

c A teaspoon can be used instead of a spatula, and a cup instead of a beaker for mixing the starch.

d See Appendix II for details of other equipment.

## Method

a The importance of frequent stirring will be obvious to pupils who have made custard and sauces. If the mixture is not stirred, water will not be available to some granules. The molecules will retain their crystalline formation, and the mass of unchanged granules will form a lump.

b While microscopic examination is not essential, it helps to explain the macroscopic observations. A *very small* drop is needed, and a coverslip should be used. Lower the coverslip carefully or air bubbles will cause confusion. Use low power first, then high power for drawing the granules. (See *Experiment 1* in both the *Teachers' Guide* and the *Pupils' Material*.)

c It is very time-consuming for one pupil to carry out the whole experiment. The apparatus will have to be modified if different pupils study the effects of different temperatures.

## Result

a The type of starch will determine the temperature at which rapid swelling begins. For cornflour it will be between 60°C and 70°C, with maximum viscosity at 90°C.

b Drawings of the microscopic appearance should illustrate swelling. It should *not* be decribed as 'bursting'.

c If a polarizing microscope is available, gelatinization is clearly (and beautifully) shown as loss of birefringence.

d If the tubes of starch paste are allowed to cool, *gelation* will be seen – formation of a gel due to hydrogen bonds between starch molecules. A continuous three-dimensional network is formed, with water molecules trapped in this solid framework.

## Suggestions for further work**

Other starches will have different gelatinization temperatures. See *Experiment 1* for the appearance of granules from different sources under the microscope.

# Experiment 30**

## Starch gelatinization (2)

### Purpose

To find the effect of sugar and acid on starch gelatinization.

### Materials

starch
sucrose
lemon juice
solution of iodine in potassium iodide

2 x 250 cm³ beakers
9 boiling tubes with stirring rods
grease pencil
test tube rack
dropping pipette (or eye dropper)
0-100°C thermometer
bunsen burner
tripod ⎤
gauze ⎬ or small pan of water on a hotplate
flameproof bench mat ⎦
microscope
microscope slides
coverslips
lens tissues

## Method

1. Suspend about 5 g starch in 100 cm³ water in a 250 cm³ beaker.

2. Put about 10 cm³ of the suspension in each of nine boiling tubes, fitted with stirring rods. Label them A, B, C, D, E, F, G, H, I.

3. Treat the tubes as follows:
   A, D, G: no additions
   B, E, H: add a pinch of sucrose
   C, F, I: add a few drops of lemon juice

4. Put tubes A, B and C into a 250 cm³ beaker half-full of water at 60°C. Stir the contents of each tube frequently. (Take care if you are using a mercury thermometer – treat any mercury spillage with sulphur and lime.)

5. At the end of 10 minutes remove the tubes from the waterbath and cool under the tap. Put a drop from each tube on to separate labelled microscope slides, looking, at the same time, for evidence of gelatinization in the tubes.

6. Observe the starch granules (stained and unstained) under the microscope (see Experiment 1). Draw what you see.

7. Repeat steps 4, 5 and 6 with tubes D, E and F at 70°C and with tubes G, H and I at 80°C.

## Result

Record the results on a chart.

### Table of results for Experiment 30

| | 60°C | | 70°C | | 80°C | |
|---|---|---|---|---|---|---|
| | macroscopic appearance | microscopic appearance * | macroscopic appearance | microscopic appearance * | macroscopic appearance | microscopic appearance * |
| Starch alone | | | | | | |
| Plus sucrose | | | | | | |
| Plus acid | | | | | | |

*draw representative granules

What effect do sucrose and acid have on gelatinization?

Relate the results to your observations in cookery, for example, the making of savoury and sweet sauces, lemon meringue pie.

58

# Experiment 30**
# Starch gelatinization (2)
## Introduction
The gelatinization (thickening) of starch is affected by:

**a** the type of starch

**b** starch concentration

**c** amount and rate of heating

**d** other ingredients such as sugar, protein and acid.

*Experiment 29* investigates **a** and **c**, and can easily be adapted to study **b**. The effect of protein is seen in batter mixtures where there are high proportions of egg and milk, but is little understood. This experiment attempts to show the effects of sugar and acid that might be observed in, for example, milk puddings, lemon meringues, custard added to rhubarb.

The term 'gelatinization' has been used for simplicity, but strictly speaking this refers only to the increase in viscosity that occurs on heating. Gel formation when the mixture is cooled should be referred to as 'gelation'.

## Materials
**a** Any starch may be used, but cornflour is probably the most readily available.

**b** Lemon juice may be fresh or preserved.

**c** Solution of iodine in potassium iodide, see *page 148*.

**d** The test tube rack must have holes large enough to take boiling tubes. See *page 155* for home-made alternative.

**e** The microscope should have x10 and x40 objectives if possible. Coverslips are not essential but the objective lens is less likely to touch the starch solution if they are used.

## Method
**a** Frequent stirring is essential to prevent the formation of lumps.

**b** It would be time-consuming for one pupil to carry out the whole of this experiment. Three pupils (or pairs of pupils) could each study one temperature.

**c** Step 6: use low power to observe the appearance of the starch granules then change to high power to draw a few representative granules. (See *Experiment 1.*)

## Result
The gelatinization temperature should increase slightly with the addition of sucrose. The sucrose competes with starch for water so swelling of the granules is delayed.

Acid should lower the gelatinization temperature. The acid causes hydrolysis of starch molecules on the surface of the granules. This makes it easier for water molecules to penetrate and hydrate the rest of the starch. However, longer heating may make the final gel thinner because of partial hydrolysis of the starch molecules to dextrin, maltose and glucose (see *Experiment 26*). This explains why some recipes for lemon meringue pie recommend addition of the lemon juice after the sauce has thickened.

# Experiment 31**

# Lipase

## Purpose

To show that lipase hydrolyzes oils to form acids.

## Materials

1% commercial lipase solution

olive oil

⚠ 50% alcohol

⚠ phenol red solution

2% sodium carbonate solution

250 cm$^3$ beaker

bunsen burner

tripod ⎤ or small pan of

gauze ⎥ water on a hotplate

flameproof bench mat ⎦

3 test tubes

test tube rack

grease pencil

dropping pipette (or eye dropper)

waterbath at 35-40°C (or pan of water
    maintained at 35-40°C).

## Method

1 Half-fill the beaker with water and bring to
   the boil.

2 Pour some lipase solution into a test tube
   (about one-third full) and place it in the
   boiling waterbath for at least 10 minutes.
   Cool thoroughly under running water before
   using the boiled enzyme solution.

3 Make an oil emulsion by shaking up about
   1 cm$^3$ of olive oil with about 10 cm$^3$ of 50%
   alcohol in a test tube. Add about 2 cm$^3$ of
   unboiled lipase solution.

4 Make up a second oil emulsion as in step 3 but
   this time add about 2 cm$^3$ of the boiled lipase
   solution as a control.

5 To each tube add 1 cm$^3$ of phenol red solution
   and just sufficient 2% sodium carbonate
   solution to give a reddish tinge. (Add the
   sodium carbonate a few drops at a time,
   shaking after each addition.)

6 Place both tubes in a waterbath at 35-40°C.

## Result

Record the results and conclusions after an hour.
Phenol red is an indicator which is red in alkaline
solution, turning yellow in acid solution.

## Suggestions for further work**

Use the method described above to test the effect
of lipase on milk. First sterilize the milk (to
prevent any bacterial hydrolysis) by boiling it
for 20 minutes. Cool the milk thoroughly before
adding the enzyme (why is this important?). Do
a control using boiled enzyme. Record your
results and conclusions.

# Experiment 31**
# Lipase

## Introduction

The lipases are a group of enzymes which hydrolyze fats to fatty acids and glycerol. This is the function they perform in human digestion, lipases being present in gastric, pancreatic and intestinal juices. A fat-lipase mixture will gradually become more acidic as hydrolysis proceeds, because of the accumulation of fatty acids, and phenol red can be used as an indicator for this reaction.

Lipases are also responsible for hydrolytic rancidity in fatty foods such as butter, cream and meats. The lipases may be from the food or from bacteria. Cooking or pasteurization inactivates the enzymes, and refrigeration slows down this type of food spoilage.

## Materials

a For method of making up percentage solutions see Appendix I.

b Lipase, *page 146*.

c The alcohol is added to stabilize the emulsion. Methanol (see *Alcohol, page 146*) is the least expensive; it is provided in different dilutions with water. Thus 70% alcohol, for example, will need further dilution. However, the precise dilution is not critical.

An alternative way of making a stable oil emulsion is to shake up equal volumes of oil and water, plus a small amount of bile salts *(page 146)*. In any case this is worth demonstrating as it emphasizes the importance of the bile salts in the bile from the gall bladder in human digestion of fats and oils.

d Phenol red, *page 148*. As alternatives, phenolphthalein (pink in alkaline solution to colourless in acid) or universal indicator solution (blue to red), could equally well be used.

e If a thermostatically controlled waterbath is not available, a beaker of water can be maintained at 35–40°C with a bunsen burner (or, indeed, a pan of water on a hotplate).

## Method

a It is a good idea for the teacher to demonstrate the indicator properties of phenol red beforehand, simply by adding a few drops to a $cm^3$ of sodium bicarbonate solution in a test tube (when a red colour will be seen) and then acidifying this solution with a weak acid, say vinegar (ethanoic) or lemon juice (citric), when the colour will change to yellow.

b When the pupil is adding the sodium carbonate (step 5), care must be taken to add the minimum amount just to produce a pinkish tinge. If the solution is made too alkaline to start with, it will take too long for sufficient fatty acid to build up to make the solution acidic, and the experiment may not be completed in the time available.

## Result

The indicator in the experimental tube will turn yellow due to enzymic hydrolysis of the fat to fatty acids and glycerol, making the solution acidic. The control will remain pink as the boiled, therefore denatured, enzyme is non-functional.

Should the teacher wish to demonstrate the presence of glycerol in the experimental tube, add a few drops of dilute copper sulphate and a few drops dilute potassium hydroxide, when a strong blue colour will be formed.

## Suggestions for further work**

The principle here is the same – the active (unboiled) enzyme hydrolysing the oil droplets in the milk. It is, of course, important to cool the milk thoroughly after sterilizing it, as if the lipase was added to hot milk it would be partially (and irreversibly) denatured and lose much of its activity.

61

# Experiment 32*

# Slip point of fats

## Purpose

To find the temperature at which fat melts.

## Materials

solid fat, eg lard, various margarines, butter

capillary tube
paper tissues
0–100°C thermometer
elastic band
retort stand and clamp
250 cm³ beaker ⎤
bunsen burner ⎮
tripod ⎮ or small pan of
gauze ⎮ water on a hotplate
flameproof bench mat ⎮
glass rod ⎦

## Method

1 Push a small amount of the fat into a capillary tube. Clean the outside of the tube.

2 Place the tube against a thermometer so that the fat is next to the bulb. Attach the two using an elastic band (Fig. 32.1). Take care if your thermometer is mercury – spilt mercury from a broken thermometer must be treated with lime and sulphur.

**Fig. 32.1**

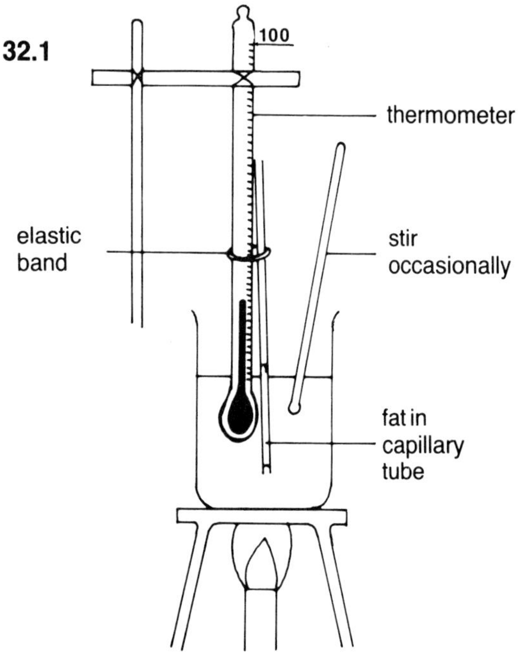

elastic band — thermometer — stir occasionally — fat in capillary tube

3 Suspend the tube and the thermometer in a beaker of cold water so that they do not touch the sides or the bottom of the beaker.

4 Heat the water gently, stirring it occasionally.

5 Note the temperature at which the fat becomes clear and begins to run out of the tube.

## Result

The slip point is the temperature at which the fat clears and begins to run out of the tube.

## Suggestions for further work*

a Repeat for other fats to compare melting points.

b An alternative way of determining melting point is to put fat and thermometer in a boiling tube and to heat in boiling water. If temperatures are taken every five minutes until the fat melts and for a further, say, 10 minutes, a graph of time against temperature may be drawn. This will show the melting point of the fat and also illustrate latent heat.

62

# Experiment 32*
# Slip point of fats

## Introduction

Fats are chosen for use in foods according to their melting points. Those used in confectionery, for example, must melt over a narrow range near to body temperature – cocoa butter is the best example. A high melting-point fat is used for flaky pastry, to form layers between the sheets of dough. Fats for cake-making should melt over a wide range, to assist creaming and rising.

Pure compounds have sharp melting points but fats consist of a mixture of triglycerides, each of which has a specific melting point.

The melting point is, strictly speaking, the temperature at which the last trace of fat melts. It is more convenient to determine the slip point, the temperature at which the fat starts to melt, which provides a good indication of the melting point of the fat.

## Materials

a  Very small amounts of the fats are needed.

b  Capillary tubes, *page 151*.

c  A pan of water on a cooker hob could be used instead of the beaker and bunsen burner, but care will be needed when using the retort stand to suspend the thermometer and capillary tube in the water. Of course, it is easier to see when the fat has melted through the glass of a beaker than when a pan is used.

## Result and Suggestions for further work*

a  Butter starts melting at about 35°C; the slip point of dripping is over 50°C.

b  The wide melting range of most fats will be clearly shown by suggestion **b.** A graph of the following type will be obtained:

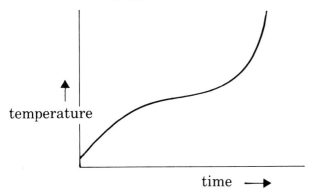

A better graph will be seen if the fat, once melted, is allowed to cool and the temperature is taken every five minutes until it has solidified.

In both cases, the slope of the graph flattens out while a change of state is taking place, from solid to liquid and vice versa. This shows the melting point of the fat, and it also shows that heat is being absorbed or given out by the fat with a reduction of temperature change. This 'invisible' heat is termed *latent* heat. It changes the state of a substance without changing the temperature. This happens, as mentioned in the *Introduction,* at a sharp temperature with a pure triglyceride, but all common fats are mixtures of very many triglycerides.

# Experiment 33*** ⚠

## Smoke point of fats

**This experiment must be carried out in a fume cupboard. Wear eye protection and have a flameproof bench mat ready in case the fat ignites. Should a mercury thermometer break, collect all the mercury, and treat the WHOLE area with a mixture of sulphur and lime.**

## Purpose

To find the temperature at which an oil or fat vapourizes.

## Materials

oil or fat samples, eg corn oil, lard, dripping

fume cupboard
crucible
sand tray
tripod
gauze
2 flameproof bench mats
retort stand and clamp
thermometer (reading to 300°C)
spatula
bunsen burner

## Method

Make sure you are wearing eye protection before starting this experiment.

1 Put the crucible in the sand tray, supported on the tripod and gauze (Fig. 33.1).

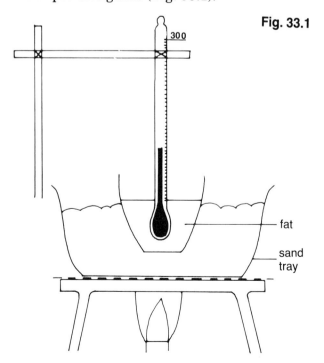

**Fig. 33.1**

2 Support the thermometer vertically so that the bulb is in the crucible.

3 Put enough fat in the crucible to cover the thermometer bulb.

4 Heat the sand tray gently until a blue haze appears over the crucible.

5 Stop heating immediately and record the temperature of the fat.

## Result

The temperature at which the fat vapourizes is the smoke point.

# Experiment 33***
# Smoke point of fats

## Introduction

One of the advantages of using fat as a heat transfer medium is that it can be heated to about 200°C, ie a far higher temperature than water. The highest temperature to which the fat can be heated before it vapourizes is called the 'smoke point' of the fat. At this temperature, fatty acids begin to split off from the glycerol (hydrolysis, Fig. 33.1), and the glycerol is decomposed to acrolein (Fig. 33.2), an irritating, acrid-smelling substance, if the temperature is raised still further.

Temperatures used for frying are usually, of course, well below the smoke point. If fats are used repeatedly, however, some hydrolysis occurs each time they are heated. The presence of the fatty acids and glycerol lowers the smoke point of over-used fat.

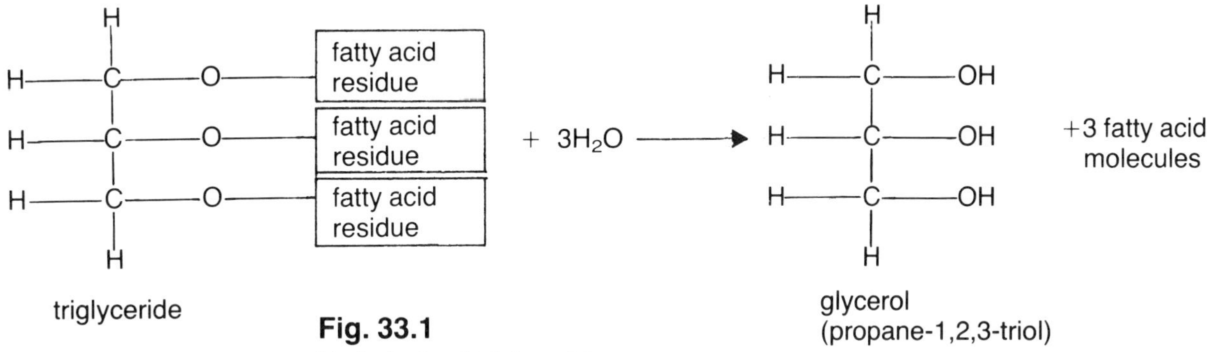

triglyceride

**Fig. 33.1**

Hydrolysis of triglycerides

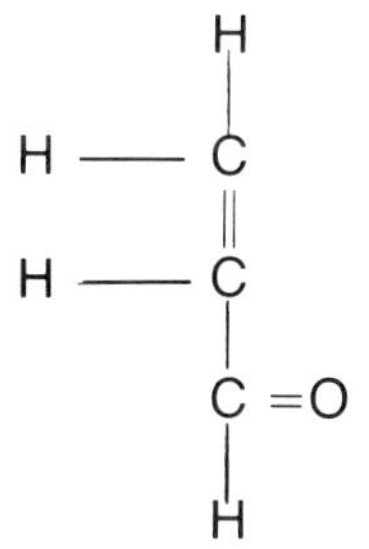

glycerol
(propane-1,2,3-triol)

**Fig. 33.2.**   Acrolein

## Materials

a  As well as a range of fresh fats and oils, it may be useful to include an over-used fat for comparison. Small amounts (about 10 g) are needed.

b  A fume cupboard is, for safety's sake, essential.

c  See Appendix II for details of other apparatus.

## Method

This is obviously a dangerous experiment. The precautions suggested in the *Pupils' Material* should be followed scrupulously to avoid the risk of fire.

## Result

Smoke points may be as low as 190°C for butter and as high as 250°C for good quality cooking oil.

# Experiment 34*

# Water content of fats

## Purpose

To compare, approximately, the water content of several fats.

## Materials

a range of fats such as corn oil, margarines, low-fat spreads, 'solid vegetable oil', dripping

balance or scales

grease pencil

boiling tubes (one for each fat to be tested)

spatula or knife

waterbath at 50°C (or pan of water on a hotplate)

## Method

1 Weigh 20 g of each fat into separate, labelled, boiling tubes.

2 Put the tubes into a water bath at about 50°C for 30 minutes. (Take care that it does not boil dry.)

3 Observe the appearance of the fats warm and after allowing to cool.

## Result

The water, if present, will have formed a layer at the bottom of the boiling tubes. Measure the height of the water layer for each fat.

---

# Experiment 35*

# Trypsin

## Purpose

To demonstrate the protein-digesting action of trypsin using agar gel containing fat-free dried milk as indicator.

## Materials

petri dish (with lid) containing a thin layer of gel prepared from fat-free dried milk, agar powder and water

5% trypsin solution

⚠ dilute hydrochloric acid

3 watch glasses

grease pencil

blotting paper

scissors *or* cork borer (1 cm diameter)

forceps (or tweezers)

dropping pipette (or eye dropper)

## Method

1 Label the watch glasses $A$, $B$ and $C$. In $A$ place about 5 cm$^3$ trypsin solution, in $B$ about 5 cm$^3$ trypsin solution plus 12 drops dilute hydrochloric acid and in $C$ about 5 cm$^3$ water.

2 With the grease pencil divide the underside of the petri dish (*not* the lid – why not?) into three segments labelled $A$, $B$ and $C$.

3 Prepare three blotting paper discs of equal size, about 1 cm diameter.

4 Using forceps, immerse the first disc into the enzyme solution in watch glass $A$. After shaking off any droplets, place the soaked disc on top of the gel in segment $A$ (Fig. 35.1).

**Fig. 35.1**

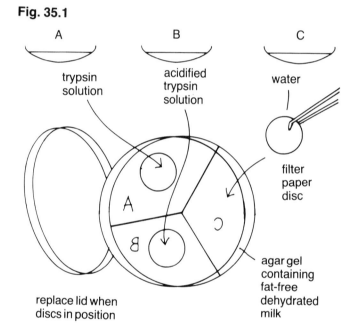

trypsin solution

acidified trypsin solution

water

filter paper disc

agar gel containing fat-free dehydrated milk

replace lid when discs in position

5 Repeat the procedure (using clean forceps), immersing the second disc in the acidified enzyme (watch glass $B$) and the third in the water (watch glass $C$), and placing them in segments $B$ and $C$ respectively of the gel. Replace the petri dish lid.

6 After a few hours examine the gel carefully.

## Result

Record the results. The solution on the blotting paper discs will diffuse into the surrounding medium.

A clear region in the milky-coloured gel surrounding a disc indicates digestion of the milk protein.

66

# Experiment 34*
# Water content of fats

## Introduction

The presence of water in certain fats may affect the use of the fats. In frying, for example, water causes spattering and increases the amount of hydrolysis (see *Experiment 33*) with consequent lowering of the smoke point.

Water is present in these fats as tiny droplets dispersed in a continuous fatty phase. Emulsifying agents, either naturally present (as in butter) or added (eg low-fat spread) are necessary to maintain the emulsion. If the emulsion is heated slowly, as described in this experiment, the fat and the water separate.

## Materials

A pan on a cooker hob could be used as a waterbath.

## Method

The weight of fat does not need to be known

exactly, nor does it need to be precisely 20 g, but similar amounts of each fat should be used for comparison.

## Result

Butter and margarine contain about 16% water. Low fat spread contains over 50% water. Whey proteins, if present, will make the watery phase of these fats appear cloudy. Lard, dripping and oils contain only a trace, if that, of water.

Results may be related to uses for the fats and to energy values, for example:

|  | % water | Energy value per 100g | |
|---|---|---|---|
|  |  | kcal | kJ |
| low fat spread | 57 | 366 | 1506 |
| butter | 16 | 740 | 3041 |
| lard | trace | 891 | 3663 |
| oils | trace | 899 | 3696 |

Note that the higher the water content, the lower the energy value.

# Experiment 35*
# Trypsin

## Introduction

Several protein-digesting enzymes (proteases) are involved in human digestion, perhaps the two best known being pepsin, present in gastric juice, and trypsin, in pancreatic juice. Both enzymes catalyse hydrolysis of the protein to smaller polypeptides with some amino acids.

In this experiment, the clearing of a previously cloudy dried milk gel is a convenient indicator of trypsin activity.

## Materials

a The gel is prepared in a 400 cm³ beaker as follows:

| | |
|---|---|
| fat-free dried milk (eg 'Marvel') | 4 g |
| agar powder | 2 g |
| water | 200 cm³ |

Stir the mixture well and bring to the boil, stirring continuously. Then, while the solution is still hot, divide it into 10–12 petri dishes so that the *thinnest possible layer* is formed. Otherwise, during the experiment, transparent zones may not be formed through the full depth of the gel, thus making it difficult to detect any change.

b The trypsin *(page 149)* solution must be freshly prepared.

## Method

a It is unwise to divide the petri dish *lid* into segments (step 2) as if the lid subsequently rotates on the base, the original labels will be confused.

b Use of a cork borer is the best way of ensuring that the blotting paper discs are of equal size. Alternatively, the pupil could draw around, say, a small coin and carefully cut out the disc.

## Result

A clear region should form around the disc in segment A (trypsin solution) but not in segment B (acidified trypsin) demonstrating that acid conditions inhibit the enzyme. In fact, conditions in the small intestine where trypsin acts have been rendered slightly alkaline by the sodium hydrogen carbonate (sodium bicarbonate) of the bile and pancreatic juice acting on the acid chyme from the stomach. The disc in segment C (water only) is a control, to demonstrate that the clear zone in A is due to the trypsin.

# Experiment 36*

# Pepsin and trypsin

## Purpose

To demonstrate the relative effectiveness of pepsin and trypsin under different pH conditions.

## Materials

hard-boiled egg

5% pepsin solution

5% trypsin solution

⚠ dilute hydrochloric acid

dilute sodium carbonate solution

250 cm$^3$ beaker ⎤
bunsen burner ⎟
tripod ⎬ or small pan of
gauze ⎟ water on a hotplate
flameproof bench mat ⎦
chopping board

knife

cork borer (0.5 cm diameter)

ruler

8 test tubes

test tube rack

grease pencil

25 cm$^3$ measuring cylinder

dropping pipettes (or eye droppers)

waterbath at 37–40°C (or a pan on a hotplate)

## Method

1  Half-fill the beaker with water and bring to the boil.

2  Put pepsin solution into a test tube (about one-third full). Add a similar amount of trypsin solution to another tube. Place both tubes in the boiling waterbath for at least 10 minutes. Cool thoroughly under running cold water before using the boiled enzyme solutions.

3  Pick away the shell from the egg. Use the cork-borer to prepare six cylinders of egg white exactly 1 cm in length.

4  Place one egg white cylinder carefully in the bottom of each of six test tubes labelled A to F, and then add the solutions indicated below:

Tube A: 5 cm$^3$ pepsin + 12 drops hydrochloric acid.

Tube B: 5 cm$^3$ pepsin + 12 drops sodium carbonate.

Tube C: 5 cm$^3$ boiled pepsin + 12 drops hydrochloric acid.

Tube D: 5 cm$^3$ trypsin + 12 drops hydrochloric acid.

Tube E: 5 cm$^3$ trypsin + 12 drops sodium carbonate.

Tube F: 5 cm$^3$ boiled trypsin + 12 drops sodium carbonate.

5  Put all six tubes in a thermostatically controlled waterbath at 37–40°C. Examine the contents of the test tubes 24 hours later and compare the amounts of protein digestion (disappearance of egg white) that have taken place. (If a thermostatically controlled waterbath is not available, just leave the tubes in a warm place.)

## Result

Express the results for each tube on a four point scale 0–3 where:

0 = no discernible change in the cylinder of egg white

1 = some digestion

2 = considerable digestion

3 = almost complete disappearance of the cylinder.

From these results state whether pepsin works best in acid or alkaline medium; similarly for trypsin.

Why were the control tubes C and F necessary?

## Suggestions for further work*

As an alternative to egg white cylinders prepared, as described above, suck egg albumen solution into a length of glass capillary tubing. On immersing the capillary in warm water the albumen will solidify. Use a file to divide the capillary tube into 1 cm lengths. What is the advantage of these albumen-filled glass cylinders over the egg white cylinders prepared in step 3 above? Alternatively, using these albumen-filled lengths of capillary tubing, devise an experiment to find the optimum temperature for pepsin (or trypsin) action.

# Experiment 36*
# Pepsin and trypsin

## Introduction

This experiment demonstrates very effectively the differing pH requirements of these two enzymes. Pepsin acts best in acid conditions, being inhbited by alkali, whilst with trypsin the reverse is the case. The results can be usefully linked with their sites of action, pepsin in the very acid conditions of the stomach (maybe as low as pH 3 or 4), trypsin in the alkaline (pH 8) conditions of the small intestine.

## Materials

a The pepsin *(page 148)* and trypsin *(page 149)* solutions must be freshly prepared.

b A cork borer is essential if exactly equal cylinders of egg-white are to be obtained for valid comparison.

## Method

a A ruler must be used to measure cylinders exactly 1 cm long.

b A thermostatically controlled waterbath is ideal. Otherwise leave the tubes in a warm place.

c Obviously it is important that the teacher arranges that the pupils are able to see and record the result for themselves the next day.

## Result

Pepsin works best in acid medium, trypsin in alkaline. Typical results after 24 hours might be:

| Tube | | Tube | |
|---|---|---|---|
| A | 2–3 | D | 0 |
| B | 0 | E | 2–3 |
| C | 0–1 | F | 0–1 |

Tube $C$ is a control to show that the pronounced hydrolysis in tube $A$ is due to the pepsin and not to the acid. Similarly tube $F$ is a control against tube $E$. Tubes $B$ and $D$ demonstrate the inhibition of pepsin and trypsin by alkali and acid respectively.

## Suggestions for further work*

The principle here is exactly the same, with the advantage that at the end (or at some intermediate point) of the experiment the albumen-filled cylinders can be removed from the test tubes, the length of unhydrolyzed albumen measured with a ruler and the results expressed quantitatively in mm rather than on a four point scale.

To demonstrate the influence of temperature on enzyme action, set up several tubes containing pepsin + acid + albumen cylinder (or trypsin + alkali + albumen cylinder) and maintain each tube at a different temperature. Record the time taken for disappearance of the egg albumen and plot a graph of rate of reaction against temperature. It may be useful to refer to the *Pupils' Worksheet, Experiment 27, Suggestions for further work, section (c)*.

# Experiment 37*

# Rennet

## Purpose

To demonstrate the coagulation of milk protein.

## Materials

pasteurized milk
commercial rennet

250 cm$^3$ beaker
bunsen burner
tripod                        } or small pan of
gauze                            water on a hotplate
flameproof bench mat
2 test tubes
test tube rack
grease pencil
dropping pipettes
waterbath at 35–40°C

## Method

1 Half-fill the beaker with water and bring to the boil.

2 Pour some rennet into a test tube (about one-third full) and place it in the boiling pan or beaker for at least 20 minutes. Cool thoroughly under running water before using the boiled enzyme solution.

3 To about 10 cm$^3$ milk add approximately 1 cm$^3$ unboiled rennet. As a control prepare another tube containing 10 cm$^3$ milk and 1 cm$^3$ boiled rennet.

4 Place both tubes in a waterbath at 35–40°C for 30 minutes.

## Result

Record your observations. Formation of a milk clot indicates coagulation of protein by the rennet.

# Suggestions for further work*

a Transfer the milk clot into a small beaker and, using a knife, break it up into small pieces. This will produce curds (solid) and whey (liquid). Heat the curds and whey and then strain through muslin. The curds can be salted slightly and the resulting 'cheese' tasted. (**CARE** – for tasting, all apparatus must be scrupulously clean.)

b Milk protein will also coagulate in acid conditions. Add 1 cm$^3$ of lemon juice to 10 cm$^3$ milk and leave for 24 hours in warm conditions. Again a milk clot will form. As a control use milk alone.

# Experiment 37*
# Rennet

## Introduction

The word 'rennet' is the commercial name for an extract of calf stomach lining which contains the enzyme rennin. It is widely used in the dairy industry to coagulate the casein in milk. The resulting curds, which consist of protein plus fat, are made into cheese. The whey, containing lactose and some soluble protein, is used for animal feed, to add to margarine, or to extract the protein.

Its chemical effect is that it causes the insoluble protein of milk, casein, to be precipitated as solid calcium caseinate. These curds (and hence cheese) are thus mainly protein but will also contain fat globules trapped as the caseinate is precipitated. Rennin is produced in all young mammals, including humans, in order that milk, the main (and often sole) source of nutrients in the early weeks, can be rendered semi-solid, thus passing more slowly along the digestive tract giving the other digestive enzymes more time to act.

## Materials

a An alternative to commercial rennet (see *page 148*) is to chop up some butterwort leaves with water, add silver sand for abrasion, grind in a mortar and filter. The filtrate contains an enzyme similar to rennin.

b If a thermostatically operated waterbath is not available, a beaker of water can be maintained at 37–40°C with a burner, or a pan of water using a hotplate.

## Method

Twenty minutes boiling of rennet is recommended in order to make certain that complete denaturation has taken place, rendering the enzyme inactive.

## Result

The casein clot will form in the tube with the unboiled rennet. No effect will be observed with the boiled enzyme.

## Suggestions for further work*

a It cannot be over-emphasized that great care must be taken to avoid any contamination, especially if the work is carried out in a laboratory.

It is useful and relevant to link up this practical work with a visit to a diary, if this can be arranged.

b Protein solubility depends on the pH of the medium. Caseinogen will precipitate in acid conditions.

# Experiment 38*

# Heat coagulation of proteins

## Purpose

To observe the temperatures at which proteins from egg, meat and milk coagulate.

## Materials

2 eggs
vinegar
minced beef
milk
sugar

boiling tube
0–100°C thermometer
400 cm³ beaker ⎤
bunsen burner ⎟
tripod ⎬ or small pan of water on a hotplate
gauze ⎟
flameproof bench mat ⎦
retort stand
clamp
filter paper
filter funnel
funnel stand
2 x 100 cm³ beakers

## Method

### Egg

1 Put about 10 cm³ egg white into a boiling tube. Insert a thermometer. (Take care if it is a mercury thermometer. Spillages of mercury from a broken thermometer must be treated with a mixture of sulphur and lime.)

2 Place the tube in a 400 cm³ beaker containing cold water. Hold the tube steady with a retort stand and clamp (Fig. 38.1).

**Fig. 38.1**

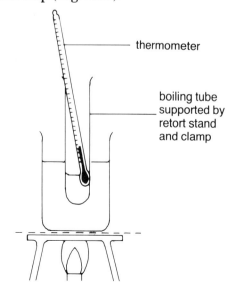

thermometer

boiling tube supported by retort stand and clamp

3 Slowly heat the water. Stir the egg white **VERY CAREFULLY** from time to time with the thermometer. Note the temperature at which the egg white begins to coagulate.

4 Repeat steps 1 to 3 with:
   a egg white + a few drops vinegar
   b egg yolk alone
   c whole egg, lightly beaten
   d whole egg and about 2 g sucrose.

### Meat

5 Soak about 30 g minced beef in about 30 cm³ water for a few hours then filter into a 100 cm³ beaker.

6 Put about 6 cm³ of the filtrate into a boiling tube. Insert a thermometer.

7 Repeat steps 2 and 3 **(CARE)**, noting the temperature at which coagulation starts, and the temperature at which the meat extract changes colour.

### Milk

8 Repeat steps 1 and 2 with about 10 cm³ milk.

9 Slowly heat the water, stirring the milk from time to time **(VERY CAREFULLY)** with the thermometer. Note the temperature at which coagulation is first observed (a 'skin').

## Result

For each food, record the temperature at which coagulation occurs. Record also the temperature at which the meat changes colour. Is this lower or higher than the coagulation temperature? Record any further observations such as whether the whole of the liquid coagulates.

What is the effect of adding sugar and vinegar to the egg?

Relate the results to what you observe in cooking, eg meat cookery and poaching eggs.

## Suggestions for further work**

Do all proteins in milk coagulate on heating? Filter the contents of the boiling tube after step 9. Test both the filtrate and the residue for protein *(Biuret test, Experiment 10)*.

Heat is one means of denaturing (altering the natural state of) proteins. In what other ways may proteins be denatured? Design experiments, using proper controls, to test your suggestions.

# Experiment 38*
# Heat coagulation of proteins

## Introduction

The secondary and tertiary structure of proteins is maintained, to a large extent, by hydrogen bonds (weak attractive forces between hydrogen in one part of the protein chain and, generally, oxygen in another part). Heating supplies energy to the protein, disrupting the hydrogen bonds. The result is a major, usually irreversible, change in protein structure and is called denaturation. It may cause visible coagulation. With some proteins the effect of denaturation may be just as important but invisible, eg. loss of enzyme activity after blanching vegetables.

Without heat coagulation of proteins there would be no scrambled eggs, omelettes or soufflés; bread and cakes would not rise; a 'cooked' steak would be very different – and milk would not boil over so easily!

## Materials

a  Any type of milk may be used as long as the pupils realise that pasteurized and homogenized milk have already been heated to 72°C for 15 seconds. Sterilized milk has already been subjected to fairly severe heat treatment: ultra-high temperature (UHT) sterilization at 135-150°C for 1-3 seconds, or traditional sterilization at 100°C or higher for at least an hour.

b  Lemon juice may be substituted for vinegar.

c  The quantities of apparatus listed are for one food. The filter funnel, stand and paper are for the meat only.

## Method

a  Note that for each food, a thermometer is used for stirring the contents of the boiling tube. This must be done **VERY CAREFULLY** to avoid breaking the thermometer. A stirring rod can be used, the thermometer being inserted from time to time.

b  The soluble proteins in meat (the albumins and globulins) are extracted for this experiment.

## Result

### Egg

Coagulation of egg-white starts at about 60°C and ends by 70°C. Egg-yolk coagulates at 65°C, becoming firm by 70°C. If heating is continued, the white becomes very hard and rubbery and the yolk appears powdery. An observant pupil will note that the temperature of the yolk does not increase when coagulation has begun – the reaction is endothermic.

## Effect of additions to the egg

Vinegar or lemon juice speed coagulation because the acid brings protein nearer its isoelectric point. This is the pH at which there is no charge on the molecules, making it easier for them to aggregate and form a coagulum or clot. Vinegar is often added to the water in which an egg is to be poached for this reason.

Sucrose raises the temperature of coagulation. An egg custard with a high level of sucrose will need a longer cooking time than one with less.

## Meat

Coagulation should begin at about 60°C. The colour should change from red to brown at about 72°C. In practice, meat cookery is very complex, the heat having varying effects on the fat, connective tissue proteins and muscle proteins. Myoglobin, the red pigment in meat, is the last muscle protein to denature. Meat, therefore, may be cooked at low temperatures: it is more tender, juicier and has better flavour.

## Milk

Heat has very little effect on casein, the major protein in milk. The soluble (whey) proteins, lactalbumin and lactoglobulin, however, coagulate on heating. They form a surface skin which traps expanding gas bubbles, causing the boiling milk to rise. The coagulated proteins may also settle on the sides and bottom of the pan, and may burn if the heating is prolonged. The whey proteins are coagulated by traditional sterilisation and this affects the temperature of the milk. UHT sterilisation, while at a higher temperature, is for such a short time that the proteins are not affected. UHT milk is, therefore, virturally indistinguishable from pasteurized milk which has also been heated for too short a time to coagulate the proteins.

## Suggestions for further work**

a  As explained above, only the whey proteins coagulate on heating. The *Biuret test* will be positive for both the filtrate and the residue.

b  Denaturation methods that are applicable to cookery are alteration in pH (eg, souring milk) and agitation (eg, whisking). Both of these can be demonstrated on raw egg.

c  Dilute egg-white with water, then add a few drops of lemon juice, acetic acid or vinegar to about 5 cm³ of the diluted egg-white in a test tube. Opaque flakes should be observed. Filter the egg-white and test the filtrate for protein.

d  If whisked egg-white is placed in a filter funnel (without paper) and left to drain for a few minutes, the foam can be tested for protein.

# Experiment 39**

# Natural pigments (1)

## Purpose

To study the effect of cooking and pH on natural pigments.

## Materials

small amounts of coloured fruits and vegetables eg cabbage (red and green), peas, parsley, carrot, tomato, beetroot, red grapes

white vinegar

1% sodium hydrogencarbonate (sodium bicarbonate) solution

pH papers

knife

chopping board

liquidizer

3 test tubes for each food tested

25 cm$^3$ measuring cylinder

250 cm$^3$ beaker

tripod

gauze

bunsen burner

flameproof bench mat

## Method

1 Cut each vegetable into very small pieces or, preferably, liquidize with a small amount of water.

2 Put portions (about 5 g) of each vegetable into three separate test tubes.

3 For each vegetable, treat the three samples as follows:
   A – add 2 cm$^3$ white vinegar
   B – add 2 cm$^3$ distilled water
   C – add 2 cm$^3$ sodium hydrogencarbonate solution

4 Observe any colour change. Test the pH of the liquid in each tube.

5 Put the tubes in a beaker of boiling water and boil for 5 minutes. Allow to stand and again note any colour change.

## Result

Record your results in a table as shown below.

### Table of results for Experiment 39

| Fruit or Vegetable | + Vinegar | | + Water | | + Sodium hydrogencarbonate | |
|---|---|---|---|---|---|---|
| | unheated | after boiling | unheated | after boiling | unheated | after boiling |
| | | | | | | |

Relate your observations to what you have seen when fruit and vegetables are pickled or cooked.

# Experiment 39**
# Natural pigments (1)

## Introduction

Although the smell of food may encourage us to taste it, appearance is the main way in which we judge food prior to eating it. Most foods are coloured, the colour being due to certain compounds in the food which may be produced during cooking (eg, the brown crust of bread) or to synthetic or natural pigments.

Many natural pigments occur in food. They are all large organic molecules which occur in various forms in the food and have varying degrees of stability to chemicals, pH changes and heat.

This experiment examines the effect of heat and pH change on the colour of fruits and vegetables.

## Materials

a Use any fruits or vegetables that are cheap or easily available. Frozen fruits are satisfactory, but frozen vegetables will probably have been blanched and therefore already heated.

b Dilute acetic acid may be used instead of white vinegar.

c Wide- and narrow-range pH papers will be needed.

d This experiment can easily be carried out in a kitchen, a pan on a hotplate being used instead of a beaker on a tripod.

## Method

a It is easier to relate the results to what is seen when food is cooked if the fruits and vegetables are chopped. Liquidizing, however, extracts the pigment from the cells.

b Use first wide-range then narrow-range pH papers to test the pH of the liquids.

## Result

The major pigments in fruits and vegetables are:

*chlorophyll:* green vegetables, eg cabbage;
*carotenoids:* orange/red fruits and vegetables, eg carrot, tomato, sweet potato;
*anthocyanins:* red, purple and blue fruits and vegetables, eg beetroot, strawberries, red cabbage.

## Chlorophyll

This is contained in chloroplasts in the cell. It is insoluble in water so does not dissolve in cooking water. It is a complex molecule, containing a magnesium atom. In the presence of weak acids (eg the acetic acid in vinegar) the magnesium atom is replaced by two hydrogen atoms. The compound is then called pheophytin and the vegetable containing it will appear a dull olive-green. The organic acids in the cells can have this effect, especially if the vegetables are over-cooked.

Traditional ways of retaining the green colour of vegetables have included adding a pinch of sodium hydrogen carbonate (sodium bicarbonate) to neutralize the acidity. However, excess alkalinity affects the flavour and texture of the vegetables. If the food is cooked without a lid on the pan, the volatile acids from the cell may escape. A copper coin has, in the past, been added to a pan of cooking cabbage. Copper replaces the lost magnesium, keeping the green colour, but the toxicity of copper makes this a potentially dangerous practice.

## Carotenoids

These, like chlorophyll, are insoluble in water and are found in chromoplasts in the cell (see *Experiment 1*). The orange-coloured fat over a stew containing carrots shows that the carotenoids are fat-soluble. Most carotenoids are precursors of vitamin A. Cooking time and the presence of acids and alkalis have little effect on these pigments. There may be some fading of the orange-red colour in, for example, tomatoes on cooking, probably due to oxidation of the unsaturated molecules.

## Anthocyanins

These are soluble, highly reactive compounds. They are affected by pH, light, oxygen, temperature, enzymes and metals. Cooking may degrade the pigment, thus dulling the colour, Anthocyanins are brightest (have the greatest intensity) and most stable at low pH. Fruits, therefore, generally retain their colour well on cooking. Red cabbage, cooked in water, takes on a bluish colour but if it is pickled in vinegar, ie at low pH, the bright red colour is maintained.

# Experiment 40**

# Natural pigments (2)

## Purpose

To find whether the colouring matter in green and orange vegetables is composed of more than one substance.

## Materials

small amounts of dark green vegetables, eg cabbage, parsley, spinach, broccoli, or of orange vegetables, eg carrot, red pepper

⚠ acetone (propanone)

pestle and mortar

filter paper or chromatography paper

scissors

paper clips

boiling tube with rubber bung for each vegetable tested

capillary tubes

hair dryer

test tube rack

## Method

1 Cut a strip of filter or chromatography paper of the same length as the boiling tube. The strip should be narrow enough to fit inside the tube without touching the sides.

2 Grind about 5 g dark green or orange vegetable with a pestle and mortar with the minimum amount of acetone (CARE). Let the mixture stand for a few minutes.

3 Using a capillary tube, put a spot of the coloured extract close to one of the narrow edges of the paper. As soon as the spot has been made, dry it with a hair dryer or by blowing on it. CARE – Before you do this, make sure all bottles of acetone are safely put away. Do not be tempted to dry the paper over a hotplate or naked flame. Put another spot in the same place and dry again. Repeat four or five times until a very dark, small spot has been made.

4 Put acetone in the boiling tube to a depth of about 1.5 cm. Bend some wire or a paper clip to the shape shown in Fig. 40.1. Fold the unspotted end of the strip so that it fits over the wire and suspend it in the boiling tube. The acetone level must be between the edge of the paper and the coloured spot. Put a rubber bung in the top of the tube and hold it upright in a test tube rack.

**Fig. 40.1**

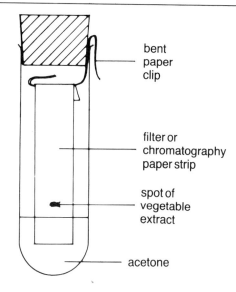

bent paper clip

filter or chromatography paper strip

spot of vegetable extract

acetone

5 Watch what happens to the extract as the acetone rises up the paper. Remove the paper when the acetone has risen almost to the top. Immediately mark the solvent front with a pencil. Hang the paper up to dry, labelling it as soon as possible.

## Result

Compare the chromatograms for each fruit or vegetable. Note the colour, the number of spots and the distance the spots have travelled from the origin.

# Experiment 40**
# Natural pigments (2)

## Introduction
This experiment serves as a simple introduction to paper chromatography (see *Experiment 41*) and investigates the pigments responsible for the attractive colour of many fruits and vegetables.

## Materials
a Very small amounts of the vegetables are needed.

b Care should be taken when using acetone (propanone) – it is highly volatile and flammable.

c A hair dryer is not essential (see step 3).

## Method
a Satisfactory results will not be obtained unless the spot of colour is very small and very dark.

b When setting up the apparatus it is *most* important to ensure that the spot is not below the acetone or the pigment will simply dissolve.

c The time taken for the acetone to rise to the top of the paper is very short, 5-10 minutes. Remove the paper just before the solvent front reaches the top.

## Result
The pigments present will be chlorophyll and carotenoids (see *Experiment 39*). Green vegetables contain two types of chlorophyll in the ratio of 3:1. Chlorophyll *a* is blue-green and chlorophyll *b* is yellow-green. Many green vegetables also contain carotenoids, in the ratio of 4 parts chlorophyll to 1 part carotenoid.

# Experiment 41*** ⚠

## Paper chromatography of food colours

This experiment is best carried out in a laboratory under the supervision of a teacher with appropriate scientific background.

## Purpose

To extract and concentrate colours from foods and to separate them by paper chromatography.

## Materials

coloured sweets, eg 'Smarties', fruit pastilles, boiled sweets

⚠ dilute ammonia solution

dilute acetic acid

⚠ solvent suitable for paper chromatography

white knitting wool

4 x 100 cm³ beakers

bunsen burner

tripod

gauze

flameproof bench mat

dropping pipette or eye dropper

blue litmus papers

chromatography paper, cut to fit jar or tank

chromatography tank or large glass jar, eg Kilner jar or coffee jar

capillary tubes

hair dryer

paper clips or stapler

## Method

Make sure you are wearing eye protection. It is best to boil the wool in a fume cupboard.

### Prepare the wool

1   Boil some white knitting wool in dilute ammonia solution to remove grease, then boil in water (Fig. 41.1).

### Extract the colour

2   Separate the sweets into sets of the same colour.

3   Extract the colour from one set with cold water (suitable for Smarties) or boiling water (for boiled sweets or fruit pastilles). Use a small volume of water – not more than 40 cm³ – and enough sweets to give a strong colour.

### Concentrate the colour

4   Decant the coloured liquid into a beaker, add a few drops of acetic acid and boil with about 20 cm of the prepared wool for a few minutes.

5   Remove the wool, discarding the liquid. Wash the wool under cold running water.

**Fig. 41.1**

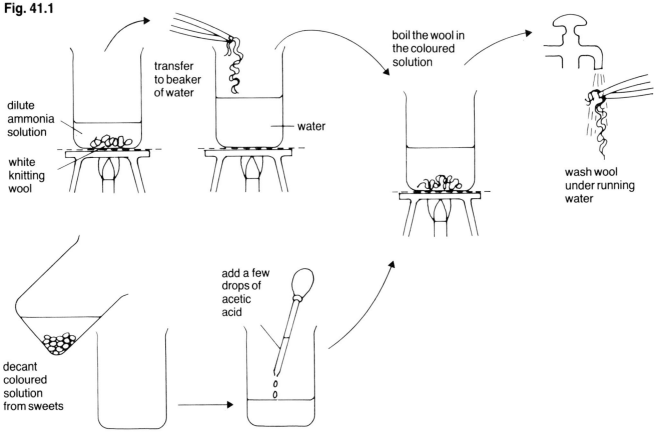

**6** In a fume cupboard, put the wool in a beaker and boil gently with dilute ammonia solution until the colour has been stripped from the wool.

**7** Remove and discard the wool. Make the liquid acidic by adding dilute acetic acid dropwise (test with litmus paper). Boil until the volume has been considerably reduced. (Fig. 41.2) Allow to cool.

**Fig. 41.2**

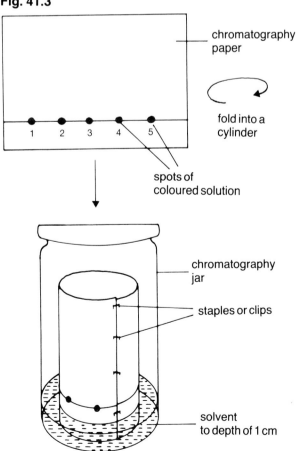

boil wool in dilute ammonia solution

remove wool

add acetic acid until solution is acidic

boil to reduce the volume

**8** Repeat steps 3 – 7 for other colours.

### Separate the colours

**9** With a pencil, draw a line 2 cm from the bottom of the chromatography paper. Put drops of the coloured solutions on the line, as shown in Fig. 41.3, from the capillary tubes.

**Fig. 41.3**

chromatography paper

fold into a cylinder

spots of coloured solution

1  2  3  4  5

chromatography jar

staples or clips

solvent to depth of 1 cm

Dry each spot with the hair dryer before adding another spot of the same colour. Keep the spots as small as possible and continue until, for each colour, a deeply-coloured spot is clearly visible.

**10** Fasten the paper into a cylinder with paper clips or staples.

**11** Put solvent in the chromatography tank or jar to a depth of 1 cm, followed by the paper cylinder. Make sure the paper does not touch the sides.

**12** Put a cover on and leave until the solvent front is about 5 cm from the top of the paper. *Immediately* mark the solvent front with a pencil.

**13** Remove the paper, take out the paper clips or staples and hang to dry, using small pegs or paper clips, on a 'clothes line' (for example, string across a fume cupboard).

**14** When dry, draw a line across the paper at the solvent front.

## Result

If the colour is stripped from the wool by ammonia (step 6), the presence of an acidic coal-tar dye is indicated.

Calculate the $R_f$ value for each colour (see Fig. 41.4), noting whether a particular colour is made up of two or more separate components.

**Fig. 41.4**

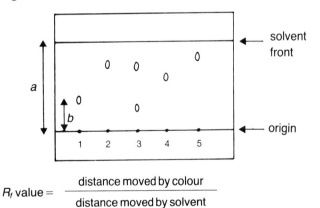

solvent front

origin

1  2  3  4  5

$R_f$ value = $\dfrac{\text{distance moved by colour}}{\text{distance moved by solvent}}$

For colour 1,

$R_f$ value = $\dfrac{b}{a}$

## Suggestions for further work***

This experiment may be carried out using cake-decorating colours. It is not then necessary to extract the colour with wool – simply acidify slightly and continue from step 9.

# Experiment 41***
# Paper chromatography of food colours

## Introduction
**This experiment must be carried out in a properly equipped laboratory. A no-eating rule must be imposed.**

Most processed foods contain added colour, generally water-soluble coal-tar colours. The colours can be detected and separated by paper chromatography. If pure samples of known colours are available, identification is also possible by comparison. The principle of paper chromatography is briefly explained in the *Result* section.

## Materials
a   Any food which is known to contain added colour may be tested, but if starch or fat are present special procedures are necessary. The colours in the suggested sweets can be extracted by simply dissolving the sweets in water. Jam may be treated in a similar way. Soft drinks are even simpler – omit steps 2 and 3 of the method in the *Pupils' Material*.

b   See *page 146* for details of ammonia solution and acetic acid.

c   Many solvents have been used to separate colours, selection depending on the main colour tested. For example, a solvent giving good separation of yellow/orange colours is:

   37 cm$^3$ iso-butanol
   37 cm$^3$ ethanol
   24 cm$^3$ water
   1 cm$^3$ ammonia solution (sp.gr.0.880)

Simpler solvents can be used, such as 2.5% sodium chloride solution, or 1 cm$^3$ ammonia (specific gravity 0.880) diluted to 100 cm$^3$. For further details of solvents see Egan, *et al* (1981).

d   A paper chromatography kit is available from large scientific equipment suppliers *(see page 156)*.

e   Capillary tubes may be bought or made, see *page 151.*

f   A hair dryer, while not absolutely essential, will ensure smaller, more concentrated spots. (Make sure all bottles of flammable solvents are safely put away before using the hair dryer.) The alternative is to blow on the spots, which is time-consuming and exhausting.

g   Special clips are available for chromatography paper but paper clips or staples are more convenient.

## Method
a   Boiling wool in dilute ammonia is a smelly task, which must be done in a fume cupboard, so it may be better for the teacher to carry out step 1, then to dry the wool and to store it in a screw-top jar for use as required.

b   The permitted water-soluble colours are all acidic. The colour taken up by the wool in acid solution (step 4) is not affected by rinsing in water (step 5) and is stripped from the wool in alkaline solution (step 6). Acid pH must be restored for concentrating the colour and for subsequent chromatographic separation.

c   The experiment may be simplified, for demonstration purposes, by omitting step 2 and so extracting several colours together. Five or six pupils can then put spots, which will be a mixture of colours, on one strip of chromatography paper.

d   It is most important to use a *pencil* to draw the line and, if necessary, to label the spot. If a ball-point or felt-tip pen is used, the ink will travel up the paper with the solvent – this looks pretty but confuses the result.

e   The spots *must* be very small (no more than 3 mm diameter) and strongly coloured. If the extract has not been sufficiently concentrated and the spot has little colour, it is pointless to run the chromatogram.

f   The solvent level must be below the pencilled line on which the spots are placed or the colour simply dissolves in the solvent.

g   The time taken for the solvent front to rise the required distance depends on the solvent, the colour separation required and the paper, but about 4 hours should be allowed. If the paper is left in the tank after a lesson it should be watched carefully. The chromatogram is useless if the solvent completely covers the paper.

h   The solvent front must be marked immediately because it is invisible once the solvent has dried.

i   **Evaporating solvent will smell and may, depending on the solvent used, be a fire hazard. A fume cupboard or a well-ventilated room should therefore be used.**

## Result
Paper chromatography is a method of separating a mixture of solids in solution. In this case the solids are molecules that appear coloured and which dissolve to differing extents in water and in a second solvent.

Chromatography paper (or filter paper) consists mainly of cellulose, which strongly absorbs water molecules because of the free hydroxyl groups. This water acts as one solvent and some molecules will tend to remain stationary, dissolved in the water.

The second solvent is placed in the chromatography tank and ascends the paper because of capillary action. Certain molecules will tend to travel with the solvent. The overall effect is that the colours that are more soluble in water will travel more slowly than those that are more soluble in the second solvent, so the colours separate. The distance travelled by the colour compared with the distance travelled by the solvent is called the $R_f$ value, and for a given pure colour in a given solvent should be constant (see Egan, H. *et al* for published $R_f$ values). In practice, however, the $R_f$ value depends on the conditions of the experiment so positive identification can only be made if the pure colour is spotted on to the paper for direct comparison.

## Suggestions for further work***
Use of cake-decorating colours simplifies the experiment because they are ready-concentrated and pure, though they may consist of more than one colour.

# SECTION D

# Assessment of food quality

## Experiment 42*

# Colours and flavours

## Purpose

To investigate the influence of colour on expectation of taste.

## Materials

gelatine

sucrose

green, red and orange food colour

lime, raspberry and orange flavouring

balance

spoon and measuring jug for making jellies

small dishes

teaspoons

## Method

1  Using 10 g powdered gelatine and 100 g sucrose to 500 cm$^3$ hot – not boiling – water, make jellies in small dishes. An example of one possible arrangement of colours and flavours is shown below, but the tasters must not be aware of the order.

| Sample | Colour | Flavouring |
|--------|--------|------------|
| A | green | lime |
| B | green | raspberry |
| C | green | orange |
| D | red | orange |
| E | red | raspberry |
| F | red | lime |
| G | orange | raspberry |
| H | orange | lime |
| I | orange | orange |

2  Set out the dishes attractively and provide the tasters with a spoon (and somewhere to rinse it between samples) and a sheet of paper on which they should write the apparent flavour of the sample tasted.

3  Collect in the papers and add up the answers.

## Result

Tabulate the answers as follows:

**Table of results for Experiment 42**

| Total number of tasters | | | | |
|--------|--------|------|-----------|--------|
| | | Number stating flavour as: | | |
| Sample | Colour | Lime | Raspberry | Orange |
| A | green | | | |
| B | green | | | |
| C | green | | | |
| D | red | | | |
| E | red | | | |
| F | red | | | |
| G | orange | | | |
| H | orange | | | |
| I | orange | | | |

*Note:* the greater the number of tasters, the more valid the results.

## Suggestions for further work*

a  Try this experiment with other flavours and colours.

b  An alternative way of assessing flavour-colour links is to colour familiar foods with various artificial colours and present the tasters with the question:

Do you
- like very much
- like moderately
- neither like nor dislike
- dislike moderately
- dislike very much

this food

(Delete statements as necessary)

Suitable foods are:   rice pudding
trifle
fish pie
blancmange
cakes

# Experiment 42*
# Colours and flavours

## Introduction

Our sense of taste is at least partly subjective. It is strongly influenced by what we *expect* to taste. Colour plays a part in this – an orange coloured drink is expected to have a taste of oranges. Some foods are rejected because their colour is not as expected. For example, the green colour must be restored to processed peas to ensure consumer acceptance.

This experiment explores, in a very simple way, the relationship between colour and flavour. It is also an introduction to sensory evaluation (see *Suggestions for further work*.)

## Materials

a The quantities of gelatine, sucrose, colour and flavouring are those for conventional jellies. The amount of colour and flavouring has not been specified: use according to taste.

b Implicit in the experiment is that green suggests lime. It may be found that peppermint is more readily associated with green food, but peppermint essence is too distinctive in both smell and taste to give satisfactory results in this type of test.

c No laboratory equipment is necessary for this experiment. In fact, **tasting should not normally ever be done in a laboratory.** Use the home economics room.

## Method

a The jellies should be made in the normal way: ensure that the texture of the individual jellies is uniform and does not influence the tasters' preference.

b It would be helpful to make a trial batch of jellies because even a small excess of synthetic flavouring can be unacceptable.

c Adequate time should be allowed for tasting, to obtain considered results.

## Result

It will be found that tasters easily recognize the flavours when accompanied by the familiar colour but they will be relatively unsuccessful when they are confused by the colour.

## Suggestions for further work*

a Other readily-associated flavours and colours are blackcurrant – dark red, or banana – yellow (though a synthetic banana flavour is difficult to identify). It is interesting to find tasters' reactions to entirely unexpected colours such as a blue jelly – very few foods are blue and it is usually found to be unacceptable.

b Milk shakes can be used in the same way as jellies in this experiment or they can be flavoured but not coloured. It should be found that tasters recognize appropriately coloured and flavoured milk shakes, are confused when the milk shakes are uncoloured, and are misled by the wrong colouring.

c Suggestion b is a more conventional, and widely-used, type of taste test, in which a hedonic scale is used to evaluate the likes and dislikes of the tasters. Just one variable colour is being assessed but it is important that the uncoloured food is also tested to establish its level of acceptability. This can then be compared with the effect of colour. If young children are the tasters, faces can be used to represent the hedonic scale:

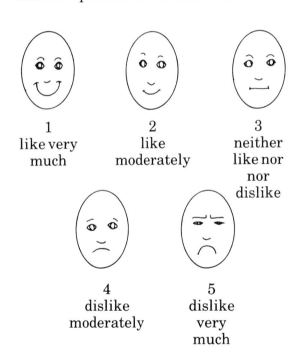

| 1 | 2 | 3 |
|---|---|---|
| like very much | like moderately | neither like nor nor dislike |

| 4 | 5 |
|---|---|
| dislike moderately | dislike very much |

# Experiment 43*

## Sensitivity to taste

### Purpose

To demonstrate that different areas of the tongue are sensitive to different tastes.

### Materials

four solutions for tasting:

    sweet – 5% sucrose solution

    bitter – 2% caffeine solution

    sour – 2% citric acid solution

    salt – 5% sodium chloride solution

drinking straws and cup

### Method

1 Work as a pair comprising subject and investigator.

2 Using a clean drinking straw to transfer each solution, the subject first tastes a few drops of each solution to find out what they taste like, rinsing out the mouth after each tasting.

3 With the subject's mouth open wide, the investigator dips a clean straw into the sugar solution and uses it to touch the tip of the subject's tongue.

4 Keping mouth *open* and tongue *still*, the subject decides whether or not the sugar can be tasted before rinsing out the mouth with water. The investigator records the part of the tongue touched and whether the response was positive (+) or negative (−).

5 Repeat 2 and 3 above on the areas of the tongue indicated in Fig. 43.1, rinsing out the mouth after each trial. Ensure that the sugar solution is placed precisely on that area of the tongue under investigation.

**Fig. 43.1**

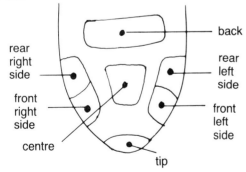

6 Finally, repeat the whole procedure with the other solutions in turn and using a fresh drinking straw for each solution.

### Result

Make a map of the tongue showing which parts are responsive to which flavours.

84

# Experiment 44*

## Taste and smell

### Purpose

To discover how taste discrimination depends upon the sense of smell.

### Materials

20 pieces of apple and 20 pieces of onion of approximately equal size on separate chopping boards.

2 pairs forceps

blindfold

nose clip

cup

### Method

1 Work as a pair comprising subject and investigator.

2 With the subject blindfolded and mouth open (but without the noseclip on) the investigator places pieces of apple or onion one by one on to the centre of the subject's tongue, using a different pair of forceps for each food. Ten pieces of apple and 10 of onion should be used in a random order drawn up beforehand by the investigator without the subject's knowledge.

3 Without chewing or biting the pieces, the subject indicates whether he or she thinks it is apple or onion on the tongue and rinses out the mouth after each piece. The investigator records whether the guess is correct (✓) or incorrect (X) but does not tell the subject.

4 Carry out a further 20 trials (again 10 apple and 10 onion but in a different pre-determined order) as above but this time with the subject wearing the nose clip (if a nose clip is not available hold the nose firmly so no air can pass through it).

### Result

Record and explain the results. Why should the subject not chew the food?

### Suggestions for further work*

As an alternative to apple and onion a solution can be made by boiling some cloves in water. When cool, a drop of this solution can be placed on the centre of the tongue with a drinking straw. The above experiment can be performed to compare the ability to distinguish the clove solution from distilled water by taste with and without the sense of smell being used.

# Experiment 43*
# Sensitivity to taste

## Introduction
There are basically four types of sensory or receptor cells in our taste buds, each responding to a different taste stimulus and concentrated at different locations on the tongue. The hundreds of subtle flavour sensations we obtain from our food are the result of the brain's differing interpretations of the varying impulse patterns coming from these sensory cells, according to the proportions of each type that are stimulated.

## Materials
As the solutions are being taken into the mouth, all containers must be scrupulously clean. Any possibility of contamination, such as putting a straw on the bench before dipping it into a solution, must be foreseen and avoided. In any case, **nothing should be swallowed.** This experiment should be carried out in the home economics room.

## Method
A negative response from the subject should be recorded if he or she cannot taste the solution when a drop of it is placed on a particular location on the tongue. In this case the natural reaction is to move the tongue in an attempt to re-locate the drop, but this must be discouraged as it will distort the results.

## Result
Although subject to individual variation, with some overlap between regions, the basic response pattern of the tongue is shown in Fig. 43.1.

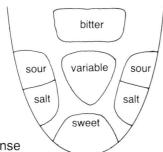

**Fig. 43.1**
Taste response
pattern of the tongue

The locations of 'sweet' and 'bitter' gustatory reception on the tongue can be used to discuss the practice of adding sugar to medicines. The unwary patient will have virtually swallowed the apparently 'sweet' medicine before the bitter taste is detected.

Professional 'tasters', of course, ensure that all areas of the tongue are exposed to the food or drink in order to appreciate fully the true flavour.

# Experiment 44*
# Taste and smell

## Introduction
We detect odours by means of sensory cells located high in our nasal cavities. These olfactory receptors can detect the odours from food in the mouth, as well as from food on the plate. The marked loss of taste experienced when these cavities are blocked with mucus during a cold is confirmation of the role our sense of smell plays in the tasting process.

## Materials
a   As in any experiment which involves taking substances into the mouth, all containers, forceps, etc., must be scrupulously clean. This experiment should carried out in a home economics room.

b   It is important that the apple and onion are chopped on different boards with different knives, and kept completely separate. Otherwise the juices from one may contaminate the other.

c   For best results, the apple should be neither too sweet nor too sharp.

## Method
A noseclip, a clothes peg will do, is desirable as it is very difficult to hold the nose firmly for the duration of each and every test.

## Result
Greater accuracy in discriminating between the apple and onion should be obtained without the noseclip on, as in this case the olfactory receptors are functioning. With the noseclip in position the subject will be less certain. In passing, note that by pure guesswork one would expect to be correct roughly half the time and, by coincidence, the figure could be higher. Therefore, it is a good idea for the teacher to collate all the results for each group, with and without the noseclip, on the blackboard so that the comparisons are based on larger numbers and 'freak' results can be seen in perspective.

The subject should not chew the food since, besides smell, other senses also play a part in the tasting process (see *Experiment 42* for the influence of sight on expectation of taste). Chewing would enable the tactile receptors of the mouth and tongue to discriminate between the foods according to texture.

## Suggestions for further work*
The advantages of using clove solution and distilled water are the ease of application and the absence of any texture difference which may give a clue to the subject.

# Experiment 45*

# Comparison of sweeteners

## Purpose

To carry out a taste test comparing the sweetness of several sugars and sweeteners with sucrose.

## Materials

5% sugar solutions, eg sucrose, lactose, glucose, fructose, icing sugar, 'raw cane sugars' (demerara, molasses, muscovado), honey, golden syrup, saccharin

$100\,cm^3$ beakers (1 for each sweetener)

grease pencil

drinking straws

cup

## Method

1 Put fractions of each of the solutions provided into small clean beakers labelled with letters or, preferably, symbols (eg △, □, ○, ◊, etc). Don't forget to retain a key for identification! In addition, include a second beaker containing sucrose, and clearly labelled 'sucrose'.

2 Arrange the beakers in any order, with a clean drinking straw in each.

3 Instruct each taster as follows:

  a Taste sucrose first by putting a few drops on the tip of the tongue, using a drinking straw.

  b Rinse the mouth with water then taste an unknown sugar in the same way.

  c Rinse again and retaste the sucrose.

  d Note the relative sweetness according to a numeric scale:

    −3 markedly less sweet than sucrose

    −2 less sweet than sucrose

    −1 slightly less sweet than sucrose

      0 indistinguishable from sucrose

    +1 slightly more sweet than sucrose

    +2 more sweet than sucrose

    +3 markedly more sweet than sucrose

  e Repeat for the other sugars but rest when fatigue is noticed.

## Result

Collate results from all tasters on a chart:

### Table of results for Experiment 45

| Code | Name of sugar or sweetener | Sweetness compared with sucrose* |
|---|---|---|
|  |  |  |
|  |  |  |
|  |  |  |

* Average the results for each sugar or sweetener.

# Experiment 45*
# Comparison of sweeteners

## Introduction
Sucrose and glucose are the main nutritive sweeteners that are added to foods. Lactose, maltose and fructose are all found in foods, and may be used commercially as sweeteners. 'Natural' sweeteners such as raw cane sugar and honey, as well as golden syrup, are used extensively in the home as sweeteners. Several non-nutritive sweeteners have been tried, the most widely used at the moment being saccharin. This experiment attempts to find whether all these substances have the same degree of sweetness by comparing the taste of equal-strength solutions with that of sucrose.

## Materials
a See Appendix I for the method of making percentage solutions.

b A sink should be available for tasters to spit into after rinsing between samples.

## Method
a This experiment should be carried out in a home economics room rather than in a laboratory.

b It is better practice in taste tests to use symbols for labelling samples, rather than letters or numbers.

c The tasters should not be able to recognize any of the sweeteners by sight. It may be necessary to cover the beakers with, for example, aluminium foil. The raw cane sugars and honey are particularly distinguishable.

d The tasters should not have eaten or drunk anything for at least half an hour before the test.

e It is unlikely that all the sweeteners suggested can be tasted without the taster experiencing loss of sensitivity – or even nausea! A rest should be taken as soon as any difficulty in distinguishing the tastes is experienced.

## Result
There are several ways of comparing a taste such as sweetness, this is probably the simplest but there are several disadvantages. For accurate results, for example, the panel should be trained, and perhaps selected for sensitivity of taste. The panel should work under controlled environmental conditions. A different way of approaching the experiment would be to match equally-sweet concentrations of the sugar solutions. However, the results of the experiment suggested should indicate the relative sweetness of the substances sufficiently to lead to discussion of their uses in cookery.

Published results of sweetness comparisons vary, but if sucrose is given a sweetness of 1, fructose is about 1.3, glucose about 0.7 and lactose about 0.25. Icing sugar should be the same as sucrose if completely dissolved; if taken in crystalline form it seems to be sweeter than granulated sugar, probably because the small crystals dissolve more easily. Similarly, the texture of raw cane sugar, honey and golden syrup affects the perception of sweetness – they usually seem sweeter than pure sucrose. The non-nutritive sweetener, saccharin, is at least 300 times sweeter than sucrose but with the disadvantage that it has a bitter after-taste.

# Experiment 46*

# Chemical raising agents (1)

## Purpose

To study gas production by chemical raising agents.

## Materials

tartaric acid (3 dihydroxybutanedioic acid)

cream of tartar (potassium hydrogen 2,3 dihydroxybutanedioate)

disodium dihydrogen heptaoxodiphosphate (acid sodium pyrophosphate)

calcium tetrahydrogendiphosphate (v) (acid calcium phosphate)

glucono*delta*lactone

sour milk

vinegar

sodium hydrogencarbonate (sodium bicarbonate)

lime water

sucrose

commercial baking powders

250 cm$^3$ beaker

bunsen burner

tripod

gauze

flameproof bench mat

at least 9 test tubes

test tube rack

pH papers

syringe or dropping pipette

at least 9 watch glasses

tongs

test tube holder

## Method

1  Half-fill a beaker with water and bring to the boil.

2  Prepare separate test tubes containing the following:

   *a*  tartaric acid
(pinch) + about 5 cm$^3$ water

   *b*  cream of tartar
(pinch) + about 5 cm$^3$ water

   *c*  disodium dihydrogen heptaoxodiphosphate
(pinch) + about 5 cm$^3$ water

   *d*  calcium tetrahydrogen diphosphate (v)
(pinch) + about 5 cm$^3$ water

   *e*  glucono*delta*lactone
(pinch) + about 5 cm$^3$ water

   *f*  sour milk
about 5 cm$^3$

   *g*  vinegar
about 5 cm$^3$

   *h*  sodium hydrogencarbonate
pinch + about 2 cm$^3$ water

Find the pH of each solution using pH papers.

3  Add a pinch of sodium hydrogencarbonate to test tubes *a* to *g*. Note any effervescence. Collect some gas from each tube in a dropping pipette and bubble it through limewater in a watchglass (Fig. 46.1). Observe the reaction.

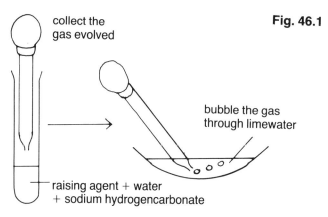

collect the gas evolved

**Fig. 46.1**

bubble the gas through limewater

raising agent + water + sodium hydrogencarbonate

4  About 5 minutes after gas bubbles have stopped appearing in the test tubes, put the tubes in a boiling waterbath. Note whether the reaction starts again.

5  Heat test tube *h* over a low bunsen flame. (**CARE** – do not point the mouth of tube at anyone.) Test any gas produced as in step 3. When gas production has ceased, test the pH of the solution, then put a pinch of sucrose in the tube. Heat again if necessary. Observe any colour change.

6  Add about 5 cm$^3$ water to a pinch of a commercial baking powder. Test any gas that may be produced. Leave for about 5 minutes, then heat the solution in a waterbath and look for renewed reaction. Repeat for other baking powders.

## Result

Record the pH of each solution and relate it to the use of each raising agent.

Sodium hydrogencarbonate reacts with acids to produce carbon dioxide, which turns limewater milky.

Some raising agents act quickly, some only after heat has been applied. Some do both ('double-acting'). State which of these applies to the raising agents used here.

## Suggestions for further work**

It has been found, in step 5, that sodium hydrogen-carbonate can be used alone to produce carbon dioxide – but the pH of the residue and its effect on sugar (and, incidentally, on flour) means that applications are limited. Discuss this in relation to the results obtained here.

# Experiment 46*
# Chemical raising agents (1)

## Introduction

The incorporation of a baking powder containing chemical raising agents into a flour mixture affects the baked product. The carbon dioxide should not be produced too slowly or the cake, for example, will not rise. Neither should it be produced too quickly or it will sink in the middle. The baking powder should be harmless, it should not leave a bitter after-taste and it should not adversely affect the texture of the product. For some baked goods, traditional ingredients such as sour milk can be used to help produce the raising action and for others sodium bicarbonate alone is sufficient.

This experiment investigates the properties of substances used to produce carbon dioxide.

## Materials

a  For details of reagents see Appendix I.

b  The pH of milk should be low enough for the reaction after being allowed to sour at room temperature for about two days.

c  Several brands of commercial baking powders should be tested.

d  For details of apparatus see Appendix II. Narrow- and wide-range pH papers should be available.

## Method

a  Test the pH of the solutions using wide-range paper first, then narrow-range.

b  The reaction produced by carbon dioxide in lime-water may be demonstrated by blowing through a straw into a small volume of lime-water in a watch glass.

## Result

a  Tubes a to g should show acid pH; h should be alkaline.

b  The reaction between sodium bicarbonate and acids may be summarized as:

$$H^+ + HCO_3^- \rightarrow CO_2 \uparrow + H_2O$$

hydrogen ions from acid  hydrogen-carbonate ions  carbon dioxide  water

The carbon dioxide reacts with calcium hydroxide solution ('lime-water') to produce a precipitate of calcium carbonate. This makes the solution appear cloudy.

c  Liberation of carbon dioxide in tubes a to g, on addition of sodium bicarbonate, depends on the pH of the solution and on the solubility of the acid. The pH of sour milk and vinegar – and of other 'traditional' substances such as fruit juice and treacle that may be used in

home baking – will vary and may, therefore, produce variable quality in the cooked products.

For reference, the formulae and speed of action of the other raising agents are shown in Table 46.1.

## Table 46.1  Action of raising agents

| Raising agent | Other names | Formula reaction<br>Note: H+ reacts with the hydrogencarbonate ion (HCO₃⁻) to produce CO₂ and H₂O | Speed of action |
|---|---|---|---|
| Tartaric acid | 2,3-dihydroxy-butanedioic acid | $HO-\overset{H}{\underset{H}{C}}-COOH$ $HO-\overset{H}{\underset{H}{C}}-COOH$ $\rightarrow$ $HO-\overset{H}{\underset{H}{C}}-COO^-$ $HO-\overset{H}{\underset{H}{C}}-COO^-$ $+ 2H^+$ | quick |
| Cream of tartar | potassium hydrogen 2,3-dihydroxy-butanedioate | $HO-\overset{H}{\underset{H}{C}}-COOH$ $HO-\overset{}{\underset{}{C}}-COOK$ $\rightarrow$ $HO-\overset{H}{\underset{H}{C}}-COO^-$ $HO-\overset{}{\underset{}{C}}-COO^-$ $+ H^+ + K^+$ | slow |
| Acid sodium pyro-phosphate | disodium dihydrogen heptaoxo-diphosphate | $Na_2H_2P_2O_7 \rightarrow 2Na^+ + P_2O_7^{4-} + 2H^+$ | slow |
| Acid calcium phosphate | calcium tetra-hydrogen di-phosphate (v) | $3CaH_4(PO_4)_2 \rightarrow Ca_3(PO_4)_2 + 4HPO_4^{2-} + 8H^+$ | quick |
| Glucono delta lactone | | produces gluconic acid as H⁺ source | gradual |

The slow-acting raising agents should show carbon dioxide production only after heating in the waterbath. When used in cake mixes, these help to prevent cakes sinking in the centre while they are in the oven by starting to produce gas when the mixture gets hot.

d  Commercial baking powders contain an acidic component and sodium hydrogencarbonate (bicarbonate). They also contain starch, as a filler. Many have both slow- and quick-acting components.

## Suggestions for further work**

Sodium hydrogencarbonate alone, on heating, produces carbon dioxide:

$$2NaHCO_3 \rightarrow Na_2CO_3 + CO_2 \uparrow + H_2O$$
sodium carbonate

This has several disadvantages, however. Sodium carbonate is alkaline, tends to make sugars yellowish-brown, increases the destruction of thiamin on heating, affects the structure of cooked flour mixtures and has a bitter taste. It is only used in strongly-flavoured foods when a brown colour and sticky texture are desired, such as gingerbread.

# Experiment 47*** ⚠

# Chemical raising agents (2)

This experiment must be carried out in a laboratory under the supervision of a teacher with appropriate scientific background

## Purpose

Qualitative tests for the constituents of baking powders.

## Materials

range of baking powders

solution of iodine in potassium iodide

⚠  dilute sulphuric acid

⚠  resorcinol

⚠  trichloroethane (NB **not** trichloroethene)

⚠  concentrated nitric acid (**CARE**)

⚠  concentrated hydrochloric acid (**CARE**)

⚠  dilute hydrochloric acid

⚠  dilute ammonium hydroxide solution

litmus paper (blue and red)

dilute acetic acid

⚠  ammonium ethanedioate (ammonium oxalate) solution

⚠  dilute nitric acid

⚠  ammonium molybdate solution

white tile (or plate)

dropping pipette (or eye dropper)

test tubes (1 for each powder)

test tube rack

spatula

bunsen burner

tongs

100 cm$^3$ beaker

waterbath

tripod

flameproof bench mat

silica rod or platinum wire

blue glass

## Method

Make sure you are wearing eye protection before starting this experiment.

1  Test each baking powder for starch by putting a pinch on a white tile and adding a drop of iodine solution. Look for a blue–black colour.

2  In a fume cupboard, test each baking powder for tartrate by the resorcinol test:
   a  Put about 2 cm$^3$ dilute sulphuric acid in a test tube.
   b  Add a pinch of baking powder and a few drops of resorcinol.
   c  Heat over a bunsen flame. (**CARE** – use tongs and do not point the tube at anyone.)
   Look for the red coloration which indicates tartaric acid.

3  To test for the remaining constituents, the starch must be removed:
   a  Put about 5 g of the baking powder in a 100 cm$^3$ beaker. Add about 50 cm$^3$ trichloroethane. Mix very thoroughly. (Avoid contact with skin, and if possible wear protective gloves.)
   b  Allow to stand until the starch rises to the top then decant it off as completely as possible. Add a further small amount of trichloroethane and repeat.
   c  In a fume cupboard evaporate off the rest of the trichloroethane over a waterbath.

4  Dissolve the residue in a concentrated nitric acid (**CARE**) and test for potassium, calcium and phosphate as described in *Experiment 16, steps 7, 8 and 13*.

## Result

Record your results on a chart.

**Table of results for Experiment 47**

| Baking powder | Starch | Tartrate | Potassium | Calcium | Phosphate | Comment |
|---|---|---|---|---|---|---|
|  |  |  |  |  |  |  |
|  |  |  |  |  |  |  |
|  |  |  |  |  |  |  |
|  |  |  |  |  |  |  |

Why is starch included in baking powders? Attempt to identify the constituents of the baking powders.

# Experiment 47***
# Chemical raising agents (2)

## Introduction

In the previous experiment, the function and use of the constituents of baking powders were investigated. The composition of the powders is now studied using simple tests that have, in the main, been encountered in earlier experiments *(Experiments 6 and 16)*.

## Materials

a For details of reagents see Appendix I.

b In home baking, cream of tartar (potassium hydrogentartrate) and sodium bicarbonate (sodium hydrogencarbonate) are sometimes used instead of a commercial baking powder. It may be useful to make a 'home-made' baking powder using these chemicals, to obtain a positive result for tartrate.

c The purpose of the waterbath is to evaporate trichloroethane. The bath may be electrically heated, or a beaker of water may be brought to the boil and removed from the heat. The vapour is flammable and so the bath should **not** be near a naked flame. This part of the experiment must be carried out in a fume cupboard. Trichloroethane must not come into contact with an aluminium container as this results in a potentially hazardous reaction.

## Method

a Rapid and simple flame tests are used to look for calcium and potassium. The production of a white precipitate in the presence of ammonium ethanedioate (ammonium oxalate) is also suggested as a test for calcium, because the yellow sodium flame may mask the red and lilac of calcium and potassium.

b Further investigation of the phosphate component may be carried out by adding about $5\,cm^3$ water to the extract, filtering and adding silver nitrate solution. A yellow precipitate shows the presence of phosphate (v) (orthophosphate) ions from calcium hydrogen diphosphate (v) (acid calcium phosphate). A white turbidity shows heptaoxodiphosphate (v) (pyrophosphate) ions from disodium dihydrogen heptaoxodiphosphate (acid sodium pyrophosphate).

## Result

a Starch will be present in all commercial baking powders. It is included as a filler, so that measurement of the active ingredients is less critical. It also absorbs moisture, preventing premature reaction. The starch may be identified by microscopic examination (see *Experiment 1*).

b See *Experiment 46, Teachers' notes* for further information about the chemical composition of baking powder ingredients.

91

# Experiment 48**

# Yeast as a raising agent

## Purpose

To examine conditions under which yeast will act as a biological raising agent.

## Materials

fresh yeast

sugar

salt

ice

limewater

2 x 250 cm³ beakers ⎤
2 bunsen burners ⎟
2 tripods ⎟ or two pans of
2 gauzes ⎟ water on hotplates
2 flameproof bench mats ⎦

400 cm³ beaker

0–100°C thermometer

100 cm³ beaker

spatula (or knife)

25 cm³ measuring cylinder

5 test tubes

grease pencil

test tube rack

balance

5 balloons

watch glass

## Method

1 Half-fill a 250 cm³ beaker with water and bring to the boil.

2 One-third fill a 400 cm³ beaker with water and heat to 37°C. Keep the water at this temperature throughout the experiment. (Take care if you are using a mercury thermometer. Spillages of mercury from a broken thermometer must be treated with a mixture of sulphur and lime.)

3 Cream about 20 g yeast in a 100 cm³ beaker with a little water, add more water to the 80 cm³ mark.

4 Put about 10 cm³ of the yeast solution in each of five labelled test tubes then set up the tubes as follows:

a yeast solution +2 g sugar, placed in boiling waterbath for 15 minutes

b yeast solution alone

c yeast solution +2 g sugar

d yeast solution +2 g salt

e yeast solution +2 g sugar

Immediately put a balloon over the neck of each test tube.

5 Put tubes a, b, c and d in the waterbath at 37°C. Put tube e in a 250 cm³ beaker of ice (Fig. 48.1).

6 Observe at 10 minute intervals for about 30 minutes.

7 At the end of the experiment, remove each balloon carefully, pinching the neck. Hold the neck under a small quantity of limewater in a watch glass. Expel the contents of the balloon through the limewater.

## Result

Inflation of the balloon shows gas production by the yeast. If the gas is carbon dioxide the limewater will turn milky.

For each tube, record:

 (i) the time at which gas production was first observed.

 (ii) whether gas production was slight or copious.

 (iii) whether the gas was shown to be carbon dioxide.

What do the results indicate about the nature of yeast as a raising agent?

## Suggestions for further work**

a After the experiment, leave tube e in the refrigerator overnight then examine for carbon dioxide production.

b Observe actively-growing yeast under the microscope (see *Experiment 1*).

**Fig. 48.1**

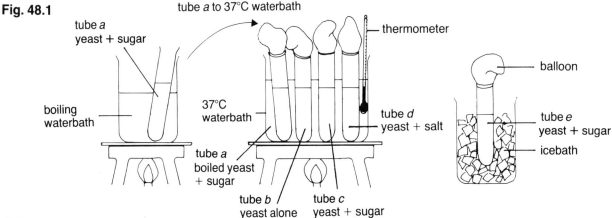

after 10 minutes transfer tube a to 37°C waterbath

tube a yeast + sugar

thermometer

balloon

boiling waterbath

37°C waterbath

tube d yeast + salt

tube e yeast + sugar

icebath

tube a boiled yeast + sugar

tube b yeast alone

tube c yeast + sugar

# Experiment 48**
# Yeast as a raising agent

## Introduction
Production of carbon dioxide by fermentation of glucose by yeast is used to raise many different kinds of flour mixture. The rapidity and quantity of gas production depend on the ingredients of the mixture and the conditions during the fermentation period. The effect of some of these ingredients and conditions are studied in this experiment.

## Materials
a If fresh yeast is not available, use about $15\,cm^3$ dried yeast but allow about 15 minutes for the yeast to activate in step 3.

b Use household sugar and salt, or laboratory sucrose and sodium chloride.

c Add a small amount of water to the ice in a beaker for the icebath (step 5). Alternatively, tube e could be placed in a refrigerator.

d In addition to the icebath, two waterbaths will be needed: one at 100°C and one at 37°C. It is suggested in the *Pupils' Material* that beakers of water may be heated over a bunsen burner, but it is difficult to maintain a temperature of 37°C. An electrically-heated waterbath, if available, is far more satisfactory.

## Method
Better results may be obtained from step 7 if the gas is collected from the balloon in a syringe from which it is bubbled through the limewater. The expected result can be demonstrated by blowing through a straw into limewater.

## Result
a Tube *a,* containing inactivated yeast, will show no inflation. Tube *c* and tube *e* should be compared – gas production is much more rapid at 37°C. If tube *e* is left in the icebath for long enough, carbon dioxide will be produced – a flour dough can be left in a refrigerator to rise overnight. Salt, in tube *d* will prevent yeast activity.

b The experiment should show that yeast, as a biological raising agent, produces carbon dioxide more readily at 37°C than at 0°C; that it is inactivated by boiling and that it is inhibited by salt. This experiment investigates only a few of the conditions that may be encountered in baking. Pupils may design their own experiments to test whether sugar is needed or whether flour alone is sufficient for carbon dioxide production, for

example. Other temperatures may also be studied.

## Suggestions for further work **
a As indicated above, carbon dioxide production should be seen when tube *e* has been left at a low temperature overnight.

b Yeasts are single-celled oval or spherical organisms. Their size varies greatly from about 10 $\mu$m to about 100 $\mu$m. Budding may be seen in some cells. The yeast can be seen without staining, under low or high power.

# Experiment 49*

# Protein in flour

## Purpose

To compare the amounts of gluten-forming proteins in various types of wheat flour and to observe some properties of gluten.

## Materials

white flour (plain, breadmaking, self-raising)

solution of iodine in potassium iodide

slimmers' starch-reduced rolls

white bread roll

balance (or scales)

$100\,cm^3$ measuring cylinder (or measuring jug)

spatula

small mixing bowl or $400\,cm^3$ beaker for each flour

sieve

boiling tube

test tube rack

baking sheet

oven

bread knife

hand lens

## Method

1 Using a spatula, mix 60 g of one flour with 40–50 $cm^3$ water to form a stiff dough. Knead until smooth.

2 Knead the dough under gently running cold water for at least 15 minutes until all the starch has been washed out, leaving insoluble gluten. To test this, squeeze a few drops of water into a boiling tube and carry out the *Iodine test (Experiment 6)*.

3 Form the gluten into a ball, squeezing out excess water.

4 Repeat with the other available flours. Compare, by appearance or by weighing, the amounts of gluten 'dough' from 60 g of each flour.

5 Knead and stretch each gluten sample. Note the elasticity (ability to stretch and then recover shape), rubbery texture and stickiness of the gluten.

6 Re-form the gluten into a ball, measure its approximate diameter, and bake in a hot oven (230°C/450°F Gas Mark 8) for about 30 minutes, until brown. Remove from the baking sheet and allow to cool.

7 Slice each gluten ball in half. Note the diameter (compared with the unbaked ball)

and texture. Observe the 'crumb' with a hand lens.

8 Compare the external appearance and the crumb of the baked gluten ball with a commercially-made slimmers' starch-reduced roll and with a normal white bread roll of similar size.

## Result

Record:

comparison of the amounts of gluten from each flour.

comments on texture and elasticity of the unbaked gluten.

comments on the diameter and texture of the baked gluten balls.

comparison between baked gluten balls, a slimmers' starch-reduced roll and a normal white bread roll.

## Suggestions for further work*

a Try steps 1 and 2 with gluten-free flour.

b Make loaves using standard recipes with the types of flour tested here. Take care that the method used is exactly the same for each flour. Compare the loaves – cut slices through the centre of each loaf and make ink prints or photocopies (putting an acetate sheet between the bread and the copier). Relate the appearance and texture of the loaves to the results of this experiment.

# Experiment 49*
# Protein in flour

## Introduction

The suitability of a flour for a particular purpose depends on the quantity and the quality of the proteins in the flour, especially the insoluble proteins that make up the substance known as gluten. In this experiment, the starch and soluble protein are washed out of a flour dough, leaving the gluten. The quantity of gluten and some of its properties are investigated.

## Materials

a It is possible to carry out this experiment on brown flours, but the bran particles remain with the gluten and may confuse the results.

b See *page 147* for details of iodine in potassium iodide.

c A kitchen measuring jug can be used instead of the measuring cylinder.

## Method

a The amount of water needed to make a stiff dough will vary with the flour used.

b Kneading is tedious, and cannot be hurried. It is sometimes recommended that muslin is wrapped round the gluten ball. This does prevent loss of gluten into the sink, but the gluten sticks to the muslin. If small pieces of gluten *are* in danger of being lost, hold the dough over a sieve in a beaker or bowl so that they can be retrieved.

c It may seem that the starch has all been washed out when the liquid is no longer cloudy, but the *Iodine test* shows starch to be present for a surprisingly long time.

d If the gluten ball is weighed, in step 4, the result must be used for rough comparisons only because the amount of water taken and squeezed out will be highly variable. The weight of dry gluten may be found after the gluten ball has been baked (step 6) or, more accurately, by cutting the wet gluten ball into 12 pieces, spreading them on a previously-weighed metal plate or small baking sheet, drying in an oven at 155°C for 30 minutes and cooling in a desiccator before weighing the gluten and the metal plate.

e If any starch is left in the gluten ball, it will not rise satisfactorily and it will have a soft wrinkled appearance.

f A well-made baked gluten ball will keep almost indefinitely, so it may be shown to future classes.

## Result

a White breadmaking flour contains, on average, 11.3 per cent protein; plain flour contains 9.8 per cent protein. Of this, about 80-85 per cent is composed of gluten-forming proteins. The intention of this experiment, however, is not to estimate accurately the percentage of gluten; a comparison of the gluten from different flours should be made to be related to the uses to which the flours will be put.

b The quality, even more than the quantity, of gluten is responsible for success in breadmaking. The elasticity – ability to stretch and recover shape – of gluten from bread making flour should be observed. This is especially important during proving.

c When the unbaked gluten balls are put in a hot oven, steam from the water causes the gluten to stretch, then the heat denatures the protein so that it 'sets' in the expanded form.

The interior of the baked, expanded, gluten ball should be light and crisp with many large air spaces surrounded by shiny walls. It is similar to a starched-reduced roll, but quite different to a bread roll because there is no starch to gelatinise.

## Suggestions for further work*

a Gluten-free flour will wash away completely, as will cornflour or flours from any other cereal except wheat and rye.

b As long as ingredients, proving and cooking conditions are constant, a very close relationship will be seen between gluten content and loaf volume.

# Experiment 50*

## Pekar test

### Purpose

To compare the colour of flours.

### Materials

range of flours, eg different brands of plain white, breadmaking, brown, gluten-free

Pekar board (rigid plastic, metal or wooden board, 5–8 cm wide, 15–18 cm long, of any thickness or colour, or a small plate)

wide-bladed spatula

large bowl

### Method

1  Fill the bowl with cold water.

2  Place about a dessertspoonful of one of the flours on the Pekar board. Slide the spatula over the flour to form it into a smooth pat with a maximum thickness of 0.5 cm. Cut the pat with the spatula to form a square at least 4 cm x 4 cm.

3  Place a similar amount of the second flour sample on the board, form into a smooth square as above, slide up to the first sample and smooth carefully with the spatula. The two flours must touch cleanly.

4  Repeat for a third flour if available (Fig. 50.1).

**Fig. 50.1**

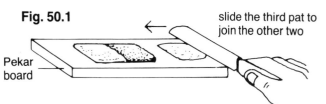

slide the third pat to join the other two

Pekar board

5  Holding the board carefully, slide it steadily under the water. The water surface should pass evenly over the surface of the flour pat (Fig. 50.2).

**Fig. 50.2**

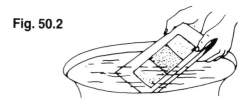

6  Hold the board under the surface of the water for a few seconds to allow a skin to form, then slide slowly out of the water.

7  Compare the colour of the wetted flours.

### Result

Comment on the colour of the flours, comparing each with one that is designated 'acceptable' for a particular purpose (such as a good quality white breadmaking flour for a white loaf).

96

# Experiment 51**

## Flour improvers

### Purpose

To detect the presence of potassium bromate and ascorbic acid flour improvers.

### Materials

white flours

2% aqueous solution of potassium iodide

⚠ dilute sulphuric acid

2% aqueous solution of iodine

2 petri dishes (or saucers)

spatula or knife

large bowl

test tube

test tube rack

### Test for bromate improver

#### Method

1  Press a small portion of flour on a petri dish.

2  Wet the flour by slowly sliding the dish under the surface of water in a large bowl, leaving it for a few seconds then sliding it out.

3  Put about 5 cm³ potassium iodide solution into a test tube, then add about 1 cm³ dilute sulphuric acid.

4  Pour this reagent over the wet flour and drain off excess.

5  Leave for a few minutes and note any colour change.

#### Result

Brown or black specks indicate bromate flour improver.

### Test for ascorbic acid improver

#### Method

6  Carry out steps 1 and 2.

7  Pour a little iodine solution over the wet flour and note any colour change.

#### Result

The whole surface of the flour will turn blue-black *except* where ascorbic acid is present.

# Experiment 50*
# Pekar test

## Introduction

The colour of flour depends on minute amounts of carotenoid pigments in the endosperm of the grain and also on specks of bran. The purpose of milling is to produce uniform grades of flour, whether they are brown or white. The *Pekar test* is used routinely in flour mills to check whether the bran particles are being screened out efficiently, but it also shows up differences in the whiteness of flours.

## Materials

a Several brands of flour, especially white flour, should be tested. If a 'special' flour is made, by adding a very small quantity of wholemeal flour to a white flour, the purpose of this test in the flour mill is illustrated.

b A special spatula is used in the flour mill, but a kitchen spatula gives good results.

c Pekar boards may be of any material as long as they are rigid. A tea-plate can even be used, but it should preferably be white or small differences in colour will be difficult to distinguish.

d A washing-up bowl or very large mixing bowl should be used.

## Method

a The thickness and size of the flour pats are not critical, but they must have a smooth surface and they must touch each other with a sharp edge.

b Similar flours should be tested together, to show *small* differences in colour. Two different brands of white flour, for instance, or a white and the 'special'.

c The flour should be held under the water until bubbles no longer rise to the surface and a skin has formed.

## Result

The colours should be compared when the flour is dry and when it is wet. Small differences are most easily seen when wet. The colour due to the presence of pigments should be distinguishable from colour due to bran specks. If possible, loaves should be made from the flours and the colour of the crumb compared.

# Experiment 51**
# Flour improvers

## Introduction

Holding flour in storage for several weeks improves its breadmaking quality. This ageing process can be accelerated by chemical 'improvers' which have the effect of making the gluten more elastic, so improving gas retention and increasing loaf volume. Permitted improvers include potassium bromate and ascorbic acid. An improving agent that also bleaches the flour is chlorine dioxide; benzoyl peroxide bleaches only.

## Materials

a A range of flours should be tested: different brands of plain, self-raising and breadmaking. For demonstration purposes, a pinch of potassium bromate and of ascorbic acid can be added to separate samples of flour.

b See Appendix I for details of reagents.

c A saucer may be used instead of a petri dish, or this experiment may be carried out immediately after the *Pekar test (Experiment 50)*.

## Method

The flour pat should have a smooth surface and should be at least 4 cm across.

## Result

a Potassium bromate is a powerful oxidizing agent (hence its flour-improving activity). In acidified solution, it releases free iodine from an iodide. This appears as a brown colour on the flour, or the spots may be darker in colour if the iodine stains the starch.

b Ascorbic acid has the opposite effect – iodine stains the starch *except* where ascorbic acid is present in the flour. The ascorbic acid prevents liberation of free iodine.

# Experiment 52*

# Composition of eggs

## Purpose

Examination of shell, white and yolk.

## Materials

2 eggs

⚠ dilute hydrochloric acid

limewater

pH papers

balance or scales

calipers

ruler

hand lens

dropping pipettes or eye droppers

watch glass or saucer

3 small beakers or cups

microscope slides

cover slips

microscope

## Method

1  Weigh the egg. Measure the diameters shown in Fig. 52.1 using calipers and a ruler.

**Fig. 52.1**

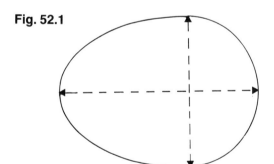

2  Examine the shell using a hand lens.

3  Put an egg into dilute hydrochloric acid and observe the reaction. Collect some of the gas in a dropping pipette and bubble it through limewater in a watch glass. Observe what happens to the limewater. When the shell has dissolved observe the membranes under the shell.

4  Break another egg and separate the white and the yolk. Weigh the shell, white and yolk.

5  Observe a drop of the white and of the yolk under the microscope. Note the difference.

6  Find the pH of the white.

## Result

Tabulate the results of weighing shell, white and yolk.

**Table of results for Experiment 52**

|  | g | % |
|---|---|---|
| Total weight of egg: |  |  |
| Weight of shell: |  |  |
| Weight of white: |  |  |
| Weight of yolk: |  |  |

Compare your results with those for the rest of your group and find the average for the class.

Note the effervescence when the shell is dissolving in hydrochloric acid. The gas should turn limewater milky, showing the presence of carbon dioxide. This indicates carbonate in the shell.

In microscopic examination, tiny fat droplets will be seen dispersed in the yolk.

The white has an alkaline pH.

## Suggestions for further work*

Note the fluorescence of egg white under ultraviolet light. This must be done with great care: do not look directly at the light.

# Experiment 52*
# Composition of eggs

## Introduction
Eggs consist of shell, white and yolk in fairly constant proportions. These proportions are investigated, and some properties of each of the constituents are studied.

## Materials
a The eggs for this experiment should be as fresh as possible.

b For details of reagents see Appendix I.

c Wide- and narrow-range pH papers should be available.

## Method
a The whole egg and the separate components should be weighed, in grams, to one decimal place.

b The diameters should be measured, in centimetres, to one decimal place.

c It is difficult to collect the gas from the reaction in step 3. One method is to place a funnel over the beaker and to collect the gas in a syringe, as shown in Fig. 52.1.

**Fig. 52.1**
Collecting
carbon dioxide

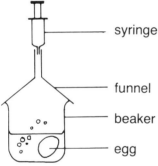

— syringe

— funnel

— beaker

— egg

d See *Experiment 1* for microscope slide preparation. The difference between yolk and white can be seen clearly under low power.

## Result
a Eggs are graded by size, but for all eggs about 10 per cent of the weight is shell, 60 per cent white and 30 per cent yolk.

b As with the experiments on raising agents, a demonstration of the effect of carbon dioxide by blowing through a straw into a small volume of limewater may be useful. If the egg is held under the acid for about 30 minutes, the shell will be removed completely, showing the shell membranes very clearly.

c The major difference between yolk and white, to be seen under the microscope, is the presence of fat in the form of tiny droplets throughout the yolk. About one-third of the yolk is fat, maintained as an oil-in-water emulsion by the emulsifying agent lecithin. The protein in both the yolk and the white (9 per cent and 16 per cent respectively) is in true, rather than colloidal, solution and cannot therefore be seen even under a powerful microscope.

d The pH of uncooked egg-white is about 9; it is the only common alkaline food.

## Suggestions for further work*
Egg-white fluoresces under ultraviolet light because of the presence of riboflavin. Viewing with ultraviolet light should be done with great care, with the light positioned in such a way that it is impossible to look directly at it, even accidentally.

# Experiment 53*

# Quality of eggs

## Purpose

To study the effects of storage on eggs.

## Materials

eggs of differing ages

10% sodium chloride solution

reading lamp

cone made from thin black card (see Fig. 53.1)

1 000 cm$^3$ measuring cylinder or similar tall glass container

wooden chopping board or large plate

## Method

Carry out the following experiments on eggs of differing ages:

1 Preferably in a darkened room, place the egg in front of a strong light as shown in Fig. 53.1 and examine the egg for:

a clarity and position of yolk.

b blemishes in yolk.

c size of air sac.

**Fig. 53.1**

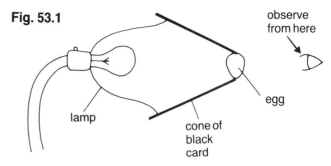

2 Fill the measuring cylinder with salt solution and carefully drop in the egg. Note the position at which the egg floats.

3 Break the egg on to a chopping board or a large plate. Note the proportion of thick to thin white.

## Result

Fig. 53.2 is a guide to the results that may be expected. Compare and explain the results for eggs of different ages.

**Fig. 53.2**

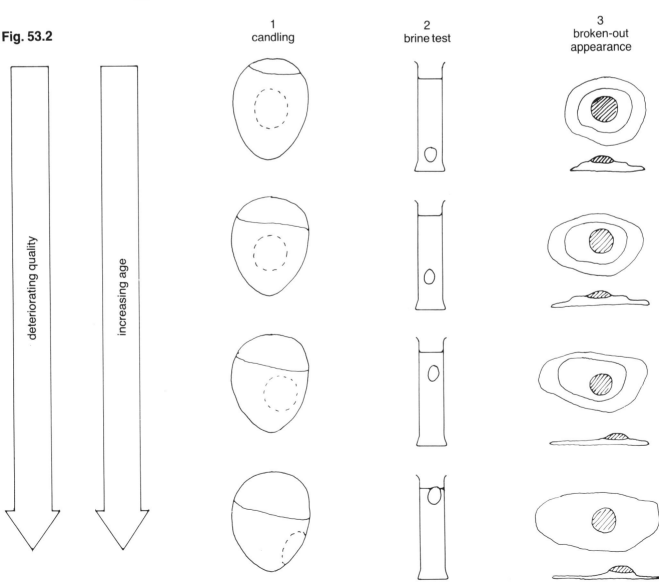

# Experiment 53*
# Quality of eggs

## Introduction

Eggs in the UK are graded for quality: *A*, *B* and *C*. Most eggs in the shops are class *A*: fresh, clean, uncracked and with a smaller air sac than class *B*. This experiment aims to demonstrate two methods for testing for freshness without breaking the egg and to compare the results of these tests with assessment of broken-out egg. Most pupils will not have seen a 'bad' egg in the home – it is interesting to look at the effects of long-term storage, especially if storage at room temperature and in the refrigerator can be compared.

## Materials

a A collection of eggs should be made so that each group of pupils can see eggs that have been stored, perhaps under varying stated conditions, for a week, a month, six months, possibly a year or more, as well as fresh eggs.

b A special candling lamp may be used, having a metal screen with a central hole screwed to the front of the lampshade, but candling is equally well carried out with the reading lamp and cardboard cone as suggested.

c A chromatography tank or a spaghetti storage jar may be used instead of the $1000 \, cm^3$ measuring cylinder. All have the disadvantage that they are large, glass and fragile.

d The chopping board or plate must be large enough for the egg-white of even the oldest egg to spread. A large frying pan is also ideal and, in the context of frying eggs, is practical. Alternatively, the eggs may simply be broken onto a wooden or plastic-topped bench or table but this is obviously messy to clean afterwards.

## Method

a Candling is best done in a completely dark room. The egg should be held against the hole in the cone and slowly revolved about the vertical axis. The outline of the air sac can be drawn on the egg with a pencil.

b Care should be taken, when breaking the egg, not to break the yolk. In old eggs, however, the membrane surrounding the yolk is sometimes so fragile that this is difficult to avoid: it should be noted as another effect of ageing.

c A diagram should be made, as in Fig. 53.2 of the *Pupils' Material,* of the broken-out appearance.

## Result

a As well as diagrams, comments should be made on the colour of the yolk and white and the smell of the egg – if any. Because of the efficient antibacterial arrangements of the egg (cuticle, shell pores, shell membranes and lysozyme in the albumen) even very old eggs may have no smell at all. In eggs of a year or more, the air sac may occupy almost all of the egg, the white and yolk having dried out. If this appears to be so on candling, there is little point in breaking the egg – ancient and venerable eggs become valuable!

b Further observations can be made on the broken-out egg, such as height of the thick white, or relative proportions of thick to thin white (thin white will drain through a sieve). The height of the yolk can be divided by its width as another index of quality. Each of these, as well as the candled and broken-out appearance, can be related to cooking tests such as cake making, foaming and even frying.

# Experiment 54**

# Methylene blue test

## Purpose

To assess the keeping quality of pasteurized milk.

## Materials

pasteurized milk (fresh, soured for 24 hours, soured for one week)

fresh pasteurized milk boiled for 10 minutes and cooled

methylene blue solution

5 sterile test tubes with cotton wool plugs

test tube rack

grease pencil

large beaker or washing-up bowl for used pipettes

sterile $10\,cm^3$ graduated pipettes

pipette filler

bunsen burner

waterbath at 35–40°C

## Method

1 First prepare the controls:

  a Take a sterile test tube, remove the cotton wool plug and pass the mouth of the tube from side to side through a bunsen flame for a few seconds (Fig. 54.1).

**Fig. 54.1**

flaming the tube

  b Using a sterile pipette fitted with a pipette filler, add $10\,cm^3$ boiled milk to the tube (Fig. 54.2).

**Fig. 54.2**

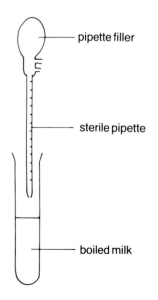

pipette filler

sterile pipette

boiled milk

  c With the same pipette, add $1\,cm^3$ methylene blue to the tube.

  d Reflame the mouth of the tube and replace the plug.

  e Carry out steps **a** to **d** using another sterile pipette and tube but using $10\,cm^3$ of the sourest milk and $1\,cm^3$ tap water instead of boiled milk and methylene blue (Fig. 54.3)

2 Into a separate labelled sterile test tube put $10\,cm^3$ pasteurized milk and $1\,cm^3$ methylene blue. Repeat for both sour milk samples, remembering to use a different sterile pipette each time and to flame the mouth of the tube as in step 1.

3 Mix the contents of all the tubes by swirling gently.

4 Place the tubes in the waterbath. Note that the waterbath must not reach temperatures higher than 40°C. Note the time.

5 Examine the tubes every 30 minutes.

## Result

The control containing the boiled milk will stay blue and the control containing tap water instead of methylene blue will remain white.

In the case of the milk samples, complete decolorization in under 30 minutes means that the milk is unfit for consumption. If the milk decolorizes methylene blue in 1–3½ hours it is of doubtful quality. If it is still blue after 4 hours it is satisfactory.

**Fig. 54.3**

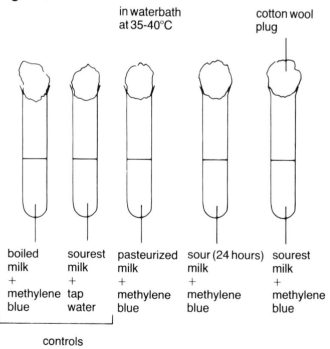

in waterbath at 35-40°C

cotton wool plug

| boiled milk + methylene blue | sourest milk + tap water | pasteurized milk + methylene blue | sour (24 hours) milk + methylene blue | sourest milk + methylene blue |

controls

# Experiment 54**
# Methylene blue test

## Introduction

Pasteurization of milk, at 72°C or more for 15 seconds, is designed to kill pathogenic microorganisms. It does not kill those bacteria that sour milk, though their numbers are significantly reduced. The milk should remain fit to drink during distribution and for a period in the home. The keeping quality of milk is assessed in the dairy by the methylene blue test, after overnight storage at about 18°C. The blue dye, methylene blue, is reduced to a colourless form by bacteria. The rate of reduction depends on the number of bacteria.

## Materials

a  To duplicate the test carried out in the dairy, only 'fresh' milk is needed – remembering that it has been stored at varying temperatures during distribution. It is more interesting, however, if a sample of milk is seen to fail the test so milk should be provided which contains large numbers of bacteria.

b  Boiled milk acts as a control; it will contain very few, if any, viable bacteria after boiling for 10 minutes.

c  For details of methylene blue solution see *page 147*.

d  To sterilize the test tubes, roll cotton wool plugs to fit the neck and insert into the tubes so that half the plug protrudes from the end of each tube. Put a set of tubes into a beaker and cover all the tubes with aluminium foil (Fig. 54.1). Place the beaker in a portable autoclave containing half a pint of water and sterilize according to the instructions on the autoclave at 15 lb pressure for 15 minutes. Cool the tubes and as long as the cotton wool is dry they will remain sterile for many weeks.
Test tubes *should* be sterile, but good results will still be obtained if they are simply spotlessly clean.

e  Pipettes may be sterilized by wrapping them, individually or in sets of 5-10, in aluminium foil and heating them in a domestic oven at about 150°C for about two hours. This may be done at any convenient time, when the oven is being used for baking. Provided there are no holes in the foil, the pipettes will remain sterile until the parcel is opened.
Although the pipettes, like test tubes, *should* be sterile, good results will still be obtained if they are simply spotlessly clean.

f  Clots in sour milk may block the end of the pipette. If the tip is removed, using a glass cutter, the milk can be drawn up the pipette though this obviously limits the use of the pipettes for other purposes.

g  A means of washing used pipettes **immediately** must be available. Once milk has dried in pipettes it is virtually impossible to remove.

h  Use an electrically-heated waterbath if possible because the temperature is critical. It is especially important that it does not rise above 40°C.

## Method

a  Since the purpose of the experiment is to assess the reduction of methylene blue by bacteria in the milk, it is important that other bacteria are not inadvertently introduced. All equipment should be sterile, and pipettes and tubes should be flamed before each operation.

b  It may be simpler to prepare the tubes with reference to the diagram rather than the text. One control contains no methylene blue, the other contains no bacteria. The other tubes, testing the milk samples, contain both methylene blue *and* bacteria.

## Result

The controls are for comparison with the samples; the result is the time for complete decolorization though partial reduction of the methylene blue will lead to useful discussion. Very sour milk will decolorize the dye in less than 30 minutes. Milk delivered on the day of the experiment should have no effect on methylene blue after four hours.

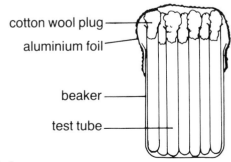

cotton wool plug
aluminium foil

beaker

test tube

**Fig. 54.1**

# Experiment 55**

# Turbidity test

## Purpose

To show that sterilized milk has been satisfactorily heat treated.

## Materials

sterilized milk
UHT milk
pasteurized milk
ammonium sulphate

balance
$100 \, cm^3$ conical flask
$25 \, cm^3$ measuring cylinder
filter paper
filter funnel
funnel stand
test tube
test tube rack
$250 \, cm^3$ beaker
bunsen burner          or small pan of
tripod                 water on a hotplate
gauze
flameproof bench mat

## Method

1 Weigh 4 g ammonium sulphate into a $100 \, cm^3$ conical flask.

2 Add $20 \, cm^3$ milk. Mix for about 1 minute to dissolve the ammonium sulphate.

3 Let the solution stand for 5–10 minutes.

4 Filter the solution, collecting at least $5 \, cm^3$ of filtrate in a test tube.

5 Boil the filtrate in a waterbath for 5 minutes then cool in cold water.

6 Examine for turbidity.

## Result

Sterilized milk, if satisfactorily heat treated, will give no turbidity. UHT milk gives faint turbidity and pasteurized milk gives a white precipitate.

104

# Experiment 55**
# Turbidity test

## Introduction
This test is performed on sterilized milk, to show that the sterilization has been efficiently carried out. If UHT and pasteurized milk are used in the experiment, as well as sterilized milk, the results form a basis for discussion of different heat treatments of milk.

## Materials
A small conical flask should be used: $50\,cm^3$ if available, otherwise $100\,cm^3$ is satisfactory.

## Method
A beaker of boiling water over a bunsen burner will serve as a boiling waterbath.

## Result
a  When the milk has been heated long enough to sterilize it (15-40 minutes at 104°C-113°C) some of the protein – the albumin – is denatured. If the heat treatment has *not* been efficient, non-denatured albumin passes through the filter paper in this experiment. It is denatured in the boiling waterbath and produces turbidity.

b  There should be no turbidity with sterilized milk, faint turbidity with UHT milk, and a precipitate with pasteurized. (If untreated milk was tested, this, as might be expected, would give a heavier precipitate still.) This can be related to the decreasing severity of heat treatment.

c  Albumin is one of the proteins to be denatured and precipitated when pasteurized milk is boiled. It forms a 'skin' on top of the milk, prevents the escape of steam, and causes the milk to boil over. It may also stick to the sides and bottom of the pan and give rise to burning.

# Experiment 56*** ⚠

# Colony count

This experiment must be carried out in a laboratory under the supervision of a teacher with appropriate scientific background.

## Purpose

To assess the bacteriological quality of milk.

## Materials

pasteurized milk

0.1% peptone water, dispensed in $9\,cm^3$ quantities in plugged test tubes and sterilized at 121°C for 15 minutes

nutrient agar, sterilized at 121°C for 15 minutes and held in a waterbath at 50°C

sterile straight-sided $1\,cm^3$ pipette with rubber teat

test tube rack

3 sterile petri dishes

grease pencil

incubator at 30–37°C

## Method

1   Using a sterile pipette fitted with a rubber teat, transfer $1\,cm^3$ of milk into a test tube containing $9\,cm^3$ peptone water. Each time a plug is removed from a tube, pass the mouth of the tube from side to side through a bunsen flame for a few seconds. This is now a $10^{-1}$ dilution of the milk (Fig. 56.1).

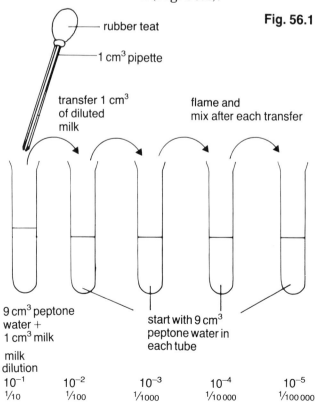

**Fig. 56.1**

2   Mix by drawing liquid into the pipette and holding the end of the pipette about 1 cm above the surface, releasing it. Repeat this twice more.

3   Using the same pipette, transfer $1\,cm^3$ from the $10^{-1}$ dilution to another test tube containing $9\,cm^3$ peptone water. Mix as in step 2. This is a $10^{-2}$ dilution of the milk.

4   Repeat for $10^{-3}$, $10^{-4}$ and $10^{-5}$ dilutions.

5   Using the same pipette, transfer $1\,cm^3$ of the last dilution to a sterile petri dish, labelled on the *base* (Fig. 56.2). Open the lid for the **minimum** time only.

**Fig. 56.2**

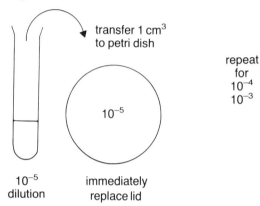

6   Transfer, in a similar way, $1\,cm^3$ of the next two dilutions to sterile labelled petri dishes. Work *up* through the dilutions: transfer first $10^{-5}$ then $10^{-4}$ then $10^{-3}$.

7   Wash the pipette *immediately,* before the milk dries in it.

8   To one petri dish containing $1\,cm^3$ of a milk dilution, add about $10\,cm^3$ sterile nutrient agar at 50°C (Fig. 56.3). Replace the lid as soon as the agar has been added and mix by gently moving the dish three times backwards and forwards, three times from side to side, three times clockwise and three times anticlockwise.

**Fig. 56.3**

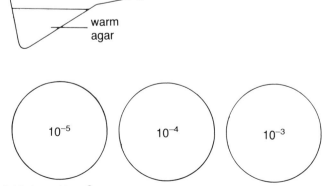

Add about $10\,cm^3$ warm (50°C) agar to each dilution replace lids and incubate at 30-37°C

9  Repeat for the other two dilutions. Allow the agar to set. Seal with two strips of transparent tape at right angles (to form a cross). **Do not re-open.**

10  Turn the petri dishes upside down and incubate at 30–37°C for 48 hours.

11  Remove from the incubator and count the colonies. **Do not under any circumstances open the dishes.** Place the dishes into autoclavable bags.

12  Proper safe arrangements must be made for the disposal of the dishes. (See *page 109.)*

## Result

Calculate the colony count by multiplying the number of colonies counted by the reciprocal of the dilution, eg

74 colonies on the $10^{-4}$ plate = colony count 74 x $10^4$ per $cm^3$.

This indicates that the original milk contained 740 000 bacteria per $cm^3$.

*Note*  The number of colonies counted on successive dilutions should differ by a factor of 10, eg

$$10^{-5} \quad 7 \text{ colonies} = \quad 7 \times 10^5 = 700\,000 \text{ cm}^{-3}$$
$$10^{-4} \quad 70 \text{ colonies} = \quad 70 \times 10^4 = 700\,000 \text{ cm}^{-3}$$
$$10^{-3} \, 700 \text{ colonies} = 700 \times 10^3 = 700\,000 \text{ cm}^{-3}$$

For greater accuracy:

a  prepare duplicate plates.

b  use a different pipette for each dilution.

c  count only those plates having between 30 and 300 colonies.

## Suggestions for further work***

Find the colony count for day-old and week-old milk, and for UHT and sterilized milk. In the former case dilute to $10^{-8}$ and plate the $10^{-6}$, $10^{-7}$ and $10^{-8}$ dilutions. In the latter case, dilute and plate only $10^{-1}$ and $10^{-2}$ dilutions.

# Experiment 56***
# Colony count

## Introduction

This test is routinely carried out in dairies on UHT milk (see *Suggestions for further work*) but it is described here for pasteurized milk. The purpose of pasteurization is to destroy pathogenic bacteria and to reduce the number of spoilage organisms, but many bacteria survive the heat treatment. These are harmless but, if allowed to multiply, will sour the milk. The colony count test uses the techniques of serial dilution and of plating in nutrient agar to find the number of bacteria in a cm$^3$ of milk.

## Note on bacteriological experiments

**a Many local authorities recommend that this type of work is not carried out in schools, and certainly not in a home economics room. Check with your Adviser before undertaking these experiments.**

**b Proper, safe, arrangements must be made for disposal of agar plates (see Method (e) overleaf) and pupils must be aware that plates are not, under any circumstances, to be opened.**

## Materials

**a** See *page 148* for details of peptone water and nutrient agar.

**b** Plug the test tubes of peptone water and sterilize them in a portable autoclave as described in *Experiment 54, page 103*.

**c** Nutrient agar may be dispensed in approximately 10 cm$^3$ quantities in test tubes, plugged, sterilized then held at 45–50°C. Each test tube then holds enough agar for one petri dish. It may be more convenient, however, to have conical flasks or Duran bottles (see *page 152*) containing 100 cm$^3$ of nutrient agar, sufficient for 8–10 petri dishes. Duran bottles are complete with screw-tops but conical flasks must be plugged with cotton wool and covered with aluminium foil (see Fig. 56.1). They must be sterilized at 121°C 15 lb pressure for 15 minutes.

**d** Once sterilized, the agar can be cooled and kept in a cool cupboard or refrigerator indefinitely. When required, melt the agar in a boiling waterbath or in a portable autoclave and hold at 45–50°C. The agar should be at a temperature as low as possible, but if it is allowed to solidify it will have to be boiled again. If the agar is too hot, bacteria from the milk will be killed.

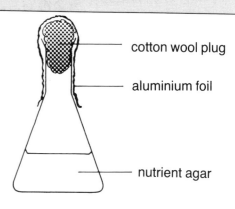

**Fig. 56.1**

cotton wool plug

aluminium foil

nutrient agar

**e** If more than one type of milk is being tested, a pipette will be needed for each milk.

**f** The tip of the pipette may need to be removed if sour, clotted milk is used.

**g** See *Experiment 54* for details of pipette sterilization.

**h** Plastic, sterile petri dishes may be purchased or glass ones can be used, but these will have to be carefully wrapped in foil or put in a special canister (see *page 151*) and sterilized in an oven at about 150°C for about two hours.

**i** If an incubator is not available, the petri dishes can be left in a warm room. The plates, once poured, must *not* be opened. Seal them with two strips of transparent sticky tape at right angles and, as an extra precaution, put in sealed plastic bags.

## Method

**a** Only the bacteria in the milk must be allowed to grow in the agar, so every precaution must be taken to keep apparatus sterile.

**b** The technique for mixing the diluted milk with the agar (step 8) may seem an unnecessary ritual, but it is the most efficient means of distributing the bacteria evenly over the plate (Fig. 56.2).

**Fig. 56.2**

colonies in efficiently mixed agar

colonies in inefficiently mixed agar

**c** The petri dishes must be inverted to incubate or drops of water fall from the lid and surface colonies will be too diffuse to count. **Under no circumstances should the dishes be opened, even for examination.**

**d** If the plates have to be stored for a week or more between classes, wrap sets of them in sealed plastic bags to prevent dehydration and store in a refrigerator.

**e  The plates must be sterilized before disposal.** Place in an autoclavable bag *(page 150)* and sterilize in a portable autoclave at 121°C 15 lb pressure for 15 minutes. The bag and contents are then discarded if plastic dishes have been used, or the dishes are washed if they are glass.

## Result

**a**  Each bacterium, by successive binary divisions, will eventually produce a separate colony which is visible to the naked eye. Each colony can consist of millions of bacteria.

**b**  The total number of bacteria in a pint of milk can be calculated from the results.

## Suggestions for further work***

This test is used in dairies for UHT milk, to check the efficiency of heat treatment. This milk is not completely sterile, hence the 'sell-by' date on the carton, but all pathogens and souring organisms should have been destroyed in the heat treatment.

It is interesting to compare results of the colony count test on fresh pasteurized, day-old and week-old milks with the results of the methylene blue test *(Experiment 54)*. Also compare the speed with which the result is obtained.

# Experiment 57*** ⚠

# Kreis test for rancidity

This experiment must be carried out in a laboratory under the supervision of a teacher with appropriate scientific background.

## Purpose

To detect oxidative rancidity in fats and oils.

## Materials

fresh and rancid fat or oil, eg margarine, corn oil, sesame seed oil

⚠ 0.1% phloroglucinol in ethoxyethane (diethyl ether)

⚠ concentrated hydrochloric acid

boiling tube

test tube rack

glass rod

## Method

Make sure you are wearing eye protection before starting this experiment, and that there are no naked flames or hotplates in the room.

1   In a boiling tube dissolve a small volume of fat (about $5\,cm^3$) in an equal volume of 0.1% phloroglucinol in ethoxyethane.

2   Add a similar volume of concentrated hydrochloric acid (**CARE**). Mix by stirring with a glass rod.

3   Leave to stand.

## Result

Development of a pink colour indicates rancidity.

# Experiment 57***
# Kreis test for rancidity

## Introduction

Oxidative rancidity is the most common cause of spoilage in fats and oils, caused by the oxidation of unsaturated fatty acid residues in the triglycerides. After oxidation, part of the molecule is split from the triglyceride and foul-smelling and -tasting substances are formed. If rancid fats are used in food production, the food will be inedible. The *Kreis test* is used to check qualitatively whether a fat is rancid.

## Materials

**a** A fresh fat should be compared with a similar one that has been allowed to become rancid. Cooking oil, for example, should be rancid after it has been left in an open dish on a window sill for a few days or longer.

**b Concentrated hydrochloric acid must be handled with great care – it is highly corrosive. Ether is highly inflammable – no naked flames or hotplates must be in the room when it is being used.**

## Method

Mixing of the fat solution and hydrochloric acid must be thorough but careful, to avoid splashing.

## Result

A red colour develops in the presence of oxidized fat, caused by a reaction with phloroglucinol acidic solution.

# SECTION E

# Fibres and fabrics

## Experiment 58**

## Microscopic examination of fibres

### Purpose

To examine and draw the microscopic appearance of fibres of different types seen in longitudinal view.

### Materials

labelled packets containing samples of yarn or fabric made up of known fibres

glycerine (propane-1,2,3-triol)

fine forceps (or tweezers)

scissors

microscope slides

coverslips

dropping pipette (or eye dropper)

mounted needle

filter paper

microscope

### Method

1   Using fine forceps take one of the yarns provided (or unravel a thread from a woven sample) and use scissors to cut off a length of a few millimetres. Immediately replace the sample in its packet. At all times handle the yarn with forceps, taking care not to mix it with other samples or contaminate it with dust or lint from clothing or other sources.

2   Place the short length of yarn on a labelled microscope slide and, using forceps and the mounted needle, tease out the fibres from the yarn as finely as possible. (Take care with your mounted needle. Your teacher will count them out to the class and count them back.)

3   Add one drop of glycerine, then once more spread the teased-out fibres so that they lie parallel without overlapping.

4   Cover with a glass coverslip – support one edge of the coverslip with a needle (see Fig. 1.1, *page 3*) and lower it very carefully on to the specimen to avoid dislodging the fibres or introducing air bubbles. Mop up surplus glycerine with filter paper.

5   Examine the appearance of two or three fibres under the microscope, first under low power and then high power. Draw what you see in each case.

6   Repeat steps 1 to 5 with the other samples in turn.

### Result

Compare the appearance of fibres of different types.

### Suggestions for further work**

Use the procedure outlined above and the drawings made of known fibres to identify samples of unknown yarns. If a woven fabric is to be identified, unravel threads from both weft and warp and examine separately.

# Experiment 58**
# Microscopic examination of fibres

## Introduction

The aim of this investigation, to demonstrate that different fibres can be identified on the basis of microscopic observation, will be best met if certain criteria are followed.

First, time should be spent beforehand ensuring that the pupils are familiar with the setting up and use of a compound microscope.

Secondly, as the synthetic fibres tend to look similar and, indeed, only certain natural fibres show obvious distinguishing features, careful observation and accurate drawing is essential.

Finally, it is suggested that only a small number of known samples are given to pupils to draw in the first instance, followed by one or two unknowns for them to identify using their own drawings (see *Pupils' Worksheet, Suggestions for further work*). This would seem to be more valuable in encouraging accuracy of observation than looking at a lot of different fibres under the microscope then copying the drawing from a book!

Take care with needles – count them out to the class and count them back.

## Materials

a New yarn or fabric is best (if possible without special finishes) as this reduces the chances of contamination with dust and other artefacts. Keep the samples in cellophane packets and only remove as required.

b It is suggested that the number of samples be restricted. The following classification indicates the range from which samples could be chosen.

### Natural fibres

*Cellulose*
　　cotton
　　linen (flax)

*Protein*
　　wool
　　silk

### Man-made fibres

*Regenerated cellulose*
　　rayon

*Acetates* (ester derivatives of cellulose)
　　eg 'Tricel'

*Synthetics*
　　polyamides, eg nylon
　　polyester, eg 'Terylene'
　　polyacrylic derivatives, eg 'Acrilan'

## Method

a If a woven fabric is provided, yarns should be unravelled from both weft and warp and examined separately.

b It is a good idea to make permanent preparations so that a collection can be built up for comparative purposes. To do this:

　i Place the fibre tuft in 80% alcohol (ethanol) for 2 minutes.

　ii Drain off the alcohol (ethanol) and replace with xylol for 2 minutes.

　iii Drain off the xylol. Respread the fibres and add a drop of Canada balsam fixative.

　iv Cover with a glass coverslip (lowering carefully to exclude air bubbles) and allow to dry and harden in a horizontal position.

c Refer to *Experiment 1* for hints on microscope technique.

## Result

It is outside the scope of this book to give illustrations of the variety of fibres available, but various specialist texts are available for reference. Ridley and Williams (1974), Taylor (1989) and Robinson (1967) contain descriptions and drawings or photographs of the microscopic appearance of a wide range of natural and man-made fibres.

## Suggestions for further work**

When unknown samples are given, ensure that the pupils can only identify the fibre on the basis of microscopic observations, rather than recognition of other features, for example colour, of the yarn or fabric.

# Experiment 59*** ⚠

## Heating and burning fibres

This experiment must be carried out in a fume cupboard.

### Purpose

To examine the effect of heat on a selection of natural and man-made fibres.

### Materials

labelled packets containing samples of yarn or fabric made up of known fibres

tongs

bunsen burner

flameproof bench mat

### Method

Make sure you are wearing eye protection before you start this experiment.

1   Twist together several yarns of one type into a tuft 2 or 3 cm long (or a 2 cm square of fabric can be twisted) and grip with the tongs.

2   Adjust the bunsen burner so that the flame is about 5 cm long and non-luminous. (A non-luminous flame is produced by closing the air intake hole at the base of the burner.)

3   Slowly advance the yarn up to the flame and observe its behaviour closely. If it shrinks and melts from the flame forming a bead it is composed of 'thermoplastic' fibres.

4   Place the sample in the flame and hold it there until burning starts. Then withdraw it and note how it burns before extinguishing (if necessary) against the flameproof bench mat.

### Result

Compare your results with the table.

### Suggestions for further work***

Use the procedure outlined above to identify samples of unknown yarns. If a woven fabric is to be identified, unravel threads from both weft and warp and examine them separately.

### Table of results for Experiment 59

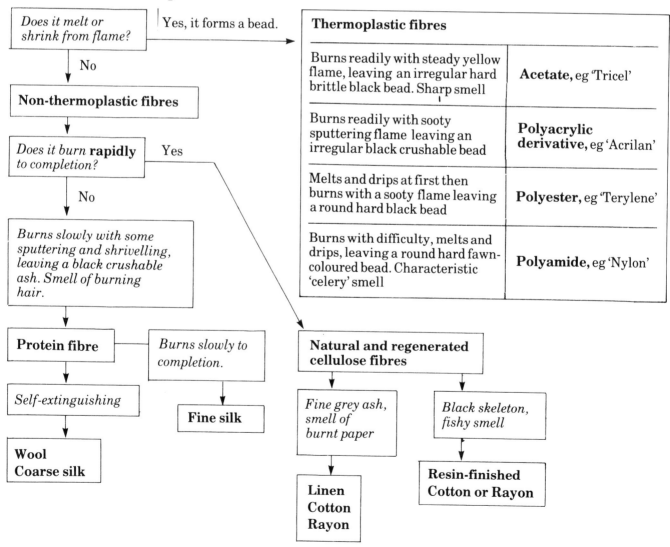

# Experiment 59***
# Heating and burning fibres

## Introduction

This is another means of identifying fibres. Besides reinforcing the concept of the division of fibres into 'natural' and 'man-made', this experiment introduces grouping based on 'thermoplastic' or 'non-thermoplastic' properties.

A good plan is initially to provide known samples in order that pupils may confirm the reactions of fibres, first to close proximity to a flame and then to burning, as indicated in the table in the *Pupil's Worksheet*. Suggestions for further work are subsequently to test unknowns for identification based on previous observation.

## Materials

The precise manner in which fibres react to heating and burning is influenced by the finish applied and whether the sample is a blend of fibres. Therefore it is advisable to use pure samples.

## Method

Sufficient time must be allowed for the effect of *heating* to be observed before the fibres are actually ignited. So the fibres must be brought slowly up to the flame and held near it for several seconds while observations are made.

## Result

It is important that pupils record their own observations rather than simply copy the table, which is for guidance only. For example 'sharp smell' may evoke a variety of subjective responses which should be recorded by the individual concerned.

The results of this experiment and *Experiment 60* can usefully be linked to a discussion or survey of materials used in the manufacture of various articles of clothing or furnishing, and the possible fire hazards.

## Suggestions for further work***

As in *Experiment 58,* the identification of unknown fibres should be on the basis of previous observations and not derived from other clues such as the colour or texture of the sample.

# Experiment 60*** ⚠

# Flammability

This is a potentially hazardous experiment. It must be carried out in a fume cupboard, and fire extinguishers (previously checked to be working) must be to hand.

## Purpose

To compare the flame-resistance of fabrics by finding the time taken for the fabric to burn over a specified distance. **Warning** – some fabrics flare unexpectedly and burn fiercely. This experiment should only be carried out under the supervision of the teacher.

## Materials

samples of fabric at least 75 cm long

metre rule

2 tall retort stands and 3 clamps

bunsen burner

flameproof bench mat

2 x approx. 10 cm lengths of stiff wire

stop clock

sheet of millimetre graph paper

## Method

Make sure you are wearing eye protection.

1   Suspend a strip of fabric 75 cm long and 5 cm wide from a retort stand clamp in a draught-free area and place a flameproof mat below the strip. Adjust the clamp until the lower edge of the fabric is 2.5 cm above the top of the unlit bunsen burner (Fig. 60.1).

**Fig. 60.1**

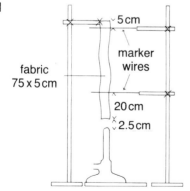

5 cm

marker wires

fabric 75 x 5 cm

20 cm

2.5 cm

## Table of results for Experiment 60

2   Use the other retort stand and clamps to position two marker wires horizontally about 2 cm in front of the strip. The lower marker wire should be 20 cm from the bottom of the fabric and the upper wire 5 cm from the top.

3   Move the bunsen burner away from the fabric and light it. Cut off the air supply and adjust the flame until it is 4 cm long.

4   Place the burner so that it is below the middle of the fabric strip and at the same time start the clock (Fig. 60.2). Turn off the burner after 12 seconds.

**Fig. 60.2**

4 cm    2.5 cm

turn off bunsen burner after 12 seconds

5   Immediately return the clock second hand to zero and, if possible, use it to measure the time in seconds from the moment the *lower* edge of the flame passes the lower marker wire to reaching the upper wire.

*Note*   If the material has been flameproofed, the flame will not spread. Therefore measure:

a   the duration in seconds of flaming and afterglow of the fabric after the bunsen burner is turned off.

b   the area of fabric charred or melted (estimate this by placing the fabric on a sheet of graph paper and counting squares).

## Result

Draw a table as shown below.

## Suggestions for further work***

### Flameproofing with borax

Take two $75 \times 5$ cm strips of a flammable fabric (eg. a cellulose fabric) and immerse in 10 g borax dissolved in 100 cm$^3$ of hot water in a 250 cm$^3$ beaker, stirring at intervals. After 5 minutes remove the strips and dry completely without rinsing. Treat a third strip similarly but using 100 cm$^3$ hot water alone. (What is the purpose of this control strip?) When the strips are dry, perform the flammability test on one of the borax-treated strips of fabric and on the water-treated control. Record the results. Finally, either hand or machine wash the remaining borax-treated strip in hot water containing ordinary household detergent. Allow to dry and carry out the flammability test once more. Record the results.

| Fabric | Non-flameproof | Flameproof | |
| --- | --- | --- | --- |
| | Time taken in seconds for flame to travel 50 cm | Duration of flaming and afterglow in seconds | Area of fabric affected (cm$^2$) |
| | | | |

# Experiment 60***
# Flammability

## Introduction

This experiment is based on an official British Standards Institute (BSI) test for the flammability of fabrics. Many tragedies have been caused in the past by accidental ignition of clothing, such as nightdresses or of fabric furnishings which have not met the BSI specifications.

This test cannot be used on fabrics which have been flameproofed and therefore do not propagate a flame. However, it is useful to provide the pupils with such fabrics for comparative purposes. In this case it is suggested (step 5) that the duration of flaming and afterglow, and the area of charred or melted fabric remaining are measured.

## Materials

Many fabrics commonly used in the manufacture of furnishings and apparel burn unexpectedly fiercely. While this can be used to promote lively discussion of the suitability of their use in view of the fire hazards involved, it also means that the pupils must be carefully supervised. **A sink or large bowl of water should be available for immersing the burning fabric. A fire extinguisher should be conveniently situated.** This should be fully checked before the experiment and the teacher must be familiar with its operation.

## Method

If flammability comparisons are to be made between different groups of pupils testing different fabrics, all dimensions must be accurately made with a rule, and a stop clock used for precise measurement of times.

## Result

These can be compared with the results obtained from *Experiment 59* and can also be linked to the necessity of flameproofing certain fabrics such as those composed of the rapidly burning cellulosic fibres, linen, cotton and rayon. Even wool and silk, which are inherently non-flammable, will burn readily where they are used in blends with other fibres such as cotton or the man-made fibres.

## Suggestions for further work***

Borax (disodium tetraborate-10-water) is a salt, the crystals of which contain a great deal of water of crystallization (this can be demonstrated by gently heating a small sample of borax in a dry test tube and noting the steam evolved). Alum (aluminium potassium sulphate-12-water) has similar properties, and a 20% solution of potash alum can also be used for flameproofing. When the treated cloth is dried its surface is covered with tiny crystals of the salt. When these come near to a flame, the steam given off acts as a protective layer, preventing oxygen reaching the fabric.

Flameproofing with borax, however, has the drawback that the flame-retardant finish is removed on laundering, and this experiment is designed to demonstrate this.

The purpose of the control is to show that it is the borax that flameproofs the fabric and not simply the effect of soaking in water. In addition, the control burning well confirms that the fabrics under test have been thoroughly dried.

117

# Experiment 61*

# Strength of fibres

## Purpose

To find the effect of moisture on the breaking load of a textile thread.

## Materials

yarns of nylon, wool and cotton

scale pan of known weight
box of weights
forceps (or tweezers)
retort stand
clamp

## Method

It is probably best to wear eye protection during this experiment. When nylon thread breaks it can have a whiplash effect and cause nasty cuts.

1 Suspend the scale pan from the retort stand using a single thread of nylon about 25 cm long (Fig. 61.1). At the same time place five or six 25 cm nylon threads in a beaker of water for 10 minutes, giving an occasional stir.

**Fig. 61.1**

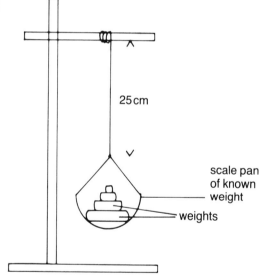

25 cm

scale pan of known weight

weights

2 Add weights to the pan until the thread breaks. (**CARE.** Mind your feet – ensure weights do not cause damage on falling.) This weight (include the weight of the scale pan) will give an approximate value of the breaking load.

3 Repeat the experiment several times on dry nylon threads adding small weights as the breaking load is approached to obtain as accurate a value as possible. Take an average of two or three accurate breaking loads.

4 Repeat the experiment using the wet nylon threads.

5 Compare dry and wet wool yarn, and dry and wet cotton yarn in the same way.

118

## Result

Record all trials in a table similar to the example shown. Calculate the wet strength of each yarn as a percentage of its dry strength.

**Table of results for Experiment 61**

| Fibre type | Breaking load (Weights added + weight of pan) Trial number | | | | | |
|---|---|---|---|---|---|---|
| | 1 | 2 | 3 | 4 | 5 | 6 |
| **Nylon – dry** | | | | | | |
| | Breaking load calculated from average of trials =......grams | | | | | |
| **Wet** | | | | | | |
| | Breaking load calculated from average of trials =......grams Hence wet strength calculated as a percentage of dry strength =......% | | | | | |
| **Wool – dry** | | | | | | |
| etc. | | | | | | |

Why cannot this experiment be used validly to compare the strength of nylon, wool and cotton? What further information is required?

## Suggestions for further work*

Using the above method as the basis, design an experiment to:

a compare the strengths of different diameters of the same yarn.

b compare the strengths of different yarns of the same diameter.

The diameter can be found by winding the yarn around a ruler. Push the turns together so that they are just touching and count the number of turns occupying a length of exactly 1 cm.

# Experiment 61*
# Strength of fibres

## Introduction

It is more convenient to use this experiment initially to compare dry and wet threads of the same textile. A comparison of the strengths of different textiles is less straightforward as the diameter (denier or tex) of the fibres will vary.

The dry-wet comparisons have a practical value in that those fibres, such as wool, which show a large drop in strength when wet will require more careful laundering.

## Materials

**a** Prior trials by the teacher with the particular threads to be used in class are advisable. This will give a rough idea of the range of weights which will be required by each group of pupils.

**b** Each group will require 10-12 threads of each material.

## Method

**a** The main hazard in this experiment is of weights falling on to the toes. It is advisable for pupils to wear sturdy shoes rather than open sandals. Also, nylon thread can have a whiplash effect when it breaks, so eye protection is advisable.

**b** The first two or three trials with each thread are simply to establish the approximate breaking load. Although these preliminary observations should be recorded, they should not be used in the final calculation. The average breaking load should be calculated from the final two or three more accurate trials when small weights can be added as the breaking load is approached.

## Result

Practical experience has shown that results, particularly with cotton, can be variable. Basically, cotton becomes stronger when wet (by about 10 per cent) and most other fibres become weaker, although to different extents. Wool gives the most consistent results, having a wet strength approximately 70 per cent of its dry strength. Nylon, theoretically, has a wet strength about 90-95 per cent of dry strength but is frequently not noticeably affected in practice.

## Suggestions for further work*

The larger the diameter the greater the strength, all other things being equal. To make comparison of different yarns valid, therefore, they must have the same diameter. The method of measuring the diameter, although simple, is sufficiently accurate for this purpose; divide 10 by the number of turns to obtain diameters in millimetres.

# Experiment 62*

# Fabrics as insulators

## Purpose

To compare the effectiveness of different fabrics as insulators.

## Materials

3 identical tin cans

samples of 2 different fabrics large enough to cover the cans

tape measure

scissors

scrap paper

needle and thread

jug

thermometer

stop clock

## Method

1 Using a tape measure, find the height and circumference of one of the cans, and cut out a rectangle of scrap paper with these dimensions. In addition, cut out a paper circle the same size as the base of the can (Fig. 62.1).

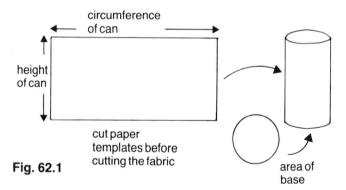

**Fig. 62.1**

circumference of can

height of can

cut paper templates before cutting the fabric

area of base

2 Using these paper templates as a pattern, cut a rectangle and a circle of each fabric to be tested. Sew the rectangle into a cylinder and then sew on each circle, thus forming a jacket into which the can fits exactly.

3 Place a can in each jacket and have an uncovered can as a control. On the inside of each can make a mark 2 cm from the top.

4 Use hot water (about 60°C) from an electric kettle to fill each can exactly to this mark (Fig. 62.2). Immediately note the starting

temperature and start the stop clock. Take care if you are using a mercury thermometer. Any spillages of mercury from broken thermometers must be treated with a mixture of sulphur and lime.

5 After 15 minutes record the temperature of the water in each can.

## Result

Present your results in the form of a table with the headings: *Fabric, Initial temperature, Temperature after 15 minutes, Fall in temperature*. Which fabric is the best insulator? Why must all results be obtained at the same time and place to be truly comparable? What is the purpose of the control?

## Suggestions for further work**

a Using the technique above compare the insulating properties of dry and wet woollen fabric and explain your results.

b Compare the effect of increasing the number of layers of a chosen fabric by enclosing cans in one, two, three and four jackets respectively (note that each succeeding jacket needs to be made slightly larger than the previous one). Plot a graph of the fall in temperature against the number of layers of material. Comment on the results.

c Compare the insulation provided by a chosen fabric in still air and in moving air (a portable electric fan or hair dryer can be used). Explain the results.

**Fig. 62.2**

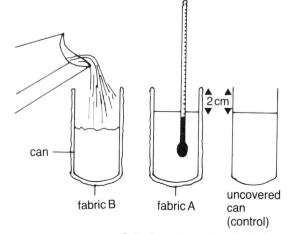

can

2 cm

fabric B

fabric A

uncovered can (control)

# Experiment 62*
# Fabrics as insulators

## Introduction

One of the major functions of clothing is to provide thermal insulation. The insulating capacity of a fabric depends not so much on the fibre itself but on it being able to trap warmed air between the fibres. The majority of clothing materials contain between 60–90% of their volume of air. The amount of air that can be held by a fabric depends upon its thickness and its bulk density (the weight of fibres per unit of volume). In general, the thicker the material and the less its bulk density, the better insulation it provides. However, the type of construction of the fabric is another factor which can affect its insulating properties.

## Materials

a  It is suggested that one of the fabric samples be a good insulator such as wool, brushed nylon or raised flannelette, where a larger percentage of the volume is air.

b  As temperature differences may be quite small, the more sensitive the thermometer the better – one with the range $-20$ to $60°C$ in divisions of $0.2°C$ would be ideal. Take care with mercury thermometers. If mercury is spilled, clear it up and treat the area with a mixture of sulphur and lime.

## Method

a  Once the fabric 'jackets' have been made, they can, of course, be re-used from year to year.

b  As already indicated, the small temperature differences involved will mean that readings must be made carefully and as accurately as the thermometer will allow.

c  Great care must be taken to ensure that the cans are subjected to as near identical environmental conditions as possible. Inadvertently placing one of the cans in a draught or near a radiator, for example, could thoroughly confuse the results.

Ideally, cans should be corked to reduce loss of heat from the water surface, with a hole bored to take the thermometer. They should also be stood on polystyrene tiles to obviate temperature differences along the bench.

## Result

Good insulators will retain heat for a longer period. The better the insulator the higher will be the temperature in the can after 15 minutes. The uninsulated control will provide a baseline temperature against which the effectiveness of the insulation can be compared.

Obviously, to be comparable, results must be made at the same time and place to reduce variables such as environmental temperature, humidity (more water from the can will evaporate into dry air, thus drawing its latent heat of evaporation from the can and producing a cooling effect), air currents, etc.

Ideally the only difference between the cans should be the insulating material, but this is difficult to achieve in practice.

## Suggestions for further work**

a  Wet wool is not as good an insulator as dry wool as the water forces the air out of the pores, and water is a better conductor of heat than air.

b  Although it would be theoretically possible to wear a single layer of clothing, this would not be flexible enough in changing conditions, hence we tend to have a multi-layer style of clothing. An added advantage is that air gaps are formed between the layers, so increasing the insulating properties. Hence, two layers of the same fabric should retain heat more than twice as effectively as a single layer of that fabric and this may be reflected in the results. There will also come a point when addition of further insulating layers has a negligible effect on the fall in temperature, that is, when the major source of heat loss is from the top surface of the can.

c  The insulating properties of a fabric depend upon the trapped warmed air within it remaining static. If this warm air is continually blown away, more heat will be lost in warming the colder air which replaces it. It has been estimated that an increase of wind speed of 10 mph is equivalent to a drop in air temperature of almost $10°C$. As an example, a woman in a light dress could have the insulation reduced to zero in a wind of 10-15 mph.

121

# Experiment 63*

# Shrinkage

## Purpose

To compare the shrinkage of a variety of yarns.

## Materials

yarns of various types in at least 100 cm lengths

scissors
retort stand
large hook
small hook
half-metre rule
forceps (or tweezers)
$250\,cm^3$ beaker
bunsen burner
tripod ⎤ or small pan of
gauze ⎥ water on a hotplate
flameproof bench mat ⎦

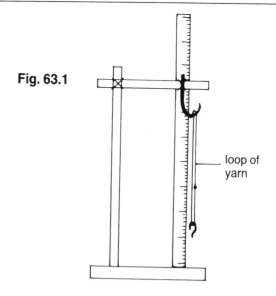

**Fig. 63.1**

loop of yarn

## Method

1 Cut three 100 cm lengths of each of the yarns provided.

2 Securely knot the ends of each length of yarn to form a loop.

3 Suspend each loop in turn from a hook supported by a retort stand. Suspend a light hook from the bottom of the loop to pull it taut, and measure the loop length using a half metre rule (Fig. 63.1).

4 Place all the samples in a beaker half-full of water, bring this to the boil and continue boiling the samples for 10 minutes.

5 Add cold water to the beaker. When the water is cool enough, remove the yarns one at a time, taking precautions to avoid them getting entangled.

6 After the yarns have been allowed to dry, repeat step 3 for each one.

## Result

Record the results as in the table below, calculating for each yarn the average of three determinations. From the average initial and final lengths, calculate the percentage decrease in length.

## Suggestions for further work*

Instead of comparing the shrinkage of different yarns to the same treatment, this experiment can be used to find how different treatments affect the same yarn. Use cotton thread and vary the length of boiling, or add detergent, bleach etc, to recreate various washing procedures.

### Table of results for Experiment 63

| Yarn | Initial length | | | | Length after boiling | | | | % decrease in length |
|---|---|---|---|---|---|---|---|---|---|
| | 1 | 2 | 3 | average | 1 | 2 | 3 | average | |
| | | | | | | | | | |

Which yarns show the least and the greatest resistance to shrinkage?

# Experiment 63*
# Shrinkage

## Introduction

When a fibre absorbs water in washing it swells, with a resulting increase in diameter. Cellulose fibres, such as cotton, can become up to 40% thicker when soaked in water; this swelling is accompanied by a shrinkage in length of the yarn. On drying, the reverse changes occur, but the yarn may not return completely to its original length. This experiment is designed simply to investigate which yarns show the greatest resistance to shrinkage. When these yarns are woven into fabrics, however, factors other than type of fibre may make a larger contribution to the shrinkability of the finished garment. For example, the degree to which the threads are stretched and strained in weaving is important, since wetting causes a tendency for the fabric to return to its normal unstretched state.

## Materials

Pieces of wire may be bent to form hooks. Obviously there are other alternatives, such as safety pins, paper clips, etc.

## Method

**a** When knotting the yarn into a loop, avoid twisting (or untwisting) it, as the degree of strain of the fibres affects the shrinkability.

**b** Ensure that the yarns are thoroughly dried before measurements are made. Use of a hair dryer, if available, will speed up the drying process.

## Result

The percentage decrease in length of each yarn can be calculated from the formula:

$$100 - \left( \frac{\text{average final length}}{\text{average initial length}} \times 100 \right)$$

Cotton and rayon, due to the high fibre swelling that takes place on wetting, tend to show a high degree of shrinkage. Untreated wool also gives high shrinkage values, partly because of its capacity to absorb water and also because wool fibres, uniquely, have a natural tendency to 'felt', that is, to close up on each other. On the other hand, synthetic fibres are immune to shrinkage due to swelling or felting.

# Experiment 64*

# Water-repellency

## Purpose

To compare the water-repellent properties of various fabric samples intended to give good protection against rain.

## Materials

samples of fabric from old raincoats, anoraks, etc.

pair of compasses

card

scissors

filter funnel

funnel stand

test tube for each sample tested

test tube rack

$10 \, cm^3$ pipette

clock

$25 \, cm^3$ measuring cylinder

## Method

1 Use a pair of compasses to draw a circle of diameter 8 cm on card and cut this out with scissors.

2 Using this card template cut out 8 cm diameter circles of the fabrics to be tested.

3 Fold each fabric into a cone like a filter paper and place it in a dry filter funnel supported by a stand and with its end in the mouth of a test tube (Fig. 64.1).

4 Use a pipette to run exactly $10 \, cm^3$ of water into the fabric cone, noting the time.

5 After one hour (or near the end of the lesson) use the measuring cylinder to find the volume of water which has passed through the fabric. If little or no water has penetrated, leave for 24 hours before measuring the volume.

## Result

Record your results in a table as shown below and state which fabric is most repellent to water.

### Table of results for Experiment 64

| Fabric | Volume of water penetrating in 24 hours ($cm^3$) | Volume of water penetrating in 1 hour ($cm^3$) |
|---|---|---|
|  |  |  |

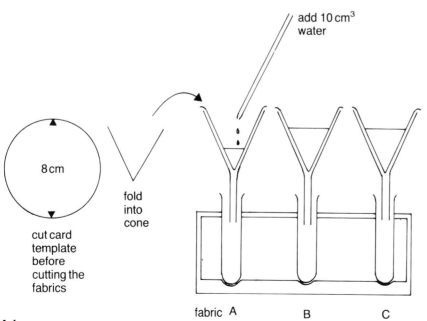

8 cm

cut card template before cutting the fabrics

fold into cone

add $10 \, cm^3$ water

fabric A    B    C

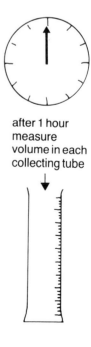

after 1 hour measure volume in each collecting tube

**Fig. 64.1**

# Experiment 64*
# Water-repellency

## Introduction

This experiment is designed to compare fabrics which are intended to give good protection against rain. It is therefore unsuitable for materials like wool which are easily wetted.

A water-repellent fabric is not necessarily waterproof (ie one which completely prevents the penetration of water), often the term 'showerproof' is used instead.

## Materials

Use fabrics which have been treated with a water-repellent finish. Pieces of PVC with no supporting fabric can also be used.

## Method

If several fabric samples are being compared, each should first be positioned in the filter funnel so that the $10\,cm^3$ water can be run into each cone at the same time.

## Result

The results can be discussed in the context of the claims made by the manufacturer of the garment concerned as to its 'waterproof', 'showerproof' or 'water-repellent' character. Water-repellency can be achieved by coating the fabric with suitable 'hydrophobic' (water hating) substances such as waxes or silicones. A spherical water droplet is attracted by untreated fibres of a cloth, and this attraction may be sufficient to separate the water molecules of the drop, which can then penetrate between the fibres. The water-repellent finish, however, does not attract the water molecules – the water droplet remains intact and does not penetrate.

# Experiment 65*

# Crease recovery

## Purpose

To compare the crease recovery of a variety of fabrics.

## Materials

fabric samples

millimetre graph paper

large pin

block of soft wood

scissors

forceps

card

weight of between 100 g and 1 kg

stop clock.

## Method

1 Stick a piece of millimetre graph paper to the face of a block of soft wood. Hammer a large pin at right angles to the wood on one of the main vertical grid lines. Exactly 2.5 cm below the pin, mark out a scale in millimetres as shown in Fig. 65.1.

**Fig. 65.1**

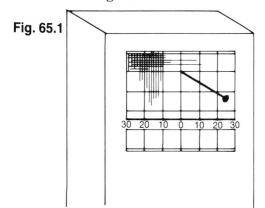

2 Cut four pieces of the first fabric to be tested each measuring 5 cm by 2.5 cm. Cut two of the four pieces with the long side parallel to the warp of the fabric and the other two with the long side parallel to the weft.

3 Using a pair of forceps, fold the first piece carefully in half to form a square of 2.5 cm side. Place this piece between slightly larger pieces of card so as to leave the ends just visible.

4 Place the weight squarely on the card, at the same time starting the stop clock. Leave for exactly three minutes then remove the weight (Fig. 65.2).

5 Using forceps, immediately pick up the fabric specimen by its ends and hang in an inverted 'V' position from the pin, close to but not touching the graph paper, and ensuring that the crease lies along the pin (Fig. 65.3).

**Fig. 65.2**

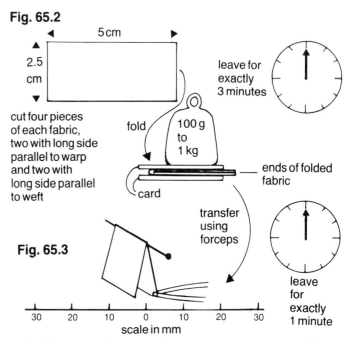

6 After exactly one minute from removal of the weight, measure the distance in millimetres between the ends of the sample as it hangs.

7 Repeat steps 2 and 3 above for the other three pieces of the fabric sample.

8 Repeat the experiment using other fabric samples.

## Result

Calculate the average result for each fabric (warp and weft) and record as shown below.

**Table of results for Experiment 65**

| Fabric | Long side parallel to warp | | | Long side parallel to weft | | |
|---|---|---|---|---|---|---|
| | 1 | 2 | average | 1 | 2 | average |
| | | | | | | |
| | | | | | | |

Which fabric tested had the best resistance to creasing?

# Experiment 65*
# Crease recovery

## Introduction

The resistance to creasing of a fabric depends to an important extent on the presence of multiple cross-linkages in its fibres. It is this feature which makes wool, for example, springy and gives good recovery from creasing. The cross-linkages are stretched without actually breaking, so that when the strain is removed they return the fibre to its original shape.

This experiment is concerned with recovery from dry creasing only. Crease recovery is also influenced by whether the fibre is wet, as water weakens cross-linkages. In this case, creasing may cause these linkages to break and re-form in different positions, thus interfering with the return of the fibres to their original shape. Fibres which absorb a lot of moisture will be less likely to recover from wet creasing.

Crease-resistant finishes can be given to fabrics such as the cellulosics, which in the main consist of long straight molecular chains with few cross-linkages.

This involves impregnating the fabric with a synthetic resin, as a result of which chemical cross-links are formed between fibre molecules.

## Materials

**a** Samples of pure fabrics such as wool and cotton can be compared. Alternatively, the same fabric with and without a crease-resistant finish can be tested.

**b** The greater the weight used, the less will be the spread of the fabric on suspending it along the pin, but the weight itself is not critical. Obviously, valid comparisons can only be made if the same weight is used for each fabric.

## Method

**a** It is important that the only source of creasing of the fabric is due to the weight. Great care must be taken in handling the samples to ensure that pressure is not inadvertently applied along the crease line.

**b** The suggested times must be adhered to exactly, and measurements must be accurately made.

## Result

The table below indicates the ability of different fibres to recover from dry creasing. It should be noted, however, that although the fibre content of a cloth is the main factor, the method of fabric construction and the finish applied may also influence the ability to resist creasing.

**Table 65.1  Recovery from dry creasing**

| **Natural fibres** | | |
|---|---|---|
| *Cellulose* | cotton | poor |
| | linen (flax) | poor |
| *Protein* | wool | very good |
| | silk | good to fair |
| | | |
| **Man-made fibres** | | |
| *Regenerated cellulose* | rayon | poor |
| *Acetate* (ester derivatives of cellulose) | eg 'Tricel' | poor |
| *Synthetics* | polyamide eg Nylon | good |
| | polyester eg 'Terylene' | very good |
| | polyacrylic eg 'Acrilan' derivatives | fair |

127

# SECTION F

# Detergents and dyes

## Experiment 66**

## Making soap

### Purpose

To make soap by reacting oil with alkali.

### Materials

olive oil

⚠ 20% sodium hydroxide solution

$250\,cm^3$ beaker ⎤
bunsen burner ⎟
tripod ⎬ or small pan of
gauze ⎟ water on a hotplate
flameproof bench mat ⎦
boiling tube

test tube holder

test tube

test tube rack

dropping pipettes (or eye droppers)

### Method

Make sure you are wearing eye protection before you start this experiment.

1 Half-fill the beaker with water and bring to the boil.

2 To $5\,cm^3$ of olive oil in a boiling tube add $5\,cm^3$ of 20% sodium hydroxide solution. **CARE.** This solution is very caustic.

3 Shake the mixture to form a white emulsion as the oil droplets are dispersed in the aqueous solution.

4 Place the tube in the boiling waterbath for 30 minutes. (Make sure it does not boil dry!) It will be necessary to shake the tube occasionally since the oil will tend to separate out on top of the aqueous solution – shaking will re-establish the emulsion. Be careful not to spill the solution on your fingers when you are shaking it.

5 After 30 minutes remove the tube and cool thoroughly under the tap. The contents should comprise an upper layer of unchanged olive oil and a lower layer of glycerine (propane 1,2,3-triol) with an intermediate layer of soap.

6 Pour away the liquids and wash the small cake of soap in cold water.

7 Place a small fragment of this soap in a test tube containing $5\,cm^3$ of distilled water and check its ability to form a lather by shaking vigorously. Note that the soap you have made is not pure enough to be applied to the skin.

### Result

Record the appearance and consistency of the soap, and its ability to form a lather with distilled water.

# Experiment 66**
# Making soap

## Introduction

The term 'detergent' refers to any 'cleansing agent' so, strictly speaking, soap is simply an example of a detergent. However, soap and detergents are often referred to separately as different types of cleansing agent. Soaps are the sodium or potassium salts of long-chain carboxylic (fatty) acids such as stearic acid (octadecanoic acid).

They are prepared by the action of strong alkali, such as caustic soda (sodium hydroxide) or caustic potash (potassium hydroxide), on a variety of oils and fats. An important aspect of commercial soap making is the choice and blending of the ingredients. The oils and fats used can be from vegetable sources, such as the coconut, palm and olive, or from animal products such as beef and mutton.

Non-soap detergents are made by reacting petroleum oils, containing long hydrocarbon chains with concentrated sulphuric acid.

## Materials

See *page 148,* for the method of preparing percentage solutions. **20% sodium hydroxide is a very concentrated solution and extremely caustic. Eye protection is essential and spillages should be immediately diluted with copious amounts of water.**

## Method

a In view of the caustic nature of the solution care must be taken when shaking the boiling tube to avoid splashing on to the fingers.

b **Note that the sample of soap produced will not be sufficiently pure to apply to the skin.**

## Result

Only a very small pellet of soap will be obtained using this simple method, but it will be sufficient to produce a good lather when shaken briskly with distilled water.

The main chemical reaction which occurs in soap making is that, upon boiling, the concentrated alkali brings about the hydrolysis and 'saponification' of the triglyceride, glyceryl tristearin, found in fats and oils.

These reactions are summarized in the equations below.

If the alkali used is sodium hydroxide, the stearic acid will form the sodium salt, sodium stearate, which is the active ingredient of most soaps.

Incidentally, the saponification reaction is made use of in oven cleaners, which are basically sticks of sodium hydroxide. The sodium hydroxide converts the grease to soap which is then easier to wipe off.

| **Hydrolysis** | | |
|---|---|---|

$$CH_2OOC(CH_2)_{16}CH_3 \qquad\qquad CH_2OH$$

$$CHOOC(CH_2)_{16}CH_3 + 3H_2O \rightleftharpoons 3CH_3(CH_2)_{16}COOH + CHOH$$

$$CH_2OOC(CH_2)_{16}CH_3 \qquad\qquad CH_2OH$$

| glyceryl tristearate (propane 1,2,3-tri-octadecanoate) | stearic acid (octadecanoic acid) | glycerine (propane 1,2,3-triol) |
|---|---|---|

| **Saponification** | |
|---|---|

$$CH_3(CH_2)_{16}COOH + NaOH \rightarrow CH_3(CH_2)_{16}COONa + H_2O$$

| stearic acid (octadecanoic acid) | sodium stearate – soap (sodium octadecanoate) |
|---|---|

# Experiment 67*

# Testing detergents for soap

## Purpose

To determine whether a sample of household detergent is soap or is soapless.

## Materials

samples of household detergents

salt

vinegar

2 test tubes

test tube rack

dropping pipettes or eye droppers

## Method

1 Add a small quantity of the detergent (a few drops if it is a liquid and a pinch if solid) to a test tube half-filled with distilled water and shake to dissolve.

2 Divide this detergent solution into two portions.

3 To the first portion add a pinch of salt and shake. With a soap a white precipitate will form and only a slight lather will be produced. A soapless detergent will form a very good lather.

4 To the second portion add a few drops of vinegar and shake. If a soap is present fatty curds will float to the top and no lather forms, whereas the soapless detergent will not be affected by treatment and a good lather will form.

## Result

Record the results and state whether the detergents tested are soap or soapless.

# Experiment 67*
# Testing detergents for soap

## Introduction

It is important to know whether a cleansing agent (detergent) is soap or is soapless. Soap forms a scum with hard water (see *Experiment 68*). In hard water areas a soapless detergent should therefore be used. Such detergents do not lose their efficiency in hard water or acid conditions and do not form a scum.

## Materials

Examples of washing products available on the supermarket shelves include:

*Pure soap* – 'Lux' flakes
*Powder mixtures based on soap* – 'Persil'
*Liquid synthetic (soapless) detergents* – 'Stergene'
*Powders based on synthetic detergents* – 'Daz'.

There are some cleansing agents such as 'Omo' which are a blend containing both soap and synthetic detergent and, to avoid confusion, these should not be used in this experiment.

## Method

The quantities of salt and vinegar needed are not critical – it is sufficient that excess of these substances are added.

## Result

The effect of the addition of household salt depends on a chemical phenomenon known as the 'common ion' effect. Soap solution contains positive sodium and negative stearate ions. When salt, sodium chloride, is added, it ionizes and the presence of excess sodium ions (the common ion) causes precipitation of sodium stearate (sodium octadecanoate) as a white solid. Insufficient ionic stearate will therefore remain to form much lather (for this reason sea water is almost impossible to wash in).

This phenomenon of the common ion effect is utilized by manufacturers to purify soap. After the hydrolysis and saponification reactions described in *Experiment 66* there will be many contaminants such as triglycerides, glycerine (propane 1,2,3-triol) etc in the vats of soap solution. So brine is added, and the precipitated sodium stearate can then be separated from these impurities before being rinsed of adhering salt.

When vinegar, acetic (ethanoic) acid, is added, the mixture will initially contain the sodium and stearate (octadecanoate) ions of the soap, positive hydrogen, and negative acetate (ethanoate) ions. In these circumstances the least soluble ion, stearate (octadecanoate), will be precipitated in association with the hydrogen ion as fatty curds of stearic (octadecanoic) acid. Once more, therefore, little lather will form.

However, soapless detergents will not be affected by addition of salt and vinegar and will continue to lather well.

# Experiment 68*

# Hard water

## Purpose

To compare the lathering ability of soap and soapless detergents in distilled water, and after hardening the water.

## Materials

soap solution
soapless detergent solution
calcium chloride
distilled water

$100 \text{ cm}^3$ conical flask
4 test tubes with corks
test tube rack
dropping pipettes (or eye droppers)
stop clock

## Method

1 Add a pinch of calcium chloride to 20 or 30 $\text{cm}^3$ distilled water in a conical flask and shake briskly to dissolve.

2 Half-fill two test tubes ($A$ and $B$) with this 'hardened' water. Half-fill two more test tubes ($C$ and $D$) with ordinary distilled water.

3 Add a drop of soap solution to tubes $A$ and $C$ and a drop of soapless detergent solution to tubes $B$ and $D$.

4 Cork all the tubes and shake vigorously for 10 seconds. Compare lather production and look for the presence of scum in the tubes.

## Result

Draw up a table of results as shown below.

## Suggestions for further work*

This experiment can be used to find out whether or not the tap water in a particular area is 'hard'.

**Table of results for Experiment 68**

| Tube | Lather | Scum |
|------|--------|------|
| A Soap and hard water | | |
| B Soap and distilled water | | |
| C Soapless detergent and hard water | | |
| D Soapless detergent and distilled water | | |

Should soap or a soapless detergent be used for washing in a hard-water area?

# Experiment 68*
# Hard water

## Introduction

Hard water is water which will not lather readily with soap. Temporary hardness is caused by the presence of dissolved hydrogen carbonates of calcium and magnesium and can be removed by boiling. Permanently hard water contains the chlorides and/or sulphates of calcium and magnesium, and cannot be softened by boiling. In this experiment distilled water is rendered permanently hard by adding calcium chloride.

Washing with soap in hard water leaves behind a scum which tends to stick to the clothes. Hard water is also a greater waster of soap, since, first of all, soap is used up in forming this scum and then more is used in the washing process.

Soapless detergents are not affected by hard water for reasons explained in the *Result* section below.

## Materials

Use for comparison a soap solution prepared using household toilet soap or pure soapflakes (eg Lux flakes) and a soapless detergent such as Stergene. The detergents should be diluted roughly 500x – this is not critical but approximates to the kind of dilution factor involved in ordinary household use.

## Method

As a lather can be obtained in hard water with excess soap solution, only one drop should be added to each test tube. This is also the reason that the soap solution needs to be diluted as indicated above.

## Result

With the soap solution, very little lather will be produced in the hardened water (tube $A$) compared with distilled water (tube $C$), and a scum will be formed in tube $A$. Hardening of the water has no effect on the lathering ability of soapless detergent (tubes $B$ and $D$), and no scum will be formed. When soap is dissolved in hard water it reacts with the calcium and/or magnesium ions present to form insoluble stearate salts which float away on top of the water as a scum. (See example below).

The essential cleansing factor in soap is the stearate anion (see *Experiment 69*). If this acid anion is not available to react with the grease and dirt (and it will not be when precipitated as an insoluble calcium or magnesium stearate scum) then the soap cannot function as a detergent. If excess soap is added, of course, all the calcium and magnesium ions in hard water can be precipitated. Subsequent addition of soap will then give soluble stearate anions available for cleansing.

On the other hand, the calcium and magnesium salts of soapless detergents are soluble in water so there is no precipitate (scum), nor is any detergent wasted in removing the calcium and magnesium ions before the detergent operation can begin.

## Suggestions for further work*

It is interesting to compare the ability of soap to form a lather using water from different areas. Use a drop of the same soap solution in each water sample and, after shaking for 10 seconds, compare the lather produced against a standard prepared using distilled water.

Obviously the use of a soapless detergent would not indicate any differences in hardness of water samples.

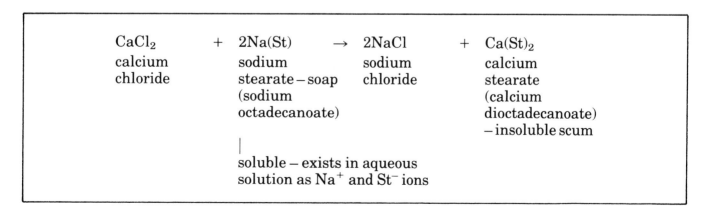

| $CaCl_2$ | + | $2Na(St)$ | → | $2NaCl$ | + | $Ca(St)_2$ |
|---|---|---|---|---|---|---|
| calcium chloride | | sodium stearate – soap (sodium octadecanoate) | | sodium chloride | | calcium stearate (calcium dioctadecanoate) – insoluble scum |

soluble – exists in aqueous solution as $Na^+$ and $St^-$ ions

# Experiment 69*

# Surface tension of water

## Purpose

To demonstrate the phenomenon of surface tension of water and to show the effect of detergent.

## Materials

detergent solution
piece of thick material
lens tissue

pins and needles
dropping pipettes
bowl

## Method

1 Place large drops of water onto a piece of thick material spread out on the bench. Note the shape of the drops and that they are slow to sink in.

2 Add one drop of detergent solution near to the water drops and observe what happens.

3 Float a lens tissue on the surface of some water in a bowl and carefully place on it some pins and needles. Observe what happens when the lens tissue sinks. Be careful not to nudge the bowl.

4 Add one or two drops of detergent solution to the water and note the effect.

## Result

Record and explain the results.

# Experiment 69*
# Surface tension of water

## Introduction

Surface tension refers to the 'skin' effect produced at a water surface as a result of intermolecular attractive forces. These forces are thus always tending to reduce the surface area to a minimum. This accounts for the spherical shape of a water droplet. The molecules near the centre of the drop are attracted equally to the surrounding molecules by intermolecular forces, but molecules on the outside of the drop can only be attracted inwards. This results in a net inward pull on the outer molecules in a particular drop and it tends to shrink away from adjacent droplets.

Detergents, either soap or soapless, are surface-active agents (surfactants) which reduce surface tension. This is explained in the *Result* section.

## Materials

The concentration of the detergent solution is not critical. Liquid detergent can be used 'neat'; for powders simply dissolve a pinch in a test tube half-filled with distilled water.

## Method

The technique of first floating a lens tissue on the water surface makes it possible to float the pins etc, since the tissue, with a little encouragement, sinks from under them. However, it is still not easy to do, care and patience are required and the water must be perfectly still.

## Result

The effect of the detergent in spreading the water droplets on the material is due to its ability to reduce the surface tension. Detergents thus make water a better 'wetting agent'. The strength of this surface tension is well shown by the floating pins which are metal and more dense than water. Again, by reducing the surface tension, the detergents cause the objects to sink.

The way in which detergents lower surface tension can be explained as follows. All detergents have the same basic molecular structure which can be illustrated diagrammatically in Fig. 69.1.

In soap, the hydrocarbon chain of the stearate (octadecanoate) ion contains 17 carbon atoms and the hydrophilic 'head' is the ionic $COO^-$ group, as shown in Fig. 69.2.

Soapless detergents have a similar structure but the 'head' is usually sulphate or sulphonate (Fig. 69.3).

The electrical neutrality of the detergent is preserved by the presence of the $Na^+$ ion. When a detergent is added to water the hydrophilic 'heads' attract water molecules but the hydrophobic 'tails' repel them. This has the effect of reducing the intermolecular attractive forces and hence lowering the surface tension.

This ability of detergents is important in their function as cleansing agents because it enables water to penetrate more readily. Another important property of detergents, their ability to remove grease, is explained in the *Teachers' notes* to *Experiment 70*.

**Fig. 69.1** Basic structure of detergent

hydrophobic ('water hating') non-polar hydrocarbon chain or 'tail'

hydrophilic polar 'head'

**Fig. 69.2** Stearate (octadecanoate) structure.

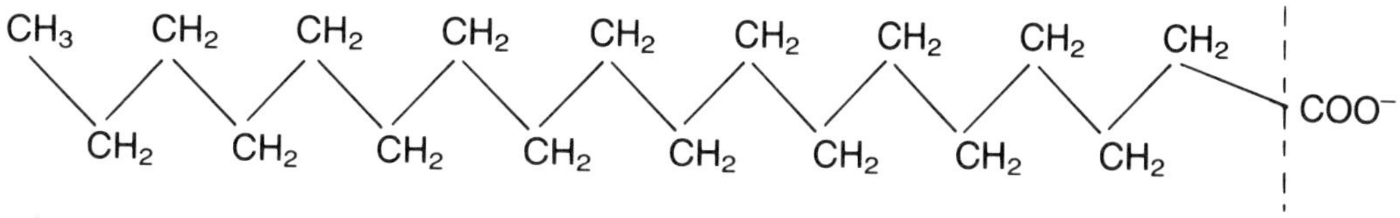

$CH_3$ $CH_2$ $CH_2$ $CH_2$ $CH_2$ $CH_2$ $CH_2$ $CH_2$ $CH_2$

$CH_2$ $CH_2$ $CH_2$ $CH_2$ $CH_2$ $CH_2$ $CH_2$ $CH_2$ $COO^-$

**Fig. 69.3** Soapless detergent

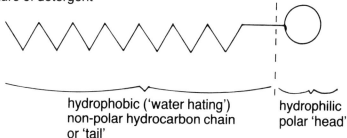

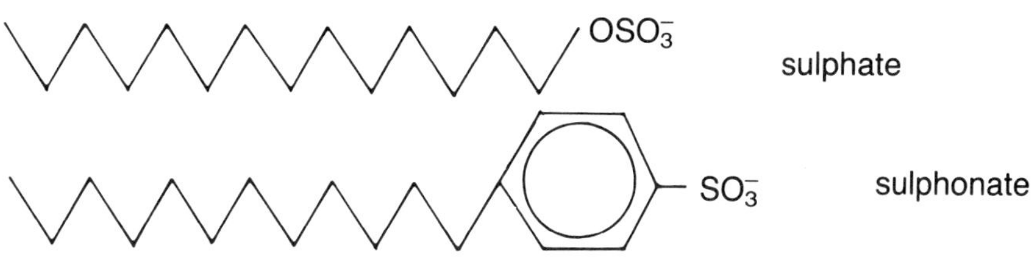

$OSO_3^-$    sulphate

$SO_3^-$    sulphonate

135

# Experiment 70**

# Effectiveness of detergents

## Purpose

To compare the emulsifying power of various household detergents.

## Materials

samples of common household detergents diluted approximately 500 times with tap water

cooking oil

graduated 10 cm$^3$ pipette

test tubes (one for each detergent) with corks

test tube rack

grease pencil

dropping pipette (or eye dropper)

stop clock

## Method

1  Accurately pipette 10 cm$^3$ of one of the samples of diluted detergent into a labelled test tube.

2  Using a dropping pipette add one drop of cooking oil. Cork the test tube and shake vigorously for exactly 10 seconds to emulsify the oil. Note that a froth also forms above the emulsion.

3  Allow the tube to stand for about half a minute. After examining the emulsion formed repeat step 2 until the detergent cannot emulsify any further oil drops – this will be when a very thin layer of oil separates out on standing and can be seen on the surface of the liquid just below the froth.

4  Repeat steps 1, 2 and 3 with the other detergent samples in turn, and finally with 10 cm$^3$ of water alone, for comparison.

## Result

Record the number of drops of oil which can be emulsified by each sample. This can be taken as a measure of the effectiveness of the detergent in removing grease.

## Suggestions for further work**

From the price of the original detergent container, and the volume of detergent it contained, calculate the cost per 100 cm$^3$ of each of the detergents tested. The results for comparative effectiveness obtained in this experiment can then provide the basis for determining the best 'value for money'.

# Experiment 70**
# Effectiveness of detergents

## Introduction

The hydrophobic 'tails' (see *Experiment 69*) of detergent molecules readily dissolve in grease molecules, and this is the basis of their ability both to lift grease from articles and to form emulsions of oil in water.

This experiment assumes for simplicity that the most effective household detergents are the ones which will best emulsify oil.

## Materials

a   A 500x dilution has been suggested for the detergents as it roughly simulates the situation in a sink when washing greasy dishes. To make comparisons valid, each detergent should be diluted by the same factor. Place $1\,cm^3$ of detergent in a $500\,cm^3$ graduated flask and make up to the graduation mark by slowly running tap water down the side of the flask to prevent excessive foaming.

b   A variety of household washing-up liquids can be compared.

## Method

a   In order to make the comparisons semi-quantitative, the same dropping pipette must be used with each different detergent sample in order to give consistently sized oil droplets.

For the same reason, results for the same detergent may vary between pupils using different dropping pipettes.

b   As far as possible, the procedure adopted for each detergent sample must be standardized, for example the shaking to emulsify the oil must be for exactly 10 seconds and of similar vigour.

## Result

The detergent which can emulsify the most drops of oil can be considered to be the most effective in dislodging grease, as the same principles apply.

In each case the non-polar 'tail' of the detergent molecule dissolves in the oil or grease, whilst the polar head dissolves in the water molecules. This separates the oil droplets forming an emulsion, or enables slight agitation to dislodge grease and carry it away in the water (dirt is removed at the same time as it usually sticks to the grease). The diagram below illustrates these actions.

**Fig. 70.1**   Action of detergent

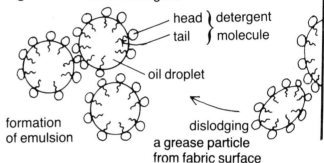

formation of emulsion

dislodging a grease particle from fabric surface

## Suggestions for further work**

The most effective detergent as indicated by the above experiment is not necessarily the 'best buy'. This will also depend on the volume of detergent and the total cost. As an example:

If a $540\,cm^3$ bottle of washing-up liquid costs 81p,

$$100\,cm^3 \text{ costs } \frac{81 \times 100}{540} = 19p.$$

If another washing-up liquid costs, say 20p per $100\,cm^3$, it may still be a better buy if the results of *Experiment 70* have shown it to be considerably more effective in its ability to dislodge grease, since less of it will need to be used for each batch of dishes.

# Experiment 71*

# Fabric conditioners

## Purpose

To show that a fabric conditioner inhibits the build up of static electricity.

## Materials

nylon
detergent
fabric conditioner

scissors
2 x 250 cm³ beakers ⎤
bunsen burner ⎥
tripod ⎥ or small pan of
gauze ⎥ water on a hotplate
flameproof bench mat ⎦
glass rod
forceps
hair dryer
piece of woollen material

## Method

1 Cut two pieces of nylon 2.5 cm square and wash them by placing both in a beaker of hot (60°C) detergent solution for 10 minutes, stirring briskly with a glass rod (Fig. 71.1).

**Fig. 71.1**

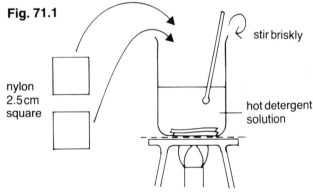

nylon 2.5 cm square

stir briskly

hot detergent solution

2 Rinse both squares under the cold water tap and then place one of them in a beaker containing a solution of fabric conditioner for 2 minutes, stirring occasionally (Fig. 71.2).

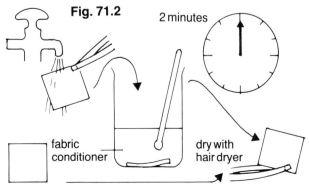

**Fig. 71.2**

2 minutes

fabric conditioner

dry with hair dryer

3 Dry both squares of nylon thoroughly by using forceps to hold them in front of a hair dryer.

4 Staple the squares of nylon to the ends of 2.5 x 5 cm strips of card and use the woollen material to rub both nylon squares vigorously for one minute (Fig. 71.3).

**Fig. 71.3**

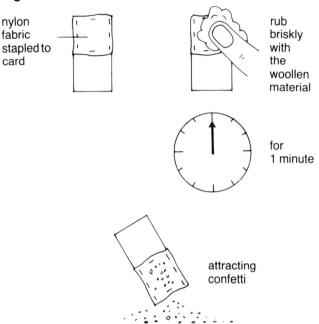

nylon fabric stapled to card

rub briskly with the woollen material

for 1 minute

attracting confetti

5 Test the effectiveness of each nylon square in attracting and picking up paper 'confetti'.

## Result

Record and explain the results.

# Experiment 71*
# Fabric conditioners

## Introduction

Conditioners are not detergents, as they do not clean. However, like detergents, they are surface active agents, carrying positive charges which neutralize the static negative charges which build up on some fabrics as a result of friction.

## Materials

A synthetic fibre, in this case nylon, is suggested for this experiment. Most synthetic fibres have a high surface resistance and are good insulators, hence wearing, washing, ironing, etc produce enough friction to generate static charge which is retained.

Natural fibres, on the other hand, have a higher moisture content, which allows static electricity to be conducted away.

## Method

a  The nylon pieces are first washed as it is important to start off with two standard clean samples. This is because any difference in the amount of particles adhering to the samples will mean a difference in their frictional resistance.

b  Both nylon pieces must, as nearly as possible, be given the same amount of rubbing in terms both of time and energy.

## Result

The effectiveness in picking up the 'confetti' is related to the amount of static charge on the sample. Therefore, the untreated sample will be more effective than the conditioned sample.

It is desirable to reduce static electricity in fabrics because dirt is not attracted as readily and they do not soil as quickly.

In addition, ironing is made easier as iron 'slip' is increased. Finally, the fibres are not so much deteriorated by static 'burn', meshing and twisting.

# Experiment 72*

# Extraction of vegetable dye

## Purpose

To extract a dye from onion skin and, using a direct dyeing method, to investigate its uptake by different fabrics.

## Materials

5 cm square samples of white material, eg wool, silk, cotton, nylon, Terylene, Tricel

skins of 3-5 onions

$250\,cm^3$ beaker
bunsen burner
tripod
gauze
flameproof bench mat
spatula
forceps

or small pan of water on a hotplate

## Method

1 Place the onion skins in the beaker and cover with about $150\,cm^3$ water. Bring to the boil and boil vigorously with occasional stirring for 10 minutes to extract the orange dye.

2 After 10 minutes drop in the fabric samples and boil for a further 5–10 minutes again stirring occasionally.

3 Remove the samples with forceps and rinse under the tap.

4 Examine the samples in daylight against a white background.

## Result

By means of a five-point scale compare the degree of dyeing of the fabric (0 = no dye uptake, up to 4 = strong colour). On the whole, do the natural fibres take up the dye better than the synthetics?

## Suggestions for further work*

Other vegetable dyes can be prepared and their uptake by different fabrics tested. A red dye can be extracted from blackberries, purple from damsons, yellow from marigolds, etc. In each case boil the crushed or chopped material with water.

140

# Experiment 72*
# Extraction of vegetable dye

## Introduction

Although many of the natural dyes have been replaced by artificial ones made from products distilled from coal tar, originally all dyes were obtained from natural sources. Using a simple method of extracting a dye from onion skins, this experiment enables dye uptake by different fabrics to be compared.

## Materials

Do not use fabrics with a size or finish as this can interfere with dye uptake.

## Method

If comparisons are to be valid, all samples must be given as nearly identical treatment as possible.

## Result and Suggestions for further work*

Compared with natural fibres, the synthetics are notoriously difficult to stain. This is because synthetic fibres have little water absorbing capacity, and uptake depends on the fibres swelling as they absorb water, allowing the dye to penetrate deep into the pores where the colour remains. Of course, the comparative dye uptakes observed for different fabrics in this experiment only apply to the particular dye and conditions employed. With other dyes and conditions very different results may be obtained.

# Experiment 73**

# Mordant dyeing

## Purpose

To compare the dye uptake of a specific fabric with and without the addition of ammonium sulphate as a mordant.

## Materials

6 x 5 cm squares of a white material such as cotton

skins of 3-5 onions

10% ammonium sulphate solution

dilute ammonium hydroxide solution

3 x 250 cm$^3$ beakers

bunsen burncr

tripod

gauze

flameproof bench mat

glass rod

forceps or tweezers

needle and thread

## Method

Make sure you are wearing eye protection for this experiment.

1 Place three of the fabric samples into a 250 cm$^3$ beaker about half-full of ammonium sulphate solution and heat gently for 15 minutes (Fig. 73.1).

**Fig. 73.1**

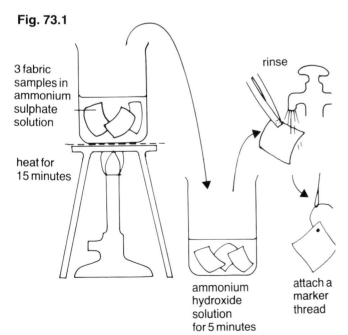

3 fabric samples in ammonium sulphate solution

heat for 15 minutes

rinse

ammonium hydroxide solution for 5 minutes

attach a marker thread

2 Remove the samples and place them in dilute ammonium hydroxide solution for five minutes. After this rinse them thoroughly with water and use a needle to attach a piece of thread to each as a 'marker'.

3 Place the onion skins in another 250 cm$^3$ beaker and cover with about 150 cm$^3$ water (Fig. 73.2). Bring to the boil and boil vigorously with occasional stirring for 10 minutes to extract the orange dye.

**Fig. 73.2**

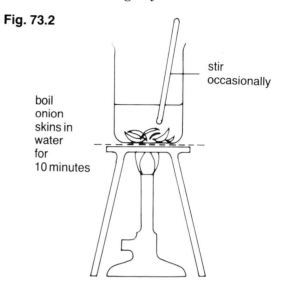

stir occasionally

boil onion skins in water for 10 minutes

4 After 10 minutes drop in all the fabric samples (the three mordanted samples and the three untouched samples) and boil for a further 5 minutes, stirring occasionally (Fig. 73.3).

**Fig. 73.3**

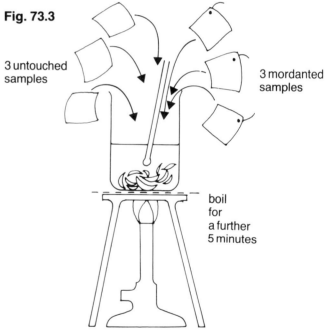

3 untouched samples

3 mordanted samples

boil for a further 5 minutes

5 Remove the samples and examine in daylight against a white background.

## Result

Score the degree of dyeing on a five-point scale. What is the effect of pre-treatment of the fabric with mordant?

## Suggestions for further work**

The effect of mordant pretreatment on onion dye uptake by other fabrics can be tested. Alternatively, the effect of the mordant on the uptake of synthetic dyes (eg methylene blue, congo red) can be investigated.

142

# Experiment 73**
# Mordant dyeing

## Introduction

There are only a few dyes which by themselves can be fixed permanently into vegetable fabrics such as cotton. In this case, the fabric is first treated with a substance called a mordant which makes the dye 'bite' (in fact, the word mordant is derived from the Latin *mordere,* to bite).

In this experiment ammonium sulphate is used as the mordant. When the dye is added, it reacts chemically with the mordant forming a complex insoluble compound, or 'lake'. This lake is permanently fixed into the fabric, giving the fabric its colour, which may be different from that given by the dye alone.

## Materials

a Do not use fabrics with a size or finish.

b See Appendix I for the method of making up percentage solutions.

c Ammonium sulphate, *page 146,* ammonium hydroxide, *page 146.*

## Method

a The purpose of standing the samples in ammonium hydroxide solution is to remove excess mordant.

b It is easy to mix up the mordanted and untreated samples once they are placed in the dye together. The suggested method of sewing a piece of thread to the mordanted pieces is the surest way of avoiding confusion.

## Result and Suggestions for further work**

The mordanted cotton samples take up the onion dye more effectively than the directly dyed material. For man-made fibres, the uptake of vegetable dyes may be so low that the effect of the mordant is negligible. Such fibres are more readily stained with synthetic dyes.

# Experiment 74**

# Fastness and retention of dye

## Purpose

To investigate the effect of washing on dye fastness and retention.

## Materials

2 x 5 cm square samples taken from a piece of uniformly dyed fabric.

$250\,cm^3$ beaker
bunsen burner
tripod          } or small pan of
gauze              water on a hotplate
flameproof bench mat
glass rod
forceps (or tweezers)

## Method

1  Half-fill the beaker with water, add some detergent and heat to 60°C.

2  Wash one of the sample squares by placing it in the beaker for 10 minutes, stirring continuously with the glass rod.

3  Observe the colour of the washing water. This will show whether any dye has been lost.

4  Rinse the washed sample thoroughly and allow to dry slowly.

5  When dry, compare the washed and unwashed samples in daylight against a white background.

6  Repeat the experiment using several sample pairs in turn, so that a variety of dyes (direct or mordanted) and fabrics can be investigated.

## Result

Score each washed sample on a five-point scale after first allocating 5 to its control. Which dyes, dyeing methods or fabrics give the fastest colours?

# Suggestions for further work**

The experimental procedure above can be used to investigate dye retention after:

a  ironing: iron the dyed samples onto a sheet of white paper and keep ironing until any dye transfer to the paper has ceased. Clean the iron carefully after each use.

b  exposure to sunlight: place the samples in sunlight for 2–3 weeks. Alternatively, if an ultraviolet lamp is available, a 6-hour exposure will simulate 3 weeks of sunshine and therefore results can be more quickly obtained. **Do not look directly at an ultraviolet lamp.** It must be set up in such a way that it is not possible to do so.

**Fig. 74.1**

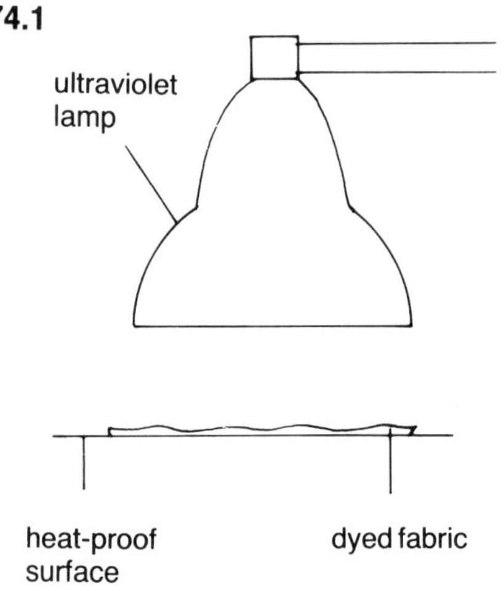

ultraviolet lamp

heat-proof surface          dyed fabric

144

# Experiment 74**
# Fastness and retention of dye

## Introduction

The fastness of a dye refers to its ability to adhere to the fabric under a variety of conditions. In this experiment the effect of washing a sample of dyed fabric is compared with a similar unwashed sample. Resistance of garments to colour loss during laundering is not only important in maintaining their appearance, but also, if colour is lost, staining of other articles in the same wash will take place.

## Materials

The fabric samples used may be the ones prepared in *Experiments 72* and *73* (with or without mordanting), or commercially dyed fabrics. In either case, control and experimental pieces must initially be uniformly dyed.

## Method

a Commercial assessment of washing fastness involves a series of five washing tests varying in severity from the equivalent of a 'hand wash' to a series of severe laundering processes at or near boiling temperature. The conditions used in this experiment are at the lower end of this severity scale.

b Ensure that the washed sample is perfectly dry – any dampness could give a misleadingly denser coloured appearance. A hair dryer, if available, saves time.

## Result

Comparison of the washed sample with the unwashed control, and scoring of results as suggested, is a simple semi-quantitative method of assessing fastness to washing. Commercially, colour changes are assessed by comparing the original and washed fabrics with standard 'grey scales'. This enables colour loss to be judged irrespective of the depth of the original colour.

## Suggestions for further work**

a Some dyes may be of good fastness to washing but be sensitive to abrasion, being removed from the fabric by either wet or dry rubbing, as in ironing. This arises when the dye is not entirely bound within the fibre but is partly on the fibre surface, and this loose surface colour may be gradually rubbed away.

b Exposure to daylight causes deterioration of all dyes to some extent. It is the ultraviolet light in sunlight which causes these photochemical changes, usually resulting in fading, or loss of colour strength. When exposing the samples, they should be in direct sunlight, as glass absorbs most of the ultraviolet rays. If an ultraviolet lamp is used it must be set up in such a way that it cannot be viewed directly, even accidentally.

# Appendix I

## Reagents

### Acetic acid
[ethanoic acid CH$_3$COOH] glacial. Causes severe burns. For dilute acetic acid, either purchase 1M acetic acid or add 58 cm$^3$ glacial acetic acid to distilled water and make up to 1000 cm$^3$ with distilled water.

### Acetone
[propanone (CH$_3$)$_2$CO]. Volatile and highly flammable. Store in a cool place.

### Acid calcium phosphate
[calcium hydrogen diphosphate(v), CaH$_4$(PO$_4$)$_2$].

### Acid sodium pyrophosphate
[di-sodium di-hydrogen heptaoxodiphosphate(v), Na$_2$H$_2$P$_2$O$_7$].

### Agar-agar
Available as powder (100 g) or in packs of 100 tablets. Store powder in refrigerator.

### Alcohol
[methanol (CH$_3$OH) or ethanol (C$_2$H$_5$OH)]. Both flammable and methanol is toxic if swallowed. Much cheaper than ethanol is industrial methylated spirits: about 95% ethanol and 5% methanol. This may be diluted with distilled water to make, for example, 70% alcohol.

### Amino acids
May be purchased in kits containing 100 mg of each of 16 amino acids, or buy L-lysine monochloride.

### Ammonium hydroxide
0.880 specific gravity [NH$_4$ OH]. Irritating to eyes, respiratory system and skin. Dilute (2M) ammonia solution may be purchased or made by adding 110 cm$^3$ 0.880 ammonia to distilled water and making up to 1 000 cm$^3$.

### Ammonium molybdate
[(NH$_4$)$_6$Mo$_7$O$_{24}$.4H$_2$O]. The solution is unstable – make up in two parts and store in separate bottles. *Solution 1:* dissolve 75 g ammonium molybdate in 50 cm$^3$ of 0.880 ammonia solution and 25 cm$^3$ of distilled water. Dilute to 500 cm$^3$. *Solution 2:* 500 cm$^3$ of 5 M nitric acid (**care –** corrosive). Mix equal volumes of solution 1 and solution 2 when required.

### Ammonium oxalate
[ammonium ethanedioate, (COONH$_4$)$_2$.H$_2$O]. Harmful in contact with the skin or if swallowed. Make solution by dissolving 3.4 g in 100 cm$^3$ distilled water.

### Ammonium sulphate
[(NH$_4$)$_2$SO$_4$]. Make 10% solution by dissolving 10 g in 100 cm$^3$ distilled water.

### Ammonium thiocyanate
[NH$_4$SCN]. Harmful if inhaled or in contact with skin and if swallowed. Make solution by dissolving 3.8 g in 100 cm$^3$ distilled water.

### Ascorbic acid
[vitamin C, C$_6$H$_8$O$_6$]. To make a 1% solution, dissolve 1 g in 100 cm$^3$ distilled water.

### Barfoed's reagent
Either buy ready-made or make by dissolving 13.3 g cupric acetate (**care –** harmful) and 2 cm$^3$ glacial acetic acid in 200 cm$^3$ distilled water.

### Barium chloride
[BaCl$_2$.2H$_2$O]. **Poison:** harmful by inhalation and if swallowed. Make solution by dissolving 6.1 g in 100 cm$^3$ distilled water.

### Benedict's solution
Qualitative. Either buy ready-made or make by dissolving 170 g sodium citrate and 100 g sodium carbonate in 800 cm$^3$ warm distilled water. In a separate beaker dissolve 17 g copper sulphate in 200 cm$^3$ cold distilled water. Add the second solution to the first, stirring constantly.

### Bile salts
[sodium tauroglycocholate], available in 100 g quantities.

### Biuret reagent
Either buy ready-made or, as suggested in *Experiment 10* in the *Pupils' Material,* use dilute sodium hydroxide solution and 1% copper sulphate solution.

### Caffeine
Buy caffeine tablets from a chemist's shop, or as a powder from chemicals suppliers. Make a 2% solution by dissolving 2 g in 100 cm$^3$ distilled water.

### Calcium chloride
[CaCl$_2$.6H$_2$O]. Deliquescent crystals – keep dry.

### Citric acid
[2-hydroxypropane-1,2,3-tricarboxylic acid C(OH)(COOH) (CH$_2$ . COOH)$_2$]. Make a 2% solution by dissolving 2 g in 100 cm$^3$ distilled water.

### Clinistix strips
Buy in a pack of 50.

## Cobalt chloride papers
Buy in packs of ten books, each book having 20 leaves.

## Copper (II) sulphate
 [$CuSO_4.5H_2O$]. Make a 1% solution by dissolving 1 g in 100 $cm^3$ distilled water.

## Cream of tartar
[potassium hydrogen tartrate; potassium hydrogen 2,3-dihydroxybutanedioate, $COOH(CHOH)_2COOK$] from chemicals supplier or grocer.

## Dichlorophenolindophenol
[DCPIP] Available in tablet form, packs of 20 tablets, or as a powder. Make a 0.25% solution by dissolving 0.5 g in 200 $cm^3$ distilled water.

## Distilled water
or deionized water should be used in experiments wherever possible.

## Ethanol see Alcohol.

## Ether
 Highly volatile and flammable – a **very dangerous** substance.

## Fructose
[laevulose, $C_6H_{12}O_6$]. Make a 1% solution by dissolving 1 g in 100 $cm^3$ distilled water.

## Gelatin
Buy in packets from grocers.

## Gluconodeltalactone
[gluconic acid, lactone, $CH_2(OH).\underline{CH.(CH.OH)_3.CO.O}$ ]

## Glucose
[dextrose, $C_6H_{12}O_6$]. Make a 1% solution by dissolving 1 g in 100 $cm^3$ distilled water.

## Glycerine
[propane - 1,2,3-triol, $CH_2OH.CHOH.CH_2OH$] Available from chemicals suppliers or buy glycerine from grocers.

## Glycogen
[$C_6H_{10}O_5$] from mammalian liver, very expensive.

## Hydrochloric acid
 [HCl]. The concentrated acid causes burns and is irritating to the respiratory system. Make dilute hydrochloric acid (2M) by pouring 172 $cm^3$ concentrated HCl into distilled water and making up to 1000 $cm^3$. The dilute solution is an irritant.

## Hydrogen peroxide
 [$H_2O_2$]. Irritating to skin and eyes. Store in a cool, dark place. Hydrogen peroxide is sold as a 20 volume solution, ie 20 volumes of the gas dissolved in 1 volume water; this is an approximate strength of 6% weight by volume.

## Invertase
[ß-fructofuranosidase]. Available in several grades – buy the cheapest.

## Iodine
 Harmful by inhalation and in contact with skin. To make a solution of iodine in potassium iodide, dissolve 1 g iodine and 1 g potassium iodide in distilled water, make up to 100 $cm^3$ with distilled water. When using in enzyme experiments, dilute 5 $cm^3$ of this solution to 100 $cm^3$ with distilled water.

## Iso-butanol
 [isobutyl alcohol; 2-methylpropan-1-ol, $(CH_3)_2CH.CH_2OH$]. Flammable and harmful if inhaled.

## Lactose
($C_{12}H_{22}O_{11}.H_2O$). Make a 1% solution by dissolving 1 g in 100 $cm^3$ distilled water.

## Lead acetate
 [lead(II)ethanoate, $(CH_3.COO)_2Pb.3H_2O$]. Harmful in contact with skin and if swallowed. Lead is a cumulative poison. Make lead acetate solution by dissolving 3.8 g of crystals in 100 $cm^3$ distilled water.

## Lemon juice
Buy from grocers.

## Lime water
Buy ready-made or make a saturated solution of calcium (II) hydroxide. Allow to settle overnight and decant off the clear liquid.

## Lipase
Store in refrigerator.

## Litmus paper
Red and blue. Packs of 10 books, 20 leaves to a book.

## Lysine see Amino acids.

## Malachite green
Available as a powder or an aqueous solution.

## Maltose
[$C_{12}H_{22}O_{11}.H_2O$]. Make a 1% solution by dissolving 1 g in 100 $cm^3$ distilled water.

## Methylene blue
Available as a powder or as a 1% solution.

## Molisch's reagent

Make by dissolving 5 g $\alpha$-naphthol in 100 cm$^3$ ethanol (or methylated spirits).

## Nitric acid

[HNO$_3$]. The concentrated acid causes severe burns. Make a dilute (2M) solution by adding 126 cm$^3$ concentrated acid to distilled water and make up to 1000 cm$^3$.

## Nutrient agar

Available as granules, tablets or – more expensive but convenient – ready-prepared.

## Olive oil

Buy from grocers.

## Peptone water

Dissolve 0.1 g peptone in 100 cm$^3$ distilled water. Dispense 9 cm$^3$ in test tubes, plug with cotton wool, cover plug with aluminium foil and sterilize at 15 p.s.i. for 15 minutes.

## Pepsin

Store in refrigerator. Make a 5% solution by dissolving 5 g in 100 cm$^3$ distilled water.

## pH papers

Available in reels: wide-range pH 1-14 and narrow-range 1-4, 4-6, 6-8, 10-12 and 12-14.

## Phenol red

Available as powder or 0.02% solution.

## Phenolphthalein

Available as 1% solution. Flammable and harmful if inhaled or swallowed.

## Phloroglucinol

[benzene-1,3,5-triol, C$_6$H$_3$(OH)$_3$.2H$_2$O]. Harmful if inhaled, swallowed or in contact with skin. Make 1% solution in diethyl ether (flammable).

## Potassium bromate

[KBrO$_3$]. For dilute (1M) solution dissolve 16.7 g in 100 cm$^3$ water. (The solid is an oxidizing agent.)

## Potassium hydroxide

[KOH]. Pellets, cause severe burns. For dilute solution, dissolve 5.6 g in 100 cm$^3$ water.

## Potassium iodide

(KI). To make a 2% solution, dissolve 2 g in 100 cm$^3$ water.

## Rennet

From calf stomach. May be bought in chemist's shop.

## Resorcinol

[benzene-1,3-diol, C$_6$H$_4$(OH)$_2$]. Harmful if swallowed and irritating to eyes and skin.

## Silver nitrate

Make dilute (0.1M) solution by dissolving 1.7 g in 100 cm$^3$ distilled water.

## Sodium carbonate

[Na$_2$CO$_3$.10H$_2$O]. Make dilute (1M) solution by dissolving 10.6 g of anhydrous salt (28.6 g if hydrated) in 100 cm$^3$ water. Store in a bottle with rubber or plastic stopper or cork.

## Sodium chloride

[NaCl]. For experiments in this book common salt can be used. Make a 1% solution by dissolving 1 g salt in 100 cm$^3$ distilled water.

## Sodium hydrogencarbonate

[sodium bicarbonate, NaHCO$_3$]. Buy from grocers.

## Sodium hydroxide

[NaOH]. Pellets cause severe burns. Make dilute solution by dissolving 4 g in 100 cm$^3$ distilled water. Make 40% solution by dissolving, adding 40 g pellets to 100 cm$^3$ distilled water. A 40% solution is caustic, **take care.**

## Sodium metabisulphite

[sodium disulphate (IV), Na$_2$S$_2$O$_5$]. Harmful if swallowed. Make a 1% solution by dissolving 1 g in 100 cm$^3$ distilled water.

## Starch

Potato, rice, maize, wheat. From chemicals suppliers.

## Starch solution

Use any starch, or cornflour. To make a 1% solution, mix 1 g starch with a small volume of water taken from 100 cm$^3$. In a separate beaker bring the rest of the water to the boil, pour on to the starch paste, stir and return the mixture to the beaker. Boil, stirring continuously, for one minute. Allow to cool. Store in refrigerator for a few days only.

## Sucrose

[C$_{12}$H$_{22}$O$_{11}$]. For the experiments in this book use sugar from the grocers. To make a 1% solution, dissolve 1 g sugar in 100 cm$^3$ water.

## Sudan black.

Available in powder form.

**Sudan III**

 Available in powder form or in 70% alcohol (highly flammable).

**Sulphuric acid**

 [$H_2SO_4$]. Concentrated acid causes severe burns. Make dilute acid (1M) by adding $54\,cm^3$ concentrated $H_2SO_4$ to distilled water and making up to $1\,000\,cm^3$. The dilute acid is an irritant.

**Tartaric acid**

 [2,3-dihydroxybutanedioic acid $(CHOH.COOH)_2$]. From chemicals supplier or grocers.

**Trichloroethane**

[$CH_3.CCl_3$]. Harmful if inhaled or swallowed. Has a violent reaction with aluminium.

**Trypsin**

Powder, from beef pancreas. Store in refrigerator. Make 5% solution by dissolving 5 g trypsin in $100\,cm^3$ water.

**Universal indicator solution** [see also *pH papers*].  Flammable and harmful if inhaled or swallowed. Colour chart supplied with bottle.

**Vinegar, white**

Buy from grocers.

**Xylene**

 [dimethylbenzene, $C_6H_4\,(CH_3)_2$]. Flammable and harmful if inhaled.

**Yeast**

Buy fresh from bakers or dried from grocers or chemicals suppliers.

*Recognised EEC hazard symbols have been used to indicate potential dangers of the chemicals used:*

 *Highly flammable or flammable: flash point below 32°C*

 *Corrosive substances*

 *Harmful substances*

 *Irritating substances*

 *Oxidising substances*

 *Poisonous substances*

# Appendix II

## Equipment

**Note:** The items are listed, as far as possible, in the way they are found in the *Materials* section of the *Pupils' Material*. For example 'Test tube rack', not 'Rack, test tube'.

*\* standard equipment in home economics room.*

### Acetate sheet
To place between bread and cake samples and photocopier. Available in packs of 50.

### Aluminium foil*

### Autoclavable bags
For culture disposal. Sold in packs of 25. Contaminated petri dishes are put in the bag, it is loosely closed with wire and sterilized in an autoclave at 121°C (15 p.s.i.) for 15 minutes.

### Autoclave
For sterilization of microbiological equipment, before use and prior to disposal. Always use 15 lb p.s.i. to produce a temperature of 121°C, and maintain this temperature for at least 15 minutes. A portable autoclave should always be used for sterilizing equipment and bacterial cultures prior to disposal. They are electrically operated and are relatively expensive pieces of equipment, but most school biology departments will possess one. In principle it is a sophisticated pressure cooker fitted with a dial which confirms the reaching of pressures of 15lb per square inch needed to ensure sterilization. It is, in fact, possible to use a pressure cooker for the purpose but inadvisable owing to the dangers of insufficient pressure being developed due to faulty seals and confusion with pressure cookers being used for food preparation.

### Baking sheet*

### Balance
For most experiments kitchen scales are sufficient but some experiments require weighing to be accurate to 0.1 g. For this a beam balance or (more expensive) a top-pan balance will be needed; see *Fig. i*.

### Balloon
From any stationer's. Carbon dioxide production is best shown if balloon is small.

### Beakers
These should be Pyrex glass, and are available singly or in packs of 12. The capacities mentioned in the experiments are 100 cm³, 250 cm³, 400 cm³ and 1000 cm³. Breakages are always a problem; polypropylene beakers are unbreakable but cannot be heated and are not transparent.

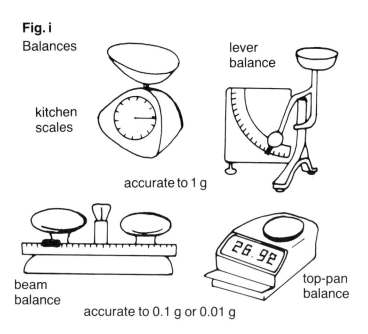

**Fig. i**
Balances

kitchen scales

lever balance

accurate to 1 g

beam balance

top-pan balance

accurate to 0.1 g or 0.01 g

### Bin, metal
For disposal of broken glass.

### Blotting paper
Filter paper may be substituted.

### Blue glass
Cobalt blue, specifically for flame tests, may be purchased from scientific equipment suppliers.

### Boiling tubes
Merely longer and wider test tubes and, like test tubes, come in different qualities and thicknesses. Soda-lime glass is the cheapest but Pyrex medium-wall tubes are less likely to crack. Boiling tubes are normally sold in packs of 144, and are 150 mm long, 25 mm wide.

### Buchner funnel
Polythene (cheapest), porcelain or glass. Use with Buchner flask and filter pump attached to tap:

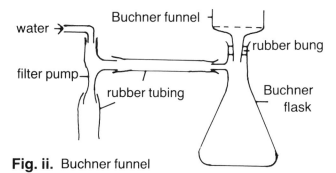

water →

Buchner funnel

rubber bung

filter pump

rubber tubing

Buchner flask

**Fig. ii.** Buchner funnel

### Bunsen burners
Normally need a special gas supply, rarely available in a home economics room. In many of the experiments, however, the bunsen burner is needed only to heat a waterbath, and a pan of water on a cooker hob will serve equally well.

### Burettes
Capacity 100 cm³, are subject to three hazards: they become blocked, the stopcock becomes

**Fig. iii**
Bunsen burner

→ to gas supply

loose and therefore leaks, or they break when being washed or stored. These may be overcome in the following ways. All solutes must be fully dissolved and filtered before filling the burette, and some fuse wire of the appropriate diameter should be available to unblock the tip of the burette. The burette always has the stopcock on the right, and it is always turned with the *left* hand, to pull the stopcock in *(Fig. iv)*: If all users

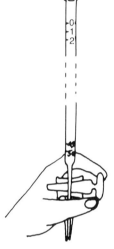

**Fig. iv**
Using a burette

do this, and the stopcock is greased periodically with Vaseline it should not stick or leak – but burettes being what they are, they will! Breakages are, like all glassware breakages, theoretically preventable. The most common cause with burettes is that their length is not appreciated (when washing) or allowed for (on storing). Two further points must be remembered when using burettes: it is not necessary to start with the liquid at zero, as long as the initial reading is recorded (to one decimal place at least), and, secondly, the tip of

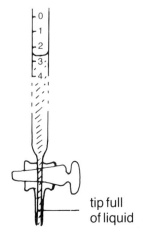

**Fig. v**
Initial reading
of a burette

tip full
of liquid

the burette must be full before taking the first reading *(Fig. v)*. If air bubbles are seen in the tip, let the liquid flow, with the stopcock open, and tap the burette sharply until the air leaves the point.

### Callipers
May be purchased cheaply from scientific equipment suppliers, but will generally be found in a woodwork room. A pair of compasses may be used as a substitute.

### Canister
For sterilizing glass petri dishes. A metal canister may be bought (specially if an autoclave is being used) but aluminium foil folded round glass petri dishes with generous overlap, will serve the purpose. Plastic petri dishes are sterile when the plastic bag is opened – note that plastic petri dishes cannot be autoclaved and re-used since the heat leaves them melted and misshapen.

### Capillary tubes
May be purchased ready-made, in packs of 100, or can be made by heating narrow glass tubing in a bunsen flame until it is red hot then pulling the ends:

**Fig. vi**

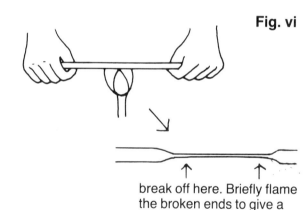

break off here. Briefly flame the broken ends to give a smooth finish.

### Card
Black. Should be thin enough to bend into a cone.

### Cellophane packets
For yarns. Any small, transparent packets may be used.

### Chopping board*

### Chromatography clips
Polythene, for securing paper cylinders, should be used, but paper clips or staples are satisfactory.

### Chromatography paper
Whatman Grade 1, 200 mm x 200 mm, from scientific equipment suppliers.

### Chromatography tank
A cylindrical glass tank is available for the purpose, but any large cylindrical glass or plastic container may be used.

**Clamp and boss**
For use with retort stand.

**Clingfilm***

**Clock glass**
A large, circular, concave sheet of glass.

**Clock** see *Stopclock*

**Compasses**
Ordinary school geometry compasses.

**Conical flask**
Available in various sizes. The most useful are narrow-mouth 50 cm$^3$ or 250 cm$^3$.

**Cork borer**
Sold in a set of six, 4 to 10 mm diameter.

**Corks**
Or use rubber bungs.

**Cotton wool**
Should be non-absorbent for microbiology.

**Coverslips**
For covering specimens on microscope slides. Not always necessary, if care is taken that the objective lens does not touch the specimen. Do not try to wash – they are cheap enough to be disposable.

**Crucible**
Porcelain. An evaporating basin may be substituted.

**Cup***

**Desiccator**
Essential for allowing glassware to cool after drying in an oven if accurate results are desired. Glass desiccators are cheap; a perspex desiccator cabinet looks neat, holds more but is ten times more expensive.

**Drinking straws***

**Dropping pipettes**
May be bought ready-made or can be made in the same way as capillary tubes:

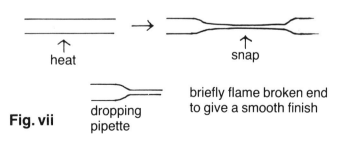

**Fig. vii**

They are difficult to clean and are best regarded as disposable. Use with a rubber teat – which should *not* be regarded as disposable!

**Duran bottles**
Wide-necked, autoclavable glass bottles for microbiological work. A conical flask with a cotton wool plug may be substituted.

152

**File**
Small, for cutting capillary tubes filled with egg-white.

**Filter funnel**
In glass or (cheaper) polypropylene.

**Filter paper**
Whatman No. 1. Fold into a cone or flute, by folding in half, making a 'fan' then opening out.

**Fig. viii**

**Fire extinguisher**
**Must** be available in every kitchen and laboratory. **Every pupil should know how to use the extinguisher.**

**Flameproof bench mat**
Reinforced calcium silicate matrix available in squares of side 150 mm, 225 mm, 300 mm. Asbestos mats must not be used.

**Forceps**
Straight, with blunt tips, are the most useful, and are the cheapest.

**Fume cupboard**
Should ideally be used wherever noxious fumes are produced, eg, finding the smoke point of fats. If no fume cupboard is available, make sure the room is well ventilated. Fume cupboards should *not* be used for permanent storage of reagents or equipment.

**Funnel stand**
Wooden – though a metal retort stand can be used.

**Gauze**
Iron wire, for use on tripod stand. Make sure there is no liquid on the outside of glassware when it is put onto hot gauze, or the glassware is likely to crack.

**Glass tubing**
Available in many diameters, in lengths of approximately 1.5 m. A useful size is external diameter 10 mm – this can be cut to size using a glass file and bent to shape by heating in a hot bunsen flame. After cutting, always smooth the ends by heating. Take *great care* when inserting tubing into corks or bungs, use glycerine as a lubricant. Insert a cork borer just larger than the tube into the cork, insert the tube into the borer, then withdraw the borer.

**Goggles**
Polycarbonate lens conforming to BS 2092. The DES and many LEAs recommend that **eye protection should be worn whenever chemicals are handled.** They **must** be used

whenever there is risk of chemical splashes or flying glass. Make sure you have some that can be worn over spectacles.

**Graduated pipettes.**
Available with capacity 1, 2, 5, 10 and 25 cm³ in two types:

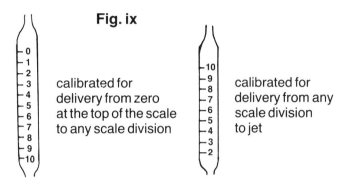

**Fig. ix**

calibrated for delivery from zero at the top of the scale to any scale division

calibrated for delivery from any scale division to jet

**Graph paper**
Millimetre and centimetre rulings.

**Graticule**
Eyepiece, horizontal scale, length 10 mm, subdivided 10 $\mu$m, and stage, length 10 mm, subdivided 100 $\mu$m.

**Fig. x**

Use graticule to measure size of cells, starch granules, etc:
a  Insert eyepiece graticule.
b  Place stage graticule on stage.
c  Choose appropriate objective lens: usually x10 or x40.
d  Focus on to stage graticule and align the lines with the eyepiece graticule. Make sure the zero of the stage graticule lies along a convenient line of the eyepiece graticule:

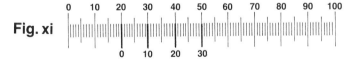

**Fig. xi**

e  Note the correspondence between the two sets of markings: in *Fig xi*
10 eyepiece divisions = 10 stage divisions
Each stage division = 0.01 mm
Therefore 1 eyepiece division = 0.01 mm
(N.B. The correspondence will not always be as neat as this, and it is important to remember that it will vary with different magnifications.)
f  Remove the stage graticule and replace with slide containing specimen to be measured. Focus and position the slide so that the specimen is in the appropriate position *(Fig. xii)*.

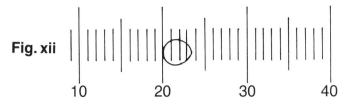

**Fig. xii**

g  Note the diameter of the specimen in terms of the number of eyepiece divisions, in this case 3.5.
h
Calculate the diameter:
1 eyepiece division = 0.01 mm
3.5 eyepiece divisions = 3.5 x 0.01 mm
= 0.035 mm
= 35 $\mu$m

**Grease pencil**
'Chinagraph', for writing on glass and polished surfaces. In black, red and blue. Writing on the surface is easier if it is slightly warm, in any case, it must be dry. Felt-tip permanent markers are even easier. Both types of writing can be removed with alcohol, acetone, etc.

**Hair dryer**
Bring from home – or, for chromatography experiment, simply blow hard through a straw.

**Hand lens**
Pocket-type folding magnifier, 19 mm diameter lens with a magnification x10.

**Ignition tubes**
Borosilicate small, narrow combustion tubes, which can be heated to red heat. **Wear goggles, take care not to point the tube at anyone. After the experiment place the hot tube on a flameproof bench mat** – and regard as disposable.

**Incubator**
Temperature range 5°C above ambient to 80°C, fitted with a thermometer. Unless a constant temperature is absolutely necesary, a warm place such as an airing cupboard may be used instead, but remember that anything placed very near a radiator may get too hot.

**Jug***

**Knife***

**Lamp**
A reading lamp, eg Anglepoise, is most suitable for candling eggs.

**Lemon squeezer***

**Lens tissues**
Esential for microscope work. Other tissues leave fibres on the lens and cloths might scratch.

**Liquidizer***

153

## Measuring cylinder
Glass or (cheaper) polypropylene. Stoppered $100\,cm^3$ cylinders are needed for some experiments.

## Metre rule
Available in wood or plastic.

## Microscope
With x10 eyepiece, x10 and x40 objective lens. Cells must be magnified at least to x100 to observe their structure.

*Hints on using a microscope*
Ensure that:
1 All lenses are clean (use lens tissues).
2 The objective lens is correctly in place.
3 The mirror (if used) is directing light into the condenser.
4 The condenser is focusing the light on to the specimen.

**Fig. xiii**

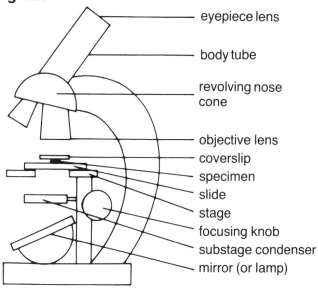

- eyepiece lens
- body tube
- revolving nose cone
- objective lens
- coverslip
- specimen
- slide
- stage
- focusing knob
- substage condenser
- mirror (or lamp)

5 The specimen is correctly positioned under the objective lens.
6 The specimen does not touch the objective lens.
7 When focusing on high power, only the fine adjustment knob is used.
8 Do not use sunlight as a light source. In certain circumstances it could be focused onto the eye, causing damage.

## Microscope slides
Clean by washing in detergent and rinsing. Wipe with lens tissue immediately before use.

## Mounted needles
Sharp needles in a wooden or stainless steel handle. A darning needle may be substituted.

## Muslin
Available in rolls or lengths from scientific equipment suppliers, or buy dressmakers'

154

muslin. A teatowel made from thin cotton will also serve the purpose.

## Needle*

## Nose clip
Available from sports shops, or use a clothes peg.

## Oven*

## Paper clips*

## Pekar boards
Small, flat wooden boards. A saucer or a petri dish may be substituted.

## Pestle and mortar
Porcelain or glass.

## Pin*

## Pipeclay triangle
Essential for use with a crucible, placed on tripod.

## Pipette
$1\,cm^3$ straight-sided. $10\,cm^3$ straight-sided.

## Pipette filler
Should always be used: **never mouth pipette.** Rubber teats may be used for small quantities or one of the following:

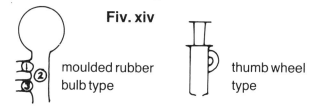

**Fiv. xiv**

moulded rubber bulb type

thumb wheel type

## Plastic bags*

## Plate*

## Platinum wire
For flame tests, fused into glass handle. It is cheaper, however, to use a silica rod.

## Polystyrene tile
Any ceiling tile.

## Pressure cooker*

## Razor blade*

## Refrigerator*

## Stopclock
Available with two hands indicating 60 minutes and 60 seconds respectively. Or use a stopwatch.

## Tape measure*

## Test tubes
Many sizes and types are available. Soda-lime are cheapest, Pyrex are better quality. The most convenient size is 125 mm x 16 mm, with a rim. For microbiology, it is best to use rimless tubes if a cotton plug is used, or tubes with a screw cap.

## Test tube holder

If care is taken that the paper is not set alight, a satisfactory test tube holder may be made from a piece of A4 paper folded lengthwise in four:

**Fig. xv**

Wooden or spring-steel holders can be purchased at reasonable cost.

## Test tube rack

An adequate rack can be made from a rectangular sheet of cardboard; fold lengthways, then cut holes as shown:

**Fig. xvi**

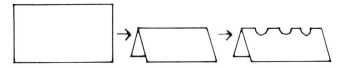

Racks are available in wood, polythene, nylon-coated, wire and aluminium. Wood and polythene racks give good all-round visibility, use for qualitative tests for nutrients where a result may take time to appear.

## Thermometer

For most purposes $-10°$ to $100°C$ is adequate but for the study of fats at high temperature a thermometer reading to $300°C$ is necessary. Care should be taken with mercury thermometers. Any spillages of mercury should be first swept up manually (do **not** use a vacuum cleaner), and the area treated with a sulphur and lime mixture.

## Thread*

## Tin cans*

## Tongs

Blackened steel crucible tongs are the cheapest and are suitable for most experiments. Do not try to hold test tubes with these tongs – use a test tube holder.

## Tripod

Triangular top with splayed steel legs. A very common laboratory accident is to touch a still-hot tripod after a bunsen burner has been turned off: take care to let it cool. Always use a tripod on a flameproof bench mat, not directly on the bench.

## Ultraviolet lamp

Bench-type or portable: both are expensive. Do not allow pupils to look directly at the bulb – the lamp must be positioned in such a way that even accidental viewing is impossible.

## Visking tubing

For dialysis: transparent, seamless viscose cellulose, 0.32 mm thick, 22 mm diameter when flat, 14 mm diameter inflated. The tubing is supplied flat and the sides may be difficult to separate: try immersing in water.

## Volumetric flasks

Available singly or in packs of 10, with capacities 10, 50, 100, 200, 250 and 500 $cm^3$.

**Fig. xvii**

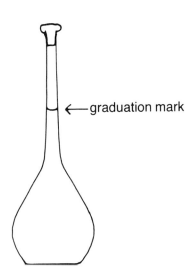

←graduation mark

## Wash bottle

250 or 600 $cm^3$. Not absolutely necessary, but useful. Fill with distilled water. A very clean beaker could be substituted.

## Washing-up bowl*

## Watch glass

The cheapest are of very thin clear glass, but use Pyrex if the glasses are to be heated.

## Waterbath

Thermostatically controlled if possible. However, these are expensive. Note that one cannot always rely on the dial setting and a thermometer must still be used as a check. As long as the temperature is *very* carefully controlled, a beaker over a bunsen burner or a pan on the stove may be used as an alternative.

## Weights

Between 100 g and 1 kg. Use laboratory balance or kitchen scale weights.

## White tile

Ceramic 100 mm x 100 mm. Use below conical flask in titrations, but a piece of white paper will serve the purpose equally well. A smooth white tile may, with care, be used instead of a spotting tile.

## Wood

Block of softwood.

## White knitting wool*

## Wire, stiff

eg thick fuse wire.

# Appendix III

List of suppliers from whom the reagents and equipment required for the experiments in this book may be obtained.

B.D.H. Chemicals Ltd., Shaw Road, Speke, Liverpool L24 9LA.
Telephone: 051 486 5023

Gallenkamp and Co. Ltd., PO Box 19, Victoria House, Croft Street, Widnes, Cheshire WA8 0NL.
Telephone: 051 424 2040

Griffin and George Ltd., PO Box 11, Ledson Road, Wythenshawe, Manchester 23 9NP.
Telephone: 061 998 5221

Oakes Eddon and Co. Ltd., Scientific House, Dryden Street, Liverpool L5 5HH.
Telephone: 051 207 3062

Philip Harris Biological Ltd., Oldmixon, Weston-super-Mare, Avon BS24 9BJ.
Telephone: 0934 413063

# Appendix IV

## References

Ministry of Agriculture, Fisheries and Food (1976) *Manual of Nutrition* 8th Ed. H.M.S.O.

Paul, A.A. and Southgate, D.A.T. (1978) *Mc Cance and Widdowson Composition of Foods* H.M.S.O. (Fourth edition).

Egan, H., Kirk, R. S. and Sawyer, R. (1981) *Pearson's Chemical Analysis of Foods* Churchill Livingstone (Eighth edition)

Ridley, A. and Williams, D. (1974) *Simple Experiments in Textile Science* Heinemann

Robinson, J. (1967) *Practical Work with Modern Materials* Edward Arnold

Taylor, M.A. (1989) *Technology of Textile Properties* Forbes (Third edition)

# Question section – Introduction

Below is a selection of GCSE and A level questions chosen for their relevance to the contents of this book. They are taken from a number of examining Boards, each denoted by initials (see key below). We are very grateful to the Examining Boards in each instance for allowing us to reproduce their copyright material.

## KEY

AEB – Associated Examining Board
MEG – Midland Examining Group
NI – Northern Ireland Schools Examinations Council
SEB – Scottish Examination Board
SEG – Southern Examining Group

## Section A – Observation of food structure

1. (i) The following diagrams show starch granules in a raw potato and a wool fibre as seen under a microscope. Label the diagrams stating which is starch and which is wool.

   (ii) Give the effect of moist heat on a:
   1. starch grain; 2. wool fibre.          *(WJEC, GCSE)*

## Section B – Tests for food constituents

2. Complete the following information relating to a food test:

   Put some egg white solution into a test tube.

   Add a few drops of ...................... Mix well.

   Add a few drops of 1% copper sulphate.

   *Result:* A...................... colour.          *(NI, A level)*

3. Discuss the functions of vitamin C in the diet and its relationship with other nutrients. With reference to the properties of this vitamin, explain the mechanisms by which it may be lost during the preparation, cooking and processing of food. Discuss the ways in which such losses can be minimised. Blackcurrants, green peppers and parsley are often quoted as rich sources of vitamin C. Comment on this in relation to the average British diet.          *(WJEC, A level)*

## Section C – Properties of food constituents

4. **a** Give an example of (i) a saturated fat; (ii) a polyunsaturated fat.

   **b** Which is considered the healthier to eat and why?          *(MEG, GCSE)*

5. **a** What are enzymes?
   **b** Give an example of a food which can show (i) enzymic browning; (ii) non-enzymic browning.          *(MEG, GCSE)*

6. Which of the following will go brown when you cook it:
   (a) a piece of steamed fish    *or*
   (b) a baked rice pudding?
   Give reasons for your answer.          *(MEG, GCSE)*

7. **a** Briefly describe the properties of starch which are used in cooking.
   **b** Explain how dishes based on a starch product vary according to the amount and type of starch used, the presence of other ingredients and the conditions used in the preparation. Give specific examples to illustrate your answer.          *(AEB, A level 1986)*

8. **a** Describe the composition of, and distinguish between, the various fats and oils currently available to the domestic consumer.
   **b** How do the physical and chemical properties of fats and oils determine their specific uses in cooking?          *(AEB, A level 1987)*

9. With reference to protein structure, explain, using examples, the process of denaturation and the factors influential upon it.
   Outline the criteria by which protein quality can be assessed. How is a knowledge of the protein quality and protein content of foodstuffs helpful in providing economical meals for a family?          *(WJEC, A level)*

10. 
```
   reddish      purple      blueish
   1 ←————————— 7 —————————→ 14
     acid         pH       alkaline
```

   **a** Name *two* watery plant foods which change colour in this way.
   **b** Name the pigment which is responsible for this reaction.          *(NI, A level)*

11. What do the following ingredients do:
    (i) Gelling agents; (ii) Antioxidant;
    (iii) Emulsifiers.          *(AEB, Nuffield Test 1987)*

12. Study the chart carefully and answer the following questions:

| Food | kJ | Protein (g) | Fat (g) | Calcium (mg) | Iron (mg) |
|---|---|---|---|---|---|
| Cheddar cheese | 440 | 7.1 | 9.6 | 230 | 0.15 |
| Eggs | 174 | 3.4 | 3.1 | 15 | 0.6 |
| Soya Bean | 465 | 10.0 | 5.0 | 50 | 2.0 |
| Chicken | 171 | 5.9 | 1.9 | 3 | 0.4 |
| Lentil | 400 | 7.0 | 0.3 | 11 | 2.0 |
| Milk | 70 | 0.9 | 1.1 | 34 | 0.025 |

*Average composition per 28g of food.*

**a** Name one pulse food from the chart above
**b** State two ways this pulse food can be used in the preparation of meals.
**c** Name two foods which provide the same amount of iron. *(SEG, GCSE 1989)*

## Section D – Assessment of food quality

**13. a** Why is yeast used in bread making?
**b** Why is *warm* water used in bread making?
**c** Give another use for yeast.
*(AEB, Nuffield Test 1987)*

**14.** Explain scientifically the action of a biological raising agent. *(NI, A level)*

**15.** Explain two physical properties of gluten in relation to breadmaking. *(NI, A level)*

**16.** You are making a rich cake mixture and the eggs have caused the batter to curdle.
**a** Explain the scientific reason for such an effect.
**b** Give one other example of curdling which has a *different* scientific explanation. *(NI, A level)*

**17. a** Which *one* of the following liquids is an example of a colloidal sol?
(i) sodium chloride and water; (ii) egg white and water; (iii) milk; (iv) cocoa in water.
**b** If cream of tartar is used with sodium bicarbonate to form a baking powder, which of the following statements is true?
(i) it produces most of its carbon dioxide when heated; (ii) it produces most of its carbon dioxide when mixed with water; (iii) it will not produce any carbon dioxide when heated unless tartaric acid is present. *(NI, A level)*

**18.** Which of the following are the result of enzymic activity?
(i) formation of milk junket
(ii) souring of milk
(iii) browning of cut apple surfaces
(iv) browning of fried chips
(v) setting of strawberry jam
(vi) softening of set jelly by fresh pineapple
*(NI, A level)*

## Section E – Fibres and fabrics

**19.** Match the following fibres with the correct longitudinal section.
(i) cotton (ii) polyamide (iii) viscose (iv) wool

*(NI, A level)*

**20.** Complete the following sentences:
**a** Cotton is a
(i) natural fibre
(ii) regenerated fibre
(iii) synthetic fibre
**b** Polyester is a
(i) natural fibre
(ii) regenerated fibre
(iii) synthetic fibre *(WJEC, GCSE)*

**21.** Answer the following questions from the pie chart showing fibre usage in the world:

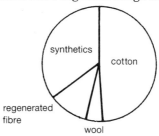

**a** Which fibre is most widely used?
**b** (i) Which fibre is least used?
(ii) Suggest two reasons for this.
*(WJEC, GCSE)*

**22. a** Name *two* vegetable fibres that are used to produce textiles.
**b** Name *one* man-made fibre made from cellulose. Name a raw material from which pure cellulose is obtained.
**c** Give *two* reasons why you would choose cotton fabric for pyjamas.
**d** Describe *two* qualities of a filament fibre.
**e** Draw a wool fibre as seen under a microscope. Label the diagram. *(MEG, GCSE specimen)*

**23.** Identify the fibres from the following burning tests.

| Approaching flame | In flame | Odour | Residue | Fibre |
|---|---|---|---|---|
| curls away from flame | burns quickly | burning hair | brittle black bead | |
| does not shrink away | burns quickly | burning paper | light, feathery | |
| melts away from flame | burns slowly | celery | hard, tough grey, bead | |
| fuses away from flame | burns rapidly | acrid | hard black bead | |

*(NI, A level)*

**24.** The table below shows some facts about three fabrics.

| | Wool | Cotton | Nylon |
|---|---|---|---|
| Wash care | Shrinks if badly washed. Slow to dry. | Can stand high temperature. Slow to dry. | Easily washed. Quick to dry. |
| Safety | Does not burn easily. | Burns easily and very quickly. | Does not burn – only melts. |
| Comfort | Very warm. Comfortable next to the skin. | Cool to wear. Comfortable next to the skin. | Not warm. Not very comfortable next to the skin. |

Which of the above fabrics would be a good choice for the following items of children clothing? Give a reason for each choice.
(i) Vest
(ii) Long nightie
(iii) Gloves

*(SEB, Standard Grade specimen)*

## Section F – Detergents and dyes

**25.** Water for washing clothes should be as soft as possible and the correct detergent should be chosen.
Comment on this statement.
Describe the International Care Labelling Code system and assess its usefulness to the busy parent of two young children.

*(AEB, A level 1986)*

**26.** In relation to the laundering of personal and household articles discuss each of the following:
**a** textile care labelling
**b** choice of detergent
**c** the effect of moisture on fabrics
**d** the effect of heat on fabrics
**e** the causes and effects of static electricity.

*(AEB, A level 1987)*